Conflict, Negotiations and Natural Resource Management

Conflicts over natural resources abound in India, where much of the population is dependent on these resources for their livelihoods. Issues of governance and management are complicated by the competing claims of parallel legal systems, including state, customary, religious, project and local laws.

Whereas much has been written about property rights, this unique collection takes a legal anthropological perspective, to explore how the coexistence and interaction between multiple legal orders provide bases for claiming property rights. It examines how hybrid legal institutions have developed over time in India and how these impact on justice in the governance and distribution of natural resources. The book brings together original case studies that offer fresh perspectives on the governance of forests, water, fisheries and agricultural land in a diverse range of social and spatial contexts.

This brand new research provides a timely and persuasive overview of the fundamental role of parallel legal systems in shaping how people manage natural resources. It will be of interest to scholars and practitioners of environmental law, property law, environmental politics, anthropology, sociology and geography.

Maarten Bavinck is Associate Professor in the Department of Geography, Planning and International Development Studies at the University of Amsterdam, the Netherlands, and President of the International Commission on Legal Pluralism.

Amalendu Jyotishi is Associate Professor at Amrita School of Business, Amrita University, India, and Coordinator of Asian Initiatives on Legal Pluralism.

Routledge Explorations in Environmental Studies

Nuclear Waste Management and Legitimacy
Nihilism and responsibility
Mats Andrén

Nuclear Power, Economic Development Discourse and the Environment
The case of India
Manu V. Mathai

Federalism of Wetlands
Ryan W. Taylor

Governing Sustainable Urban Renewal
Partnerships in action
Rory Shand

Employee Engagement with Sustainable Business
How to change the world whilst keeping your day job
Nadine Exter

The Political Economy of Global Warming
The terminal crisis
Del Weston

Communicating Environmental Patriotism
A rhetorical history of the American environmental movement
Anne Marie Todd

Environmental Justice in Developing Countries
Perspectives from Africa and Asia-Pacific
Rhuks Temitope Ako

Climate Change and Cultural Heritage
A race against time
Peter F. Smith

'Looking at natural resources from the perspective of legal pluralism provides important insights into the possibilities and constraints of governance. Showing how actors navigate through the confusing webs of law in their struggles for land, water, forest, and fisheries, the book is a must for anyone interested in natural resource management.'

Keebet von Benda-Beckmann, Max Planck Institute for Social Anthropology, Germany

'Bavinck and Jyotishi have brought together an excellent group of authors who offer critical perspectives and new insights into the relevance of the legal pluralism perspective in the context of conflict over natural resources in India. This edited volume contributes to the debate on critical questions arising in the field of natural resource governance and will be of enormous value to scholars, practitioners and policy makers across the world.'

Merle Sowman, University of Cape Town, South Africa

'This book is a timely focus on issues of conflict and governance over forests and fisheries in India. Several case studies examine legal pluralism as an alternative perspective for both the cause of conflicts and a potential solution, suggesting governability to diffuse potentially damaging social and environmental consequences. Recommended reading for law-makers and law-breakers.'

Minoti Chakravarty-Kaul, University of Delhi, India

A Global Environmental Right
Stephen Turner

The Coming of Age of the Green Community
My neighbourhood, my planet
Erik Bichard

Fairness and Justice in Environmental Decision Making
Water under the bridge
Catherine Gross

Carbon Politics and the Failure of the Kyoto Protocol
Gerald Kutney

Trade, Health and the Environment
The European Union put to the test
Marjolein B.A. van Asselt, Michelle Everson and Ellen Vos

Conflict, Negotiations and Natural Resource Management
A legal pluralism perspective from India
Maarten Bavinck and Amalendu Jyotishi

Conflict, Negotiations and Natural Resource Management

A legal pluralism perspective from India

Edited by
Maarten Bavinck and
Amalendu Jyotishi

Routledge
Taylor & Francis Group
LONDON AND NEW YORK

First published 2015
by Routledge

2 Park Square, Milton Park, Abingdon, Oxon OX14 4RN
711 Third Avenue, New York, NY 10017, USA

Routledge is an imprint of the Taylor & Francis Group, an informa business

First issued in paperback 2016

British Library Cataloguing in Publication Data
A catalogue record for this book is available from the British Library

Library of Congress Cataloging in Publication Data
Conflict, negotiations and natural resource management : a legal pluralism perspective from India / edited by Maarten Bavinck and Amalendu Jyotishi.
pages cm
1. Legal polycentricity—India. 2. Environmental law—India. 3. Right of property—India. 4. Natural resources—Law and legislation—India. 5. Natural resources—Government policy—India. I. Bavinck, Maarten, 1954- editor of compilation. II. Jyotishi, Amalendu, editor of compilation.
KNS469.5.C66 2014
344.5404'6—dc23
2014019986

ISBN: 978-0-415-83480-3 (hbk)
ISBN: 978-1-138-22598-5 (pbk)

Typeset in Goudy
by Swales & Willis Ltd, Exeter, Devon, UK

Contents

Illustrations

Figures

Tables

Box

Contributors

Editors

Maarten Bavinck is Associate Professor in the Department of Geography, Planning and International Development Studies at the University of Amsterdam, the Netherlands, and President of the International Commission on Legal Pluralism.

Amalendu Jyotishi is Associate Professor at Amrita School of Business, Amrita University, India, and Coordinator of Asian Initiatives on Legal Pluralism.

Contributors

D. Parthasarathy is Professor in the Department of Humanities and Social Sciences at the Indian Institute of Technology, Bombay, India.

Ajit Menon is Associate Professor at the Madras Institute of Development Studies, Chennai, India.

Sashi Sivramkrishna is Professor in the School of Business Management at the Narsee Monjee Institute for Management Studies, Bangalore, India.

Satyapriya Rout is Assistant Professor in the Department of Sociology at the University of Hyderabad, Hyderabad, India.

Pampa Mukherjee is Associate Professor in the Department of Political Science at Panjab University, Chandigarh, India.

Derek Johnson is Associate Professor in the Department of Anthropology at the University of Manitoba, Winnipeg, Manitoba, Canada.

Prateep Kumar Nayak is Assistant Professor in the School of Environment, Enterprise and Development (SEED) at the University of Waterloo, Canada.

Svein Jentoft is Professor at the Norwegian College of Fishery Sciences, University of Tromsø, Norway.

Preface

This volume finds its origin in the biennial conferences of the international Commission on Legal Pluralism (CLP) that have been circulating around the world. Two of these conferences (Chiang Mai, 2000 and Jakarta, 2004) were noteworthy for they offered scholars in Asia the chance to gather and engage with the academic tradition of legal pluralism. A selection of these scholars established a chapter called the Asian Initiative on Legal Pluralism (AILP) in 2000, consolidating the group in subsequent gatherings at regular intervals. The two-day seminar on legal pluralism and natural resources organised at Amrita University in Coimbatore, India, in April 2012 by the Asian Initiative on Legal Pluralism was one of a kind, bringing together scholars young and old from all sides of India and other parts of Asia. For many of those taking part, legal pluralism was an exciting new concept, pertinent to the issues they study. The debates that resulted were therefore spirited and convivial. A sizable number of these scholars were attracted to legal pluralism, providing fresh perspective and opportunity to plan this volume.

Although many of the papers in this volume were originally presented in Coimbatore, they have been added to from various sources. First, the editors decided to include a few reprints of articles that had already been published in niche journals, but had not yet received the attention they deserve. In each case, these articles have been updated with recent insights. Second, the editors invited contributions from a few scholars who had not been able to attend the Coimbatore seminar, but whose work is relevant to the topic.

While the original intention was to include papers from South-East Asia too, the editors eventually decided to limit the book's ambit to India. Readers will also notice that fisheries and forestry receive relatively more attention than other natural resource sectors. This 'sectoral bias' is, however, not the result of deliberate choice, but merely of chance.

The seventeenth international conference of the CLP will take place in Mumbai, India in December 2015. We hope that this volume will add to the debate that takes place there and generally contribute to the scholarship on legal pluralism and natural resources.

Maarten Bavinck
Amalendu Jyotishi

Acknowledgements

The editors have incurred many debts in the process of realising this volume. We are grateful to Dr Sushanta Mahapatra for his help in not only organising the seminar that lies at the source of this volume, but also for his support in the initial phase of its realisation. We thank Phil van der Krogt for his careful language-editing work. Ajit Menon provided counsel at various points of time. The following persons of Routledge have facilitated the publication process, largely through their patience: Bethany Wright, Charlotte Russell, Helena Hurd and Louisa Earls; also Tamsin Ballard of Swales and Willis.

Maarten Bavinck acknowledges the support of the Governance and Inclusive Development (GID) group of the University of Amsterdam and the international Commission on Legal Pluralism.

Amalendu Jyotishi acknowledges the funding support of the Netherlands Organisation for Scientific Research (NWO) and WOTRO Science for Global Development and CLP and the intellectual contribution of several members of the Asian Initiative on Legal Pluralism. Amrita University, and especially the faculty, staff, students of Amrita School of Business, deserves a special mention and acknowledgement in organising the seminar where the idea of this volume first germinated.

Both editors would also like to thank all of the contributors to this volume, who had to put up with a stream of emails and requests for additional information.

1 Introduction

The legal pluralism perspective

Maarten Bavinck and Amalendu Jyotishi

Preliminary remarks

Conflicts over natural resources are by no means a new field of study in India (Shiva 1991). The question of to what extent a legal pluralism perspective has something new to offer is therefore worth raising. Does legal pluralism help us understand why conflicts emerge and how they develop? Is it at all relevant for those who are interested in governance and in providing solutions? Although legal pluralism shares interests with other disciplines and approaches, in this chapter and volume as a whole, we will argue that its contribution is not only original, but also a necessity.

Legal pluralism – understood here as multiple sets of norms and rules applied to similar situations (Vanderlinden 1972; Benda-Beckmann 2002) – is recognised to be an intrinsic element of India's makeup (Eberhard and Gupta 2005). Scholars firstly identify Indian legal pluralism as a result of the colonial and pre-colonial legacy, a consequence of the overlaying of prevailing legal systems by those of new conquerors (Mommsen and de Moor 1992). Legal pluralism obviously also follows on from the geography of the country and its cultural heterogeneity. The plurality of personal laws that relate to issues of marriage and inheritance, for example, is a consequence of the division of the population into various religious groupings with different legal traditions (Larson 2001). Finally, legal pluralism can be explained through the crisis of the Indian legal system (Baxi 1981; Mendelsohn 1981), which is not only less effective, but also less legitimate than desired and gives rise to alternative methods of dispute resolution (e.g. Vatuk 2013).

This volume is concerned with a specific dimension of the legal pluralism landscape in India. For rural 'ecosystem people' (Gadgil and Guha 1995), who depend on their surroundings for basic necessities such as firewood, water, fodder, food and livelihoods, natural resources are of eminent importance. Such resources, however, are under increasing pressure for at least two reasons. The Millennium Ecosystem Assessment (2005) has estimated the extent of environmental degradation on a global scale, and its conclusions are relevant also for India (Millennium Ecosystem Assessment 2005, sub-global assessment India). In addition to environmental pressures, there are the pressures of 'ecological marginalisation' that follow in the wake of economic development (Gadgil and Guha 1995;

Nadkarni, 2002). These push vulnerable populations off the lands on which they have historically depended, to make way for hydropower dams, special economic zones, mining complexes and aquaculture farms. Social conflict, here, is accompanied by opinions on the legality and the fairness of new claims that are profoundly divergent.

This chapter traces the relevance of the legal pluralism perspective in the context of conflict over resources, as well as governance, and thereby provides an introduction to the themes of following chapters. Zips and Weilenmann (2011: 7) observe that 'governance and legal pluralism belong to separate academic idioms,' and it is only recently that the interface between them is being explored. Analysis suggests that legal pluralism poses special governance challenges, and often affects the governability of societal systems negatively (Bavinck et al. 2013). Where legal systems meet, bricolage – or institutional tinkering – is often the result (Cleaver 2012). In the following sections we briefly consider the debates on legal pluralism, conflict, governance and bricolage respectively.

Legal pluralism and natural resources

Legal pluralism is a sensitising concept that emerged in the interstices of the disciplines of law and anthropology (Pandey and Pathak 1995; Benda-Beckmann 2002; Tamanaha et al. 2012; Twining 2010). Its adherents challenge the inherent superiority of statutory law and argue that societies are characterised by plural sets of norms and values.

More than a state of being, legal pluralism is a process in which 'intricate processes of adaptation, appropriation and vernacularisation take place' (Benda-Beckmann and Benda-Beckmann 2006: 8). People change, societies change and so too does law. Interactions between legal systems therefore deserve to be followed in the context of time (Moore 1978). Several contributions to this volume testify to this effort.

Although natural resources have always been within legal pluralism's range of vision, particularly in studies on rural society, they have achieved focus only recently. The volume edited by Spiertz and Wiber (1996) on the role of law in natural resource management is a frontrunner in this regard. The biennial conferences organised by the Commission on Legal Pluralism (CLP)[1] have formed a platform for debates on this topic since the mid-1990s, with publications on a variety of resource types and dynamics. Many of these publications have concentrated on the concept of property and its deconstruction as 'bundles of rights' (Benda-Beckmann et al. 2006; Schlager and Ostrom 1993).

In India, scholarly attention in the field of legal pluralism has mainly gone to dispute resolution, with authors alternatively highlighting the role of actors in the state judiciary (Holden 2005; Kidder 1974), new mechanisms such as the Lok Adalat (Baxi 1985; Galanter and Krishnan 2003), women's courts (Vatuk 2013), and the workings of caste and village councils (Hayden 1999; Randeria 2002; Sbriccoli 2013; Vincentnathan 1992). Natural resources too are now becoming a fruitful field of enquiry. Many studies have appeared in the field of water and irrigation (Meinzen-Dick and Pradhan 2002; Roth and Vincent 2013), forestry (Rangarajan, 2002; Saberwal et al. 2001; Sivaramakrishnan 1999), pastoralism (Chakravarty-Kaul 1996; Saberwal 1999), fisheries (Bavinck 2001; Bavinck et al. 2013b) and mining (Lahiri-Dutt 2007). It is to this body of scholarship that this volume aims to contribute.

Law is closely connected to power play, and – when it is focused on the environmental field – to the concerns of political ecology. Political ecology emphasises that the allocation of environmental resources is decided in the realm of politics and that actors with more power are often able to shape policy choices (Adams 2009). It investigates how the allocation of resources affects people unequally, and additionally how losers may contest the practices that undermine livelihoods and their notions of fairness (Ribot 2004). Finally, political ecology is interested in the creation, legitimisation and contestation of environmental narratives (Stott and Sullivan 2000) and in processes of creating governmentality (Agrawal 2005).

Scholars recognise that power contributes to the realisation of aims and the implementation of law (Benda-Beckmann and Benda-Beckmann 2009), but also to conflict, inequalities and injustice. It plays out at different levels: between individuals, groups and nations. Legal systems function because of the distribution of power over decision-making, adjudication and implementation (Jentoft 2007a). They may also, however, be impaired by disagreement and power struggle. In contexts of legal pluralism, power differentials between legal systems and the people that adhere to them obviously influence events (Berman 2009).

In the scholarship on legal pluralism, state law is often considered dominant and even hegemonic (Merry 1988). In practice, however, this is not always true; scholars therefore argue that the social significance of any type of law is an empirical question and not something to be decided in advance (Benda-Beckmann and Benda-Beckmann 2006). Where state law does dominate, as Tamanaha (2008) points out, state agencies respond differently to the availability of legal systems, varying from neutrality to repression. Those affected respond in kind, generally making use of the social space provided, sometimes accepting subjugation but also choosing to rebel. This brings us to the area of conflict studies.

Conflict

Conflicts over natural resources are analysed from different quarters (Bavinck et al. 2014; Ratner et al. 2013). The main polemic of the recent past was whether conflicts should be explained as a result of increasing environmental scarcity (Homer-Dixon 1999) or of human greed (Collier 2003). Subsequent research has noted that these theories are too straightforward and actually deal with different problem fields. The environmental scarcity literature thus tends to focus on situations involving renewable resources, while the greed literature highlights the plight of high-value mineral resources. Both approaches have subsequently been nuanced to the degree that Frerks et al. (2014: 17) conclude: ‘At present, scholarship tends to promote a multi-causal, multi-level and multi-actor perspective in which the role of environmental factors is mediated through or combined with other factors, often of a socio-political nature.'

Institutions are of a 'socio-political nature', and it is in this direction that authors dealing with the origin and continuation of conflict now often point (Ratner et al. 2013). Institutions include values, norms, rules, rights and organisational structures (Jentoft 2007b), which are also the ingredients of law defined in a social science sense. It is therefore reasonable to also assume a connection between legal pluralism and conflict.

Scholarship suggests that legal pluralism is a distinct source of social strife, as the parties involved differ with respect to their sets of values. As Rapoport (1975) pointed out four decades ago, conflicts that take place between such systems – so-called exogenous conflicts – differ substantially from endogeneous conflicts, often being more intense and long lasting. This is best visualised in relation to conflicts over property. When parties to a conflict agree on the basic rules of property rights, agreement is more easily reached than when the premises are fundamentally at odds. If common mediation structures are then also unavailable – as is often the case where legal pluralism prevails – such tensions endure and gain in strength. This is the 'cauldron of conflict' reported on by Gadgil and Guha (1995) in their classic on environmental struggles in India. The issues they report on involve large-scale appropriations of resources and displacements of people, such as now occur in the Maoist-dominated tribal belt of the country (Kapur et al. 2012). However, conflict also takes place both in the drudgery of work and processes of forum shopping (where individuals or groups seek out the best legal forum for their problem) or shopping forums (where legal forums seek out and appropriate problems) (Benda-Beckmann 1981).

Although legal pluralism is easily associated with conflict, conflict is not the only way in which legal systems relate. Discussing the varying conditions of legal pluralism in the capture fisheries of India's coastal states, Bavinck et al. (2013b) distinguish between four types of interaction that can occur between legal systems: indifference, conflict, accommodation and mutual support. Similar patterns are found in other sectors, such as forestry, and these too shift over time. Interactions between legal systems often bring about institutional change, as we will discuss further in the Bricolage section.

Governance and governability

Although the contributors to this volume are mainly interested in the analysis of legal pluralism in particular societal fields, they are all at the very least indirectly concerned with how pluralism affects governance. Governance, as it is understood today, includes the steering done by civil society, the private sector and the state alike (Torfing et al. 2012). As governing actors are numerous, the interactions between them as well as with society are an important constituent of the governing process (Kooiman 2003). Governance can then be defined as 'the whole of interactions taken to solve societal problems and to create societal opportunities' (Kooiman and Bavinck 2005: 17).

This definition does not detail whose problems and opportunities are actually being addressed, or who is being left out of the process – the concerns of political ecology. It also leaves aside the question of whether governance objectives are actually being attained. In fact, there are many limitations to governance (Jentoft 2007b), and many natural resource systems therefore possess a low level of governability (Bavinck et al. 2013a). 'Governability' in this context refers to 'the overall capacity for governance' (Kooiman et al. 2008: 3), which is argued to vary greatly from system to system.

We contend that legal pluralism contributes significantly to the problems of governance, creating societal divisions over the values that are to be pursued, as well as parallel sets of institutions and tools for doing so (Jentoft 2011). Under such conditions, the legitimacy of governance is a prime concern. But governance theory also points a way forward: through purposive interaction. It is to this topic that we now turn.

Bricolage

Interaction is a basic constituent of human society, taking place all the time and at all societal levels. Like other forms of social identity, legal pluralism creates particular patterns of interaction, facilitating certain flows and limiting others. It is thus logical to assume that people adhering to a particular system communicate more and in different ways with each other than they do with 'outsiders' (at least in the situation to which the legal system pertains). As a result, one can distinguish, in addition to domains of intense communication, places where interaction is lacking. Such 'institutional voids' (Hajer 2003) or 'ambiguities' (Tatenhove 2013) can be a problem for successful governance, sometimes to be addressed through the creation of new interaction platforms. This is the co-management approach ventured by Jentoft et al. (2009) in the context of Indian capture fisheries. Needless to say, such platforms function only in a context of mutual trust and respect.

Competing claims for natural resources that are rooted in legal pluralism have a great potential for strife and therefore considerable urgency. Where one social group, and one legal system, lacks the power of imposition – a situation that applies almost generally (Elias 1978) – competing claims are addressed through negotiation. Negotiation can occur between individuals, such as when representatives of a dominant group try to bribe leaders of the other side, but also on a collective level (Ratner et al. 2013). The latter constitutes an attempt to decide on new rules of the game. It can result in institutional conversion (Tatenhove 2013), or bricolage (Cleaver 2012), whereby old practices and accepted norms are patched together with new arrangements. Where legal systems rub shoulders, however, their accommodation is not always a result of conscious negotiation. After all, as Sousa Santos (2002) points out, people do not always experience situations of legal pluralism as fractured wholes, but as a 'natural' condition of interlegality (cf. Simon Thomas 2013). Institutional change and adaptation is then often a gradual and unintentional process. Hybridisation of law is a common outcome thereof. This is a reminder that legal pluralism is best thought of as alternative cycles of 'pluralisation' and 'depluralisation' (Benda-Beckmann and Benda-Beckmann 2006).

The contributions to this volume

The book is organised as follows. Chapters 1 and 2 are of a general nature, providing a perspective on legal pluralism and natural resources in the context of the region as a whole. Chapters 3 to 6 focus on a variety of forest-related issues, while Chapters 7 to 9 turn to fisheries. The final chapter broadens the perspective again to discuss legal pluralism and governance of natural resources at a theoretical level.

Chapter 2 by Parthasarathy takes a critical legal pluralism stance on natural resource use in colonial and post-colonial India. The author argues that the legal pluralism approach has three major weaknesses. The first is the assumption that social practice – such as rebellion against, for example, the state – necessarily reflects the existence of a separate normative regime. Second, he suggests that the notion of a semi-autonomous social field (Moore 1973), a common departure point for scholars in the area of legal pluralism, tends to focus attention on 'internal matters' rather than considering the multiple relations between the field and its exterior. Third, Parthasarathy points out that governments – with activists and academics in their wake – have generally taken a too-restricted, sectoral perspective on natural resources. Drawing on examples from various domains, he concludes that 'a central task of legal scholars and activists in India would be to develop a better understanding of legal pluralism issues in India as applicable to ecological regimes'.

Chapter 3, by Menon, makes use of a court judgment to explore the history of land use in the forests of Gudalur in the Nilgiri hills. The Supreme Court's Godavarman judgment, as it has become known, is argued to be based on the assumption that more forests are to be preferred and that the state is best equipped to protect them. His analysis of the complex forest landscape suggests, however, that the state's priorities have shifted over time and that small farmers, who were instrumental to realising the state's earlier revenue objectives, are now victimised for the sake of conservation. Plurality of normative visions is argued to underlie many decisions about land use in the region.

Sivramkrishna and Jyotishi (Chapter 4) use a legal pluralism approach to consider the changing historical position of tribal iron smelters in India's deep forests. They argue that iron smelters probably played an important role in the war economy of the pre-colonial and early colonial period, making substantial use of forest resources for conversion to charcoal in the process. The authors note that in the later colonial period the iron smelters faced reduced demand due to decline in warfare as well as competition from colonial foundries. The colonial state's need for charcoal is suggested to have been one of the important causes for the subsequent protection of forest through statutory law.

Chapter 5, by Rout, looks at the genesis and outcome of a conflict over mining in the Niyamgiri hills of Odisha. A forested hill that occupies a central position in the cosmology of a tribal community called Dongaria Kondh became the locus of a conflict with a private bauxite mining company. The corporate interest aligned well with the state's interest in investment and industrialisation. The tribal community was, however, supported by civil society organisations interested in preserving the natural ecology of the tract as well as the cultural and religious sentiment of the community. Rout analyses this conflict over the (forest) land and (mineral) resource from a legal pluralism perspective.

Mukherjee (Chapter 6) takes us to the forests of Uttarakhand and the various property regimes that prevail there. She highlights the role of the so-called *van panchayats* that were established in the first decades of the twentieth century in the context of community forest management, and were functioning until 2005. These decentralised, largely self-governing organisations were remarkably effective, mainly because of their local legitimacy. Two new developments threaten their continued performance, however: the inauguration of a new style of *van panchayats* under the direction of the Revenue Department, and village forest joint management by the Forest Department. Both initiatives – and others as well – have contributed to a fragmentation and centralisation of forest policy that contradicts the ideals of participatory management.

Bavinck (Chapter 7) shifts attention to legal pluralism in marine fishing. Departing from an example of violent conflict that emerged between three fishing villages in Chennai over a 'law' that had been drawn up by the fishing population, he examines the manner in which governmental authorities looked for an appropriate solution. The 'street-level bureaucrats' entrusted with this task, whose major aim was to maintain the peace, built their case largely outside the realm of state fisheries law. He concludes that the two legal systems largely lead a separate existence, with state law ending where fisher law begins. But where they do intersect, such as in the case of this particular conflict, government officers engage in bricolage in order to solve the problem at hand.

Johnson (Chapter 8) brings us to Gujarat where marine fisheries suffer from overcapacity and the effects of overfishing. These fisheries possess two major sources of regulation: state law and fisher law. Making use of a combination of political ecology, interactive governance and legal pluralism theory, Johnson explores the obstacles for achieving better governance, defined in terms of social justice and environmental health. The 'defective legal pluralism' he encounters in Gujarat is argued to be the result of a variety of historical and cultural factors, including the vegetarian ethos that prevails in the state. The root of the problem, however, is 'a striking lack of vision and capacity to transform these various elements into an enduring and adaptive governing system for the fishery'.

Chapter 9, by Nayak, uses the small-scale fisheries of Chilika Lagoon in Odisha as a case to analyse how critical gaps in governance may even occur in situations of 'institutional plenty'. The context is one of increasing incursion of aquaculture enterprises and state regulation that together undermine the effectiveness of fisher institutions. Nayak asks how the present situation could possibly, if at all, be converted into a workable polycentric governance system (Ostrom 2010). His conclusion reads that fishers' marginalisation can only be countered through 'a process of empowerment of appropriate institutions that can help revive fishers' collective strength to negotiate their rights with multiple contesting stakeholders'.

We noted earlier in this chapter that according to scholarly observers 'governance and legal pluralism belong to separate academic idioms' (Zips and Weilenmann 2011: 7). Jentoft's final chapter takes on the challenge of establishing a connection between the legal pluralism and interactive governance perspectives, taking fisheries as a reference point. 'Governability' is a hinge concept in his analysis, with legal pluralism constituting a possible threat as well as an opportunity for governance. He concludes that interactive governance provides a useful framework for diagnosing the role of legal pluralism, with the first step being a search for the diversity, complexity, dynamics and scale of normative orders.

Conclusion

The contributions to this book make clear that legal pluralism, as an empirical phenomenon, is varied, and that its role in Indian natural resource settings cannot be defined unequivocally. It is instead the subject of meticulous analysis and comparison. Our studies do indicate, however, that at a general level plurality of normative orders plays a role in generating and perpetuating social conflict, thereby impeding governance. Governors – whether they belong to the state, civil society or market – therefore would do well to pay attention to legal pluralism as a relevant factor in situations of natural resource use. Legal pluralism is, however, not constant but in flux, with bricolage and hybridisation taking place at the interface of constituent legal systems. Their interactions are argued to offer threats but also opportunities for better governance.

Note

The CLP was established in 1979 and is attached to the International Union for Anthropological and Ethnographical Sciences (IUAES) as well as the International Association of Legal Science (IALS). For more information see www.commission-on-legal-pluralism.com.

References

Adams, W.M. (2009) *Green Development: Environment and Sustainability in a Developing World* (3rd edition), London: Routledge.

Agrawal, A. (2005) *Environmentality – Technologies of Government and the Making of Subjects*, Durham, NC: Duke University Press.

Bavinck, M. (2001) *Marine Resource Management: Conflict and Regulation in the Fisheries of the Coromandel Coast*, New Delhi: Sage Publications.

Bavinck, M., R. Chuenpagdee, S. Jentoft and J. Kooiman (eds) (2013a) *Governability – Theory and Applications for Fisheries*, MARE Publication Series, Dordrecht: Springer.

Bavinck, M., D. Johnson, O. Amarasinghe, J. Rubinoff, S. Southwold and K.T. Thomson (2013b) 'From indifference to mutual support: a comparative analysis of legal pluralism in the governing of South Asian fisheries', *European Journal of Development Research*, vol. 25, no. 4, pp. 621–640.

Bavinck, M., L. Pellegrini and E. Mostert (eds) (2014) *Conflict Over Natural Resources in the Global South – Conceptual Approaches*, Oxford: CRC Press/Taylor & Francis.

Baxi, U. (1981) *The Crisis of the Indian Legal System*, New Delhi: Vikas Publishing House Ltd.

Baxi, U. (1985) 'Popular justice, participatory development and power politics: the Lok Adalat in turmoil', in Allott, A. and G.R. Woodman (eds), *People's Law and State Law: The Bellagio Papers*, Dordrecht: Foris Publications, pp. 171–186.

Benda-Beckmann, F. von (2002) 'Who's afraid of legal pluralism?', *Journal of Legal Pluralism*, vol. 47, pp. 37–82.

Benda-Beckmann, K. von (1981) 'Forum shopping and shopping forums: dispute processing in a Minangkabau village in West Sumatra', *Journal of Legal Pluralism*, vol. 19, pp. 117–159.

Benda-Beckmann, F. and K. von Benda-Beckmann (2006) 'The dynamics of change and continuity in plural legal orders', *Journal of Legal Pluralism*, vol. 53–54, pp. 1–43.

Benda-Beckmann, F. von and K. von Benda-Beckmann (2009) 'Rules of law and laws of ruling: law and governance between past and future', in Benda-Beckmann, F. von and K. von Benda-Beckmann (eds), *The Power of Law in a Transnational World*, New York: Berghahn, pp. 2–30.

Benda-Beckmann, F. and K. von Benda-Beckmann and M.G. Wiber (eds) (2006) *The Changing Properties of Property*, Oxford: Berghahn.

Berman, P. (2009) 'The new legal pluralism', *Annual Review of Law and Social Science*, vol. 5, pp. 225–242.

Chakravarty-Kaul, M. (1996) *Common Lands and Customary Law – Institutional Change in North India Over the Past Two Centuries*, Delhi: Oxford University Press.

Cleaver, F. (2012) *Development Through Bricolage? Institutions and Natural Resource Management*, London: Earthscan.

Collier, P. (2003) *Natural Resources, Development and Conflict: Channels of Causation and Policy Interventions*, Washington DC: World Bank.

Eberhard, C. and N. Gupta (2005) 'Legal pluralism in India: an introduction', *Indian Socio-Legal Journal*, vol. 31, pp. 1–10.

Elias, N. (1978) *What Is Sociology?*, London: Hutchinson.

Frerks, G., T. Dietz and P. van der Zaag (2014) 'Conflict and cooperation on natural resources: justifying the CoCooN programme', in Bavinck, M., L. Pellegrini and E. Mostert (eds), *Conflict Over Natural Resources in the Global South – Conceptual Approaches*, Oxford: CRC Press/Taylor & Francis, pp. 13–34.

Gadgil, M. and R. Guha (1995) *Ecology and Equity – The Use and Abuse of Nature in Contemporary India*, New Delhi: Penguin Books.

Galanter, M. and J.K. Krishnan (2003) 'Debased informalism: Lok Adalats and legal rights in modern India', in Jensen, E.G. and T.C. Heller (eds), *Beyond Common Knowledge: Empirical Approaches to the Rule of Law*, Stanford, CA: Stanford University Press, pp. 96–141.

Hajer, M. (2003) 'Policy without polity? Policy analysis and the institutional void', *Policy Sciences*, vol. 36, pp. 175–195.

Hayden, R.M. (1999) *Disputes and Arguments Amongst Nomads: A Caste Council in India*, Oxford: Oxford University Press.

Holden, L. (2005) 'Official policies for (un)official customs: the hegemonic treatment of Hindu divorce customs by dominant legal discourses', *Journal of Legal Pluralism*, 49, pp. 47–74.

Homer-Dixon, T.F. (1999) *Environment, Scarcity and Violence*, Princeton, NJ: Princeton University Press.

Jentoft, S. (2007a) 'In the power of power: the understated aspect of fisheries and coastal management', *Human Organization*, vol. 66, no. 4, pp. 426–437.

Jentoft, S. (2007b) 'Limits of governability? Institutional implications for fisheries and coastal governance,' *Marine Policy*, vol. 31, pp. 360–370.

Jentoft, S. (2011) 'Legal pluralism and the governability of fisheries and coastal systems', *Journal of Legal Pluralism*, vol. 64, pp. 149–172.

Jentoft, S., M. Bavinck, D.S. Johnson and K.T. Thomson (2009) 'Fisheries co-management and legal pluralism: how an analytical problem becomes an institutional one', *Human Organization*, vol. 68, no. 1, pp. 27–38.

Kapur, D., K. Gawande and S. Satyanath (2012) 'Renewable resource shocks and conflict in India's Maoist belt', CGD Working Paper 302, Washington DC: Center for Global Development. See www.cgdev.org/content/publications/detail/1426377.

Kidder, R.L. (1974) 'Formal litigation and professional insecurity: legal entrepreneurship in South India', *Law and Society*, Fall, pp. 11–37.

Kooiman, J. (2003) *Governing as Governance*, London: Sage Publications.

Kooiman, J. and M. Bavinck (2005) 'The governance perspective', in Kooiman, J., M. Bavinck, S. Jentoft and R. Pullin (eds), *Fish for Life – Interactive Governance for Fisheries*, Amsterdam: Amsterdam University Press, pp. 11–24.

Kooiman, J., M. Bavinck, R. Chuenpagdee, R. Mahon and R. Pullin (2008) 'Interactive governance and governability: an introduction', *The Journal of Transdisciplinary Environmental Studies*, vol. 7, no. 1.

Lahiri-Dutt, K. (2007) 'Illegal coal mining in Eastern India: rethinking legitimacy and limits of justice', *Economic & Political Weekly*, 8 December, pp. 57–66.

Larson, G.J. (2001) *Religion and Personal Law in Secular India – A Call to Judgement*, Bloomington, IN: Indiana University Press.

Meinzen-Dick, R. and R. Pradhan (2002) 'Legal pluralism and dynamic property rights', CAPRi Working Paper No. 22, Washington, DC: International Food Policy Research Institute.

Mendelsohn, O. (1981) 'The pathology of the Indian legal system', *Modern Asian Studies*, vol. 15, pp. 823–863.

Merry, S.E. (1988) 'Legal pluralism', *Law & Society Review*, vol. 22, no. 5, pp. 869–896.

Millennium Ecosystem Assessment (2005) See www.millenniumassessment.org/en/index.html.

Mommsen, W.J. and J.A. de Moor (eds) (1992) *European Expansion and Law: The Encounter of European and Indigenous Law in 19th- and 20th-century Africa and Asia*, Oxford: Berg.

Moore, S.F. (1973) 'Law and social change: the semi-autonomous social field as an appropriate subject of study', *Law & Society Review*, vol. 7, pp. 719–746.

Moore, S.F. (1978) *Law as Process: An Anthropological Approach*, London: Routledge and Kegan Paul.

Nadkarni, M.V. (2002) 'Commons, development and the poor', in Marothia, D. (ed.), *Institutionalising Common Pool Resources*, New Delhi: Concept Publishing Company, pp. 79–91.

Ostrom, E. (2010) 'Polycentric systems for coping with collective action and global environmental change', *Global Environmental Change*, vol. 20, pp. 550–557.

Pandey, V.N. and A. Pathak (1995) 'Sociology of law in India – postscripts and prospects', *Economic & Political Weekly*, vol. 30, no. 31/32 (5–12 August), pp. 1974–1977.

Randeria, S. (2002) 'Entangled histories of uneven modernities: civil society, caste solidarities and legal pluralism in post-colonial India', in Elkana, Y., I. Krastev, E. Macamo, and S. (eds), *Unraveling Ties: From Social Cohesion to New Practices of Connectedness*, Frankfurt: Campus, pp. 284–311.

Rangarajan, M. (2002) *Fencing the Forest: Conservation and Ecological Change in India's Central Provinces 1860–1914*, New Delhi: Oxford University Press.

Rapoport, A. (1975) *Conflict in Man-made Environment*, Harmondsworth: Penguin.

Ratner, B.D., R. Meinzen-Dick, J. Hellin, E. Mapedza, J. Unruh et al. (2013) 'Addressing conflict through collective action in natural resource management: a synthesis of experience', CAPRi Working Paper No. 112, Washington, DC: International Food Policy Research Institute, http://dx.doi.org/10.2499/CAPRiWP112.

Ribot, J.C. (2004) *Waiting for Democracy: The Politics of Choice in Natural Resource Decentralization*, Washington DC: World Resources Institute.

Roth, D. and L. Vincent (2013) *Controlling the Water: Matching Technology and Institutions in Irrigation Management in India and Nepal*, New Delhi: Oxford University Press.

Saberwal, V.K. (1999) *Pastoral Politics: Shepherds, Bureaucrats, and Conservation in the Western Himalaya*, Delhi: Oxford University Press.

Saberwal, V.K., M. Rangarajan and A. Kothari (2001) *People Parks & Wildlife: Towards Coexistence*, New Delhi: Orient Longman.

Sbriccoli, T. (2013) 'Legal pluralism in discourse: justice, politics and marginality in Rajasthan, India', *Journal of Legal Pluralism and Unofficial Law*, vol. 45, no. 1, pp. 144–165.

Schlager, E. and E. Ostrom (1993) 'Property-rights regimes and coastal fisheries: an empirical analysis', in Anderson, T.L. and R.T. Simmons (eds), *The Political Economy of Customs and Culture: Informal Solutions to the Commons Problem*, Lanham, MD: Rowman & Littlefield, pp. 13–41.

Shiva, V. (1991) *Ecology and the Politics of Survival: Conflicts Over Natural Resources in India*, New Delhi: Sage Publications.

Simon Thomas, M. (2013) 'The challenge of legal pluralism – local dispute settlement and the Indian-state relationship in Ecuador', unpublished PhD thesis, University of Utrecht.

Sivaramakrishnan, K. (1999) *Modern Forests: State-Making and Environmental Claims*, Stanford, CA: Stanford University Press.

Sousa Santos, B. de (2002) *Toward a New Legal Common Sense: Law, Globalization, and Emancipation*, London: Butterworths LexisNexis.

Spiertz, H.L.J. and M.G. Wiber (eds) (1996) *The Role of Law in Natural Resource Management*, Gravenhage: VUGA Uitgeverij.

Stott, P. and S. Sullivan (eds) (2000) *Political Ecology: Science, Myth and Power*, London: Arnold.

Tamanaha, B. (2008) 'Understanding legal pluralism: past to present, local to global', *Sydney Law Review*, vol. 30, pp. 375–411.

Tamanaha, B.Z., C. Sage and M. Woolcock (eds) (2012) *Legal Pluralism and Development – Scholars and Practitioners in Dialogue*, Cambridge: Cambridge University Press.

Tatenhove, J. van (2013) 'How to turn the tide: developing legitimate marine governance arrangements at the level of the regional seas', *Ocean and Coastal Management*, vol. 71, pp. 296–304.

Torfing, J., B.G. Peters, J. Pierre and E. Sørensen (2012) *Interactive Governance: Advancing the Paradigm*, Oxford: Oxford University Press.

Twining, W. (2010) 'Normative and legal pluralism: a global perspective', *Duke Journal of Comparative & International Law*, vol. 20, pp. 473–517.

Vanderlinden, J. (1972) 'Le pluralisme juridique: essai de synthèse', in Gilissen, J. (ed.), *Le pluralisme juridique*, Brussels: Editions de l'Université de Bruxelles, pp. 19–36.

Vatuk, S. (2013) 'The "women's court" in India: an alternative dispute resolution body for women in distress', *Journal of Legal Pluralism and Unofficial Law*, vol. 45, no. 1, pp. 76–103.

Vincentnathan, S.G. (1992) 'The social construction of order and disorder in two South Indian communities', *Journal of Legal Pluralism*, vol. 32, pp. 65–102.

Zips, W. and M. Weilenmann (2011) 'Introduction: governance and legal pluralism – and emerging symbiotic relationship', in Zips, W. and M. Weilenmann (eds), *The Governance of Legal Pluralism: Empirical Studies from Africa and Beyond*, Wien: LIT Verlag GmbH & CoKG, pp. 7–34.

2 Law-breakers and law-makers

Critical legal pluralism, normative subjects and ecological regimes in India[1]

D. Parthasarathy

The Indian social science debates on environmental concerns have been characterised by a fair degree of consensus on the conceptualisation of conflict and equity. It is largely agreed that the politics of resource governance is as much, if not more, a problem of social conflict, as it is of conservation, efficiency and sustainability. In historicising Indian debates, struggles, conflicts and 'social movements' around natural resources, assessments of the conditions under which groups gain and lose control over resource access, management and rights have led historians, sociologists, anthropologists, geographers and political scientists to pay attention to law-breakers *and* law-makers. Deriving from an approach that critiques individual interest and the nation-state as the only or major sources of rule-making, sociologists and anthropologists in India have sought to comprehend the 'complex matrix through which the narratives of the modern nation state are implicated in creating and sustaining local codes' (Das 2006: 195), which are themselves implicated in diverse power structures. Such an approach, combined with the sociological notion that 'Indians' 'do not radically separate the moral from the natural order, act from actor, person from collectivity' (Appadurai 2006: 187), necessitates a focus on normative orders that are not distanced from the logic of practice in studying natural resource governance and conflicts. This partly propelled me to look at critical legal pluralism approaches to assess their utility for helping to explain issues of law-making and law-breaking across colonial and post-colonial Indian history, resource regimes and governmentalities. The meagre literature on legal pluralism in India largely ignores the important research on resource conflicts in the colonial period, while the theoretically significant and empirically rich investigations of the colonial period (e.g. Guha 2000; Rangarajan 1996; Sivaramakrishnan 1995; Washbrook 1981[2]) rarely utilise insights from the legal pluralism debates of the past three or four decades. A key arena of continuity across both periods in India has been the operationalisation of the state's control over law- and policy-making and its role in generating institutional mechanisms for management, ownership, access and utilisation of natural resources (Grove, Damodaran and Sangwan 1998; Guha and Gadgil 1992, 1995; Jewitt 1995; Kumar 1990). Not surprisingly the law-making and implementing role of the state has generated a large number of conflicts over resources between various fractions of the 'omnivores', 'ecosystem people' and 'ecological refugees'

(Guha and Gadgil 1995), and between the state and various resource dependent communities. In the process, similarly constituted groups of law-breakers have been created – groups of people attempting to access and use resources as part of their survival and livelihood strategies, and using normative regimes[3] of rights and liberties that pre-date the emergence of the modern state.[4]

A deeper reading of the history of resource conflicts in India sensitised me to the need to look for alternate theoretical perspectives, not least because much of the literature is empiricist in nature, and/or lacks frameworks that are derived from legal-philosophical approaches and paradigms.[5] Also, I wished to avoid essentialist[6] readings of law and legal pluralism approaches. In addressing such concerns I became aware of the emergence of critical legal pluralism as an approach within the broader discourse on legal pluralism. This approach has helped re-focus debates on issues related to normativity in general, and more specifically on the themes of normative subjects, normative interaction and normative regimes. This chapter posits that much of the discourse – including perspectives that inform environmental and social activism – suffers from three shortcomings. The first pertains to the definition and valorizations of the notion of normativity, which include the identification and definition of normative subjects. Despite standing the traditional legal pluralism discourse on its head, the critical legal pluralism approach confuses normativity and practice; it ignores normative regimes that are embedded in social-environmental practices in ways that do not create normative subjects, and hence misrepresents legal issues in natural resource regimes. The second limitation derives from the first, by giving greater value to the idea of law as an autonomous or semi-autonomous social field. Norms, rules and laws regulating ownership of, access to and management of natural resources may have evolved from or linked to practices of kinship, caste, clan or simply to broader economic relations. While sociologists and social anthropologists in India have largely ignored resource law issues in ethnographic research, legal and legal pluralism scholars have neglected the social embeddedness of resource practices and regimes. The third is generic to legal pluralism approaches in general, and to much of social science theorising, policy studies and activism – the conceptualisation of resources in purely instrumentalist, as well as narrow, sectoral terms.[7] Using illustrations from environmental debates and movements in India, the chapter argues that reconceptualising natural resources in terms of ecological regimes is central to the task of developing a better understanding of legal pluralism issues in India.

Critical legal pluralism: prospects and problems

Kleinhans and Macdonald (1997) have significantly contributed to the evolution of the critical legal pluralism approach by rejecting 'the characterisation of law as an external force obeyed by legal subjects' (Adams 2012: 1). Rather than reifying or accepting legal subjects as law-obeying, they are seen as law-creating, subjects who are implicated in generating 'their own legal subjectivity and establishing normative authority as a knowledge process of creating and maintaining reality' (Adams 2012: 1).

Critical legal pluralists imagine 'law as improvisation', as a process of 'legal meaning-making'. They argue that describing law as arising from obligatory tendencies of law-making, rather than originating from law-obeying subjects makes us decrease the undue emphasis on the issue of how laws come to be enforced and obeyed or disobeyed. A key advance of critical legal pluralism lay in asking questions about the processes by which normative authority is generated by legal subjects themselves. Scholars advocating a critical legal pluralism approach suggested that 'legal subjectivity is not externally imposed but is instead called into being by the legal subject itself' (Adams 2012). Social constructionist[8] perspectives are deployed in seeking to comprehend the processes whereby legal subjects construct legal meaning.

Further, Kleinhans and Macdonald (1997: 42) define critical legal pluralism as a 'continuing autobiography of meaning', pushing scholars to recognise 'law as its own discourse with unique links to other forms of thought and expression' (Piper 2010). This essentially delimits the sphere of law's influence as conventionally understood; it demarcates a boundary for law as a social field, while simultaneously forcing us to rethink the idea of autonomy in formulations of law as an autonomous or semi-autonomous social field (Moore 1973) hence, the origins of normative regimes and how these create normative subjects also have to be reassessed. Macdonald challenges the 'neatness' inherent in traditional legal pluralism approaches whereby legal pluralism is defined in terms of an interaction between clearly defined 'official and unofficial normative orders in one social field' (Eberhard and Gupta 2005). Pointing to the absence of stability, the presence of ambiguity, and the fluid and porous nature of normative regimes, Macdonald states that critical legal pluralism abandons these limitations, and instead 'suggests that the sites of normative interaction operate on several levels at once, often taking the form of a broad zone of adjustment, in dynamic evolution and redefinition. These levels include the individual, the group and the societal' (Macdonald 1998: 18). Critical legal pluralism begins with how individuals and members of groups approach and react to law, how they create laws, rather than as entities whose behaviour is governed by law. Particularly in the case of ecological regimes or resource use and management systems, critical legal pluralism helps us to better comprehend the interaction between different normative systems (and their effects and outcomes), instead of emphasising only the consequences or implications of how resource-based communities are governed. The term 'ecological regime' in this chapter follows its elaboration by Baerlocher and Burger (2010: 88–89) as a conceptual scheme rather than a concept, and refers to the 'level of institutional structures which not only allows us to integrate the biophysical environment into social theory at the aggregated organised action level, but also to demonstrate empirically the mutual influence that biophysics and societies exert upon each other'. As such the term is used to refer not just to rules and regulations concerning a particular ecological domain (e.g. forests and water), but also to the entire social structure comprising of organisations, institutions and political processes that impinge on 'socio-biophysical interrelations' (Baerlocher and Burger 2010 : 89), as well as the complex set of resource interactions between a particular ecological domain (e.g. water) and other domains (e.g. agro-forestry, pastoral livestock systems).

The theoretical advance of critical legal pluralism is not insignificant, but it is in attempting to deploy its key arguments in understanding the plight of so-called law-breakers – groups labelled as criminal for their extraction of and participation in resource management *against* state-enacted laws and normative regimes – that its limitations emerge. A first limitation is the confusion between norms and practice. The colonial period witnessed a large number of peasant and tribal revolts across the South Asian subcontinent (Guha and Gadgil 1989; Guha 1999), as much to do with exploitative agrarian relations and revenue maximising strategies of the colonial state, as with new resource regimes and governmentalities that excluded large sections of the population from resource access and marginalised their livelihoods and resource dependencies. The bureaucracies and institutions that evolved during the British colonial rule used colonial science to monopolise natural resources to feed into economic growth in metropolitan centres (Kumar 1990); these colonial institutions and strategies persisted even after independence, and continued to impose state bureaucracies on resource dependent communities, excluding and criminalising historical, indigenous strategies of resource extraction and management (Jewitt 1995; Sivaramakrishnan 1995; Sundar 2000, 2011; Warhaft 2001). While the critique offered by critical legal pluralism helps us in going beyond simplistic colonial or state law approaches in law-making and law-breaking, it nevertheless carries forward a key limitation – of assuming that communities necessarily had their own normative regimes that were subsumed, overthrown or simply ignored by new colonial resource regimes.[9]

This chapter argues against the tendency to presume that all legal subjects are normative subjects; normativity is not a 'natural' proclivity of subjects, but in fact is bound up with practical reason (Bourdieu 1998), environmental *phronesis* (Gunder 2003) and practice. In the Indian context, Sivaramakrishnan (1995) provides an elaboration of such an approach using a Foucauldian lens to analyse historical shifts in 'technologies of power' that affected forestry in colonial India. Linking discourses of rule and resistance, and hence 'consciousness and politics' to do with forestry to the central problem of power, he advocates the use of a theory of practice 'to be applied to the state-making process by inserting culture into a larger historical program of interpretation and analysis' (Sivaramakrishnan 1995: 4). Relations of power and domination create and sustain politics, institutions and processes that provide the basis for norms to evolve and get transformed. Absence and presence of conflict, competition, domination or exploitation influence the need for and the strength of normative regimes in resource management. Resource use, management and governance within specific ecological regimes are experiential and place-based, and evolve through long-term human and non-human relationships that transform and generate practical 'deep ecology'[10] environmental ethics, which may be value-based rather than norm-based. Normative regimes have a historicity and are more likely to emerge under conditions of impending or actual scarcity, conflicts over sharing of resources and in contexts that require dealing with specific or broader issues of governance and management, and social inequalities. Scale of resource use and management, technology and population density defined intensity of resource use (Jodha 1985), and regimes of control from above also have a role in the evolution of normative systems.

That marginalised communities in the past have revolted and rebelled against the colonial and post-colonial state is no reason to presume that they had a normative subjectivity different from the one imposed by the state, or that they had evolved normative regimes that were or were not better, efficient or more egalitarian. We need to pay attention to the nature and characteristic of indigenous state formation, the type of resource that is of concern and interaction with other communities in the use and management of a resource. All these are of importance in determining the emergence of normative regimes, and whether in fact resource management practices remain at the level of practice or evolve to a level of some kind of normativity. That human beings become normative subjects ought to be shown as a matter of historical fact rather than human inevitability deriving from a state of nature. The definition and valorization of the notion of normativity, the identification and definition of normative subjects, cannot be a priori acts. Confusing normativity and practice makes us forget that normative regimes may be and are in fact embedded in social-environmental practices in ways that do not or may not create normative subjects, and hence may lead us to misunderstand legal issues in natural resource regimes. Robbins et al. (2009), point to the pragmatic attitude of law-breakers who routinely do not comply with governance arrangements in Rajasthan. This non-compliance may be interpreted in normative terms, but their study also shows the extent to which such practices are historically and structurally rooted, and constitute 'conservation realities – that is, conservation as it is'. Robbins et al. are pessimistic about the future of effective resource governance being determined either by 'a self-organised, local, non-state, collective choice institution' or by 'a draconian state resource monopoly' (2009: 574). Instead 'conservation as it is' conceives of resource governance being rooted in actual rules and practices that result from negotiations between local actors, the local state and local formal and informal institutions; in addition to normative ideas, such rules are also affected by the specificities of local household economies, and features of the natural habitat. The crisis of the commons demonstrates in no small way, the failure of smaller, local groups to adapt and evolve normative or legal mechanisms to sustainably manage resources and environmental systems. Further Robbins et al. (2009) and several others have shown that the disappearance of local, informal institutions for resource management, or the breakdown of sustainable practices may be attributed to the power, resource commitments and influence of an 'intrusive' state and other powerful actors (Agrawal and Gibson 1999; Bromley and Cernea 1989; Ghai 1993; Meinzen-Dick and Knox 1999).

A second limitation pertains to the idea of law as an autonomous or semi-autonomous[11] social field. Practices of kinship, caste, clan or changing agrarian relations and class formation affect the creation of norms, rules and laws regulating ownership of, access to and management of natural resources. In India, sociologists and social anthropologists have largely neglected resource law issues in ethnographic research (with some exceptions e.g. Brara 2006), while scholars and activists using rights-based, legal approaches have failed to notice the sociality of resource practices and regimes. Whether kinship, caste or clan rules affect resource norms or resource-related practices affect kinship and clan practices is essentially a chicken and egg question. Studying natural resource issues in terms of normative regimes and normative subjects needs to account for the exact nature of 'normativity', whether in fact one is confusing normativity with practice, and whether norms or practices influencing resource use and ecological governance are actually norms/practices of kinship, clan, community, etc., and not those of resource management. Recent studies have brought out the role of kinship and caste in agricultural transformation in the semi-arid tropics in India (Padmaja 2012), and the role of intra- and inter-clan inequalities in affecting socio-environmental transformation and migration related socio-ecological relationships (Walling 2011). Bavinck (2001: 1088) explores how non-state 'caste' panchayats ('fishermen panchayats') regulate marine resource management, 'regulating to and usage of fish resources' along the Coromandel Coast in Tamil Nadu. The work of Agrawal (1999) and Brara (2006) in Rajasthan shows the ways in which caste and caste-place-based village power structures can exclude nomadic or migrant communities from accessing the pastoral commons despite the best intentions of democratic devolution processes, a point that is also made by Sundar (2000) in critiquing the failure of devolution-based forest management strategies in India. However, Bavinck in his discussion of conflicts between small-scale and large-scale fishers, shows that caste councils or *uur* panchayats do have rules to conserve fish stock, and ensure fairness 'within communities and with regard to outside fishers' (2013: 117), but their success in enforcing the rules to outsiders depend on a range of factors including issues of the scale of governance, and the nature of the 'administrative divide' (2013: 132). An ecological interpretation of kinship or caste practices is a valid exercise, but is severely restricted by having too much of a materialist approach (e.g. Harris 1965). To what extent can we think of normative regimes in structural terms linked to kinship practices, human cognition or simply ways of relating to and surviving on natural resources? Do subjects themselves have a consciousness of norms and normativity? When communities rebel and revolt, are they rejecting specific legal-normative regimes, are they rejecting the act of being subjected to specific legal norms, or are they rejecting being subjected to regimes of normativity itself? In other words, to what extent can we state that law-breaking is not just rejecting specific legal-normative regimes in favour of alternative ones,[12] and to what extent is such behaviour a rejection of normative regimes in favour of regimes of practice, of practical reason, of environmental *phronesis*? As Mosse (1997) argues in his study of water institutions in Tamil Nadu, governance and institutions evolve in response to both ecological characteristics and historical courses of action in adapting to environmental systems and ecological-social change. In light of the critiques of Robbins et al. and Sivaramakrishnan outlined earlier, it is vital that we understand when practices become normativised, when they don't and under what conditions of control, expropriation, governance or conflict. We need to separate out particular environmental practices and norms that evolved as a response to resource management concerns, from those related to the exercise of social power rooted in caste, class, regional or gender inequalities and domination.

There is also a hint of an assumption in critical legal pluralism that normative subjects' attitude towards law and law-making is shaped by individual factors of socialisation. Issues of sociality, in other words aspects of mutuality, dependency, sharedness and also exploitation shape law-creation, affect the generation of subjects' legal subjectivities, and construct/maintain a social reality in which knowledge production and practical reason are the foundations of normative authority.[13] Legal subjectivities and normative regimes to do with natural resources may then be a reflection of other aspects of sociality such as kinship, caste, community etc., which would lead us towards Moore's construction of law as a 'semi-autonomous social field'. While not disagreeing with Moore, the critique in this chapter is to add the focus on practice, and to think of Moore's 'larger social matrix', which affects rule-making within the 'semi-autonomous social field', as a social field that is defined as much by practice as by norms.

The third limitation deals with the instrumental or sectoral approach to research and policy-/rule-making on natural resources. The very active environmental movement in India that has clearly linked with livelihood and subsistence issues has put enormous pressure on the post-colonial state to reform laws, policies and institutions that are seen to be exploitative, exclusive and marginalising. Despite the innovative theorising and critique by scholars and activists, the state and its institutions have usually found ways and means of obstructing the intent of new laws and policies. This chapter argues that these problems arise due to the nature of theorising and instrumentalising resources, which is as much a feature of the state and market forces, as of policy- and law-making processes. Resource-dependent communities, or 'ecosystem people' in Guha and Gadgil's (1995) words, perceive specific resources (forest, pasture, minerals, water) in ecological terms, not merely as livelihood resources, and hence a central task of legal scholars and activists in India would be to develop a better understanding of legal pluralism issues in India as applicable to ecological regimes. The term 'ecological regime' is preferred here precisely for this reason. While activists tend to use 'balance of nature' and conservationist frameworks in understanding and supporting indigenous notions and management of resources, academic research has tended to compartmentalise the environment into different resources that are the subject of study. Commodification and governance imperatives with or without the push from activists and the research community ultimately lead to resource specific laws, rules and management systems or design principles (Ostrom 1990). Ecological regimes are complicated by the presence of multiple resources that are mutually linked with multiple users and uses for the same resource. Temporality, seasonality and the spatiality of resource use by multiple users make it difficult for institutional and normative arrangements to evolve and sustain; hence, historically at local levels, ad-hoc arrangements, bargaining, negotiation and common-sense approaches have characterised multiple resource use, with normative approaches providing more of a backdrop.

The colonial and post-colonial states in India have instrumentalised natural resources by defining, legislating and institutionalising them in very narrow terms. The environmental movement's frequent demands for more inclusive, participatory, sustainable and egalitarian legal and normative systems in the arena of resource extraction and management have, despite their clear ecological focus, tended to mimic the state in terms of conceptualising mechanisms and institutions that imitate the state's own instrumentalist view of resources. Thus the achievements of the past few decades have failed to yield major results as new policies and laws are linked to older forms of institutions that are largely bureaucratic and single resource-centred (forestry, surface water, pasture, groundwater, fisheries). The various lower level bodies – forest committees, water users committees, etc. – despite their significant participatory nature, are also single-resource focused. They become subject to the larger normative regime of the state, and are divorced from both the local ecological regime and structures of sociality.

These critiques of critical legal pluralism are exemplified through cases pertaining to minerals, forests, pasture and fisheries in India, in the final section of this chapter.

Ecological regimes, resource conflicts and critical legal pluralism

The emphasis on figuring out the legal subjectivity of law-makers and law-breakers has been put forward as a key advance in our understanding of legal pluralism. The considerable and high-quality research on resource-related conflicts in India does not much reflect the significant theoretical developments on legal pluralism, with the possible exception of the research on coastal fisheries and water management. This section of the chapter applies the legal subjectivity theorisation of critical legal pluralism to the debates and discussions on resource-related conflicts and struggles in India; while doing so, it recasts the critical legal pluralism approach to incorporate the three sets of limitations outlined above.

The evolution of new forms of citizenship that began during the colonial period, and that largely expropriated the majority of the resource-dependent population in India from their customary rights over resources, continued after independence, despite reformist legislation in the areas of land reform, property rights and constitutional obligations of equality and development (Sivaramakrishnan 2008; Sundar 2011). As the examples show, the form, content and implementation of resource regulations, judgments and laws need to be critiqued both in terms of the advances of critical legal pluralism and its theoretical limitations. Simply enacting more socially sensitive laws, or supporting pluralist approaches, may not work for the resource-dependent ecosystem people, unless the practices deriving from the functioning of the state and its institutions, and power issues inherent in caste/kinship/community practices, are adequately addressed.

The long struggle over forest rights culminated in the Forest Rights Act of 2006; its final shape owes as much to the conflicts between the state and forest-based communities and their activist representatives, as to internal conflicts between communities and groups for whom forests are a crucial livelihood resource.

However the experience of activists, non-governmental organisations (NGOs), and forest-based communities, and the evidence of recent scholarship, is revealing in the nature of obstacles that the forest bureaucracy sets up, sometimes even going against the elected political leadership functioning at the ministerial level. The case of Lekha-Mendha in Gadchiroli district of Maharashtra is illustrative. The first documented case (Pathak et al. 2003) of a village community seeking to use the new act to get access to forest resources revealed a long battle with the Forest Department, which went to great lengths, even to the extent of changing the biological classification of bamboo from that of grass to that of timber, in denying local people from cutting bamboo for their subsistence use, defying a Supreme Court of India judgment in the process. Similar cases are reported from around the country.

The forest committees[14] have similarly been hindered in their functioning, or have become power centres in themselves, denying access to other groups who have traditionally enjoyed access. The formation of forest committees has ignored traditional kinship and clan rules – some of which promoted equity norms while others were discriminatory. Rather than addressing the latter, the combination of colonial origin institutions and new powers has created new powerful groups that have displaced old elites in expropriating access to and ownership of resources (Baviskar 2001). Access to forest land for cultivation, enabled by specific clauses in the Forest Rights Act, has faced similar obstacles (Sathyapalan and Reddy 2010). Narrowly defined conservation objectives and economic growth imperatives drive state attitudes while issues of livelihood, sustainability and equity drive the quest for better access to forest resources on the part of the poor. This clash of objectives highlights the distinction between a normative subjectivity and an approach that largely is influenced by practice on the part of the state as well as the ecosystem people.

The need to think in normative terms to design or develop norms-based governance is usually contingent upon scarcity or conflict events, and is not a regular feature of environmental or resource management. For instance, fisherfolk in Mumbai did not have many norms beyond an informal monsoon ban to protect fish during the breeding season. As such they have found it quite difficult to deal with all sorts of infringements and invasions by 'outsiders' who threaten artisanal fishing, simply because a strong tradition of normative rule-making does not exist (Chouhan 2012). Agriculture is a particularly good example of how resource use was linked to larger ecosystems, but common rules were rarely formulated or enforced, owing to the nature of privatised and compartmentalised agricultural activity. Particularly in the case of new practices requiring common, coordinated practices such as integrated pest management or cooperative water use, the absence of normative regimes is clearly evident, notwithstanding romanticised notions of the cooperative and environment-friendly peasant or farmer. Studies of success and failure in the case of common pool resources, and commonly managed institutional arrangements for forests, water or pasture – these show both the presence and absence of normative regimes; they also show the conditions that are conducive for normatively defined institutions to evolve and flourish, as well as conditions that hinder or obstruct normative subjects who can move beyond individual self-interest, or beyond pragmatic and experiential approaches to resource management.

Such 'conditions' are often related to structural inequalities in India, as evident in the studies on pasture and grassland, which (along with diverse commons and state-owned resources classified as 'wasteland' in India) have historically supported livestock-based livelihoods in India both for sedentary and nomadic groups (Brara 2006; Jodha 1985). Access to these has become increasingly scarce, except in areas where NGOs, activists and social movements have launched a struggle to protect these and ensure access to dependent communities. The absence of clear institutional mechanisms to both provide access and ensure that appropriate systems of management function efficiently is particularly felt in the case of these commons, many of which are in fact state-owned in India. Studies by Brara (2006), Agrawal (1999) and others show that issues of peasant and class differentiation, the inequality between sedentary and nomadic pastoralists, and between different agrarian classes, determine the impacts of decentralised common pool resource-management policies and laws. The seventy-third amendment to the Indian constitution granting greater power and rights over village commons has tended to exclude the nomadic groups who do not 'belong' to any village, and whose access in earlier times was negotiated, not on the basis of normative considerations of rights, justice and citizenship, but through bargaining over shared economic benefits. Gendered access is another key issue that is rarely brought into institution development, policy design and normative guidelines for the pastoral commons.[15] The politics of democratisation, the ownership status of pasture, grassland and wasteland (public, common, state-owned, privately owned) also affect new institutional forms aimed at enabling greater access and equity for pastoralists. Practices related to kinship, caste, nature of resource dependence, or agrarian class structure deeply implicate normative regimes and law-making with reference to the pastoral commons; the imperfect nature of our understanding of these practices as applicable to resource management and the failure to consider these in law-making exercises create new classes of law-breakers.[16] It is only those scholars with an explicit focus on gender or kinship who have recognised the significance of such issues in their studies, which in India are few and far between. Conversations between those who study family, caste and kinship and those who research resource management are as yet limited to a few regions and sectors. Similarly, in tracking recent environmental-economic transformations, the problems of crop/livestock interactions, new trade linkages and the growth of agro-processing industries that create new livelihood patterns and chains of exploitation, have not been adequately recognised in simplistic legal attempts to create new normative-legal regimes.

The case of the commons particularly creates complications for understanding problems of normativity, legal pluralism and law-making subjects. As Jodha (2001) has shown extensively through a lifetime of research in India, the decline of commons has been greatly facilitated by the market economy, assisted by legal changes enacted by the state. In theory this has created new legal systems, but for the commoners, the essential consequence has been to cease or reduce their normative capacity to govern themselves, to make rules or practices for resource management. When the commoners become law-breakers, they assert their right to law-making, they seek to reclaim their earlier status as 'law-creating subjects', who wish to reject their legal subjection to the state and the market and instead claim the power to craft their own 'legal subjectivities'. The critical legal pluralism approach becomes alive and contributes new insights once we begin to study legal subjects as law-breakers and not just as law-makers. The fact that commoners constitute a huge proportion of law-breakers around the world ought to force scholars to rethink the very idea of the meanings of law, and of the processes of law-making in such a way as to valorize law-breaking as a significant process in itself, so that one is not complicit in the neo-liberal strategy of treating law-breakers as criminals.

The case of fisheries-related legislation and regulatory changes constitutes one illustration of the failure to consider ecological (as opposed to resource) regimes in attempts to protect the livelihoods of traditional fisherfolk. While the story of small-scale fishing in India is one of continuous marginalisation (Bavinck 2001; Kurien 1991; Warhaft 2001), the limited attempts to consider their interests and mitigate impacts of larger 'development' policies indicate an instrumentalist approach to fisheries resources. Breeding and spawning areas for fish (e.g. mangroves adjacent to fishing grounds) are not part of proposed solutions to protect and provide livelihoods for small-scale fish workers (Chouhan and Parthasarathy 2013). The larger idea of an ecological habitat is absent in the proposed Traditional Coastal and Marine Fisherfolk (Protection of Rights) Act. The various definitions of terms in the Bill (e.g. 'traditional'), and the applicability of provisions and clauses for protection of fisheries livelihoods clearly indicate that the state has no interest in making this a dynamic sector, but wishes to create restrictions so that there is little competition with commercial large-scale fishing. The policies on coastal regulation zone (CRZ), the various enactments, rules and amendments to CRZ notifications – these also have been largely ineffective in the face of a lack of institutional mechanisms for monitoring and implementation, and in a context of increasing encroachment of small fisheries zones (Chouhan 2012).

As in the case of pasture, one perceives a lack of fit between new normative regimes and the attempt to create new normative subjects on the one hand, and fisheries as a social and ecological practice on the other. Ongoing fieldwork by this author and by Chouhan (2012) in Mumbai seeking to assess the urban development and CRZ violation impacts on fishing communities provided an interesting insight about the normative perceptions of fisheries resources and livelihoods. While entitlements, rights and justice frameworks do influence their strategies and legal struggles, fisherfolk and their leaders pitch the environmental or ecosystem contribution of artisanal fisheries in a strong way in order to seek support for their struggles against developmental marginalisation, land grab and threats from large-scale, commercial fishing. Hence, rather than arguing for better laws or norms, they argue for greater autonomy in fisheries and resource management, and the role of 'traditional' practices in sustainable resource use, in the prevention of resource degradation. Small-scale fishers' struggles in Mumbai and other parts of India go beyond livelihood threats; and the focus on the protection of mangroves indicates both subsistence aspects (protection of fish-breeding areas) as well as ecosystem function aspects (flood protection, coastal erosion, biodiversity).[17] The normative authority that fisherfolk assert derives not merely from a desire to refashion their legal subjectivities, but also from a fusion of older and newer forms of environmental citizenship that originates less in political philosophy and ideas of modern democracy, and more in environmental *phronesis*.

Licensing and extraction of minerals have been among the most controversial developments in recent times in India, with huge implications for displacement of populations, loss of livelihoods and ecological degradation (Parthasarathy 2007). Mining is also a good illustration of the problems of a narrow instrumental definition of a single resource without linking the resource to its larger ecological and social context. India does have laws and policies to prevent environmental damage from mining activities and for environmental restoration post mining closure. However these policies do not recognise the subsistence nature of ecological regimes in mining areas, the livelihood dependence of local communities on local ecological complexes, and the changing social dynamics of mineral extraction in a context of old and new social divides. Hence impact assessment and rehabilitation exercises and policies are ameliorative at best and destructive at worst. In an interesting analysis of the politics of cultural identity, ecological degradation and environmental regulation in mining areas of the north-eastern state of Meghalaya, Das (2007) points to the complexity of conflicts of interests, emerging class divides and an emerging moral economy that undergird so-called identity-based conflicts. Demands over customary rights in the name of livelihoods are seen to mask elite appropriation of resources, even as regulations for environmental sustainability are violated by the poor as these vary from their traditional normative regimes or practices of resource appropriation.

Whatever perspective on law and society one utilises, the relationship between local normative strands and the plurality of ecological regimes is rarely the subject of study, as disciplinary and academic orientations make it easier to link particular resource regimes to issues of law and governance. Persons representing the environmental movements in India (Narmada, Tehri, Chipko and countless other local, lesser-known movements and struggles) have argued for reconceptualising natural resources in more ecological terms; it is argued here that this will have to be a central task for developing a better understanding of legal pluralism issues in India as applicable to ecological regimes. The failure to implement the Samata judgment[18] (Parthasarathy 2007), which explicitly linked mineral resources to other environmental-livelihood relationships, is in part an outcome of neoliberal growth policies. But the failure can also be seen in terms of an absence – the failure on the part of activist groups and communities themselves to come up with appropriate institutional mechanisms to implement the judgment. Since the state's approach to resources is always instrumentalist, the Samata judgment opened up a window of opportunity to evolve alternate institutions that would be based on an explicit awareness of ecological regimes rather than resource regimes. Part of the problem goes back to the distinction between normativity and practice. The opposition to mining projects is a normative one though rooted in pragmatic livelihood struggles; however the alternatives (including retaining indigenous livelihood systems) are rooted in practice related to everyday usage and access, even if normative elements can be observed in resource allocation and management within communities. Institutional mechanisms that emerge *are* attached to normative regimes, which are easier to develop for single-resource regimes than for more complex ecological regimes.

The problems with the failure to consider complex ecological regimes in technologies of governance can also be observed in water-related conflicts. The controversy over the Mullaperiyar dam[19] is an apt example. The making of the conflict into an inter-state issue is essentially to do with the dam itself as a particular technological solution for water-related problems. Dams are notoriously anti-ecological, in giving primacy to its own flows, levels and maintenance needs, rather than paying attention to ecological problems engendered in their river basins, canal systems and reservoirs. A group of scholars/activists has called for an alternative imagination in terms of reviving and restoring the traditional South Indian village water tanks as an alternative to the Mullaperiyar dam (Baviskar et al. 2011). Village tanks are much more intimately and intricately linked to local ecological health, and have also formed a basis for institutional development of a very different kind from the hydrological bureaucracies of large irrigation systems (von Oppen and Subba Rao 1980). In the case of watersheds, ignoring the needs of livestock owners is quite common (Rai 2007). A number of similar illustrations and cases can be drawn upon to prove the narrow definition[20] of resources by the legal system, and hence the tendency to neglect the larger socio-ecological complex within which resources are used and governed, and within which legal (pluralist) approaches to resource governance evolve.

The developmentalist state's failure to develop 'a more historically grounded understanding of landscapes, rights, and rules for resource use' (Mosse 2003) is mirrored (as in the case of pastoral commons) in gendered analysis of water issues as well. Cleaver's (1998: 347) insights on gender and informal institutions in water management are applicable to other resources as well. Criticising 'economism' and the 'abstraction of the individual from a life world', he takes to task the conceptualisation of institutions purely in organisational terms, and hence the focus is more on 'formal manifestations of collective action: contracts, committees, and meetings' (1998: 347), rather than informal manifestations such as norms, practices and conventions. Cleaver goes on to show the significance of women's reproductive concerns and 'the minor exigencies of daily life (as well as from productive concerns)' for appropriate design of alternative institutional models that better fit with local contexts (1998: 347). Likewise, the need for factoring in differential levels of power and differential abilities (between men and women) to make decisions over family resources including labour are shown to affect the efficiency and sustainability of water programmes in the Asia-Pacific region (Lahiri-Dutt 2006). Gender and inequality introduce power as an element that influences normative orders, or even the very definition of the 'legal', and alerts us to beliefs and perceptions about what normative regimes can achieve.

The treatment of different resource regimes in this chapter has been selective, and does not do justice to the richness of debate that exists on each theme. The purpose here has been to illustrate the possibilities of applying critical legal pluralism approaches to the struggles and conflicts over resources and environmental issues in India. This preliminary exercise, it is hoped, would provide a launch pad for a fuller analysis of specific resource sectors by locating them within larger ecological regimes, and by giving equal credence to issues of normativity and environmental *phronesis*.

Conclusion

In developing a critique of critical legal pluralism for analysing resource-based conflicts, inequalities and normative regimes in India, this chapter makes a case for more attention to practices that appear to be, but are not necessarily normative, and for taking the role of communities and individuals as law-breakers more seriously. The latter implies trying to understand whether law-breaking is a symptom or a solution, whether it derives from the law-making subjectivities of individuals and groups, or simply reflects their survival strategies and livelihood practices. At the same time, it is also essential that we be aware of a 'retreat from critical theory' and its substitution 'by a pragmatic empiricism' (Johnson 2004) that is to be observed in the new institutionalism of Ostrom (1990), North (1989) and others. The focus on collective action, common pool resource management and institutional arrangements that has resulted from environmental movements and struggles has of course alerted us to the normative capacities of resource-dependent ecosystem people, their role as law-making subjects and their ability to create new meanings for law and legal systems. However, despite the clear normative concerns of new institutionalism, it also reflects a 'retreat from normative theorizing' (Johnson 2004). The modest aim of this chapter is to bring in some criticality to the topic through an emphasis on critical legal pluralism and its flaws, the normative subjectivities of law-breakers as much as law-makers, the distinction and relationship between practice and norms, and the ecological regimes within which struggles around specific natural resources are located and find resonance.

The limited success of activists, policy-makers and scholars in making a difference on environmental equity issues in India is usually explained as an outcome of colonial and post-colonial instrumentalist approaches to resources (Grove, Damodaran and Sangwan 1998; Guha and Gadgil 1989; Jewitt 1995; Ranagarajan 1996; Sivaramakrishnan 1995). This chapter argues that policies, laws and institutions that aim to effect greater equity in resource sharing (such as with regard to water, forests, fisheries, minerals, pasture) need to be informed by a comprehension of broader ecological regimes and livelihood dependencies that are embedded within social structures. The latter give rise to socio-environmental practices whose normative basis cannot be easily captured without first comprehending strategies of survival and forms of sociality and subjectivity. If critical legal pluralism is to contribute even if in a small discursive way to a larger emancipatory project, it must, as Sousa Santos (1995: 582) insists, find ways of confronting and addressing the issues of 'emergent subjectivity and sociability'. The logic of practice, the relationship between practice and the evolution of norms, and the idea of an integrated ecological regime are some of the schemes that can aid us in capturing how resource-dependent subjects generate and establish a legal subjectivity and normative authority.

Acknowledgements

I wish to thank Maarten Bavinck for a critical and thorough review and comments on the chapter that has vastly improved the content and arguments. I also thank an anonymous reviewer and Amalendu Jyotishi for comments and suggestions, as well students of my Law and Governance course through the years who have helped me learn along the way by asking interesting questions and contributing to discussions.

Notes

1 The ideas presented in this chapter largely emerged from teaching a course on 'Law, Governance, Rights, and Development', especially the modules pertaining to natural resource management and governance. The course was offered as a graduate-level elective for the students of M.Tech. (in different engineering disciplines), M.Phil. (Planning and Development), and PhD (in social science disciplines), at the Indian Institute of Technology, Bombay. It has been taught from 2002 to 2012 with breaks in 2009 and 2011. This chapter also benefited from discussions with doctoral students working on natural resource themes, specifically on the problems of interpreting data in the Indian context using theoretical perspectives largely derived from legal/philosophical approaches that have originated in other social contexts. In particular I would like to acknowledge discussions with Wati Walling, Dibesh Deb Barma and Soma Kishore Parthasarathy.

2 Washbrook's explicit focus on law and agrarian society precludes a discussion of legal pluralism. Most environmental historians of colonial India generally look upon law as an instrument of imperial control and domination; where customary laws are discussed, this is usually from a perspective of conservation; the legal pluralism debate is usually not specifically cited or used.

3 By 'normative regime', I refer to the standard definition of normative orders enunciated by scholars of legal pluralism, namely the formal and informal systems that provide and give legitimacy to 'processes of establishing rules, securing compliance to these rules, and punishing rule-breakers', and which appear to be 'natural and taken for granted' (Merry 1988: 870–871).

4 For an overview of some of these movements and struggles, see Sundar 2011, and Parthasarathy 2003; resource-dependent communities, occupational groups and individuals involved in law-breaking in an urban context are discussed in Parthasarathy 2011.

5 Nationalist, Subaltern and Marxist represent the three significant theoretical strands deployed in understanding resource conflicts and environmental struggles in colonial and post-colonial India. Few of the studies derive their theoretical approaches or frameworks from legal-philosophical strands of social science theorising.

6 That is, deriving definitions, interpretations and explanations of legal and normative problems purely from a priori or other definitions of the 'legal'. See Tamanaha 2000 and Kleinhans and Macdonald 1997, for an elaboration of the critique of essentialism in legal anthropology and legal pluralism studies.

7 In terms that are purely utilitarian in the short term, especially in terms of the anthropogenic use of resources, without factoring in larger issues of ecosystems, deep ecology and socio-cultural and spiritual approaches to the resources of nature.

8 The reference here is not only to the classic sociological perspective of the embeddedness of knowledge, concepts and theories, and perceptions of reality in specific social contexts and structures of social relations and interactions, but also beliefs and perspectives about observed facts.

9 Such assumptions are to be found in the post-modernist or romanticised environmental critiques of colonial modernity e.g. Shiva, Alvares. Bayly provides a counter-argument to point out continuities across pre-colonial and colonial periods in resource governance regimes (Bayly 1999 cited in Sivaramakrishnan 2008). On the influence of an imagined past on later critiques of colonial and post-colonial environmental policies, see Sivaramakrishnan 1995.

10 Deep ecology refers to an environmental philosophical ethics that believes in the inherent worth of non-living beings. It has been popularised and theorised in India by environmentalists such as Sunderlal Bahuguna.

11 The idea of law as a semi-autonomous social field was theorised by Sally Falk Moore as a social field that 'can generate rules and customs and symbols internally, but that … is also vulnerable to rules and decisions and other forces emanating from the larger world by which it is surrounded. The semi-autonomous social field has rule-making capacities, and the means to induce or coerce compliance; but it is simultaneously set in a larger social matrix which can, and does, affect and invade it, sometimes at the invitation of persons inside it, sometimes at its own instance' (Moore 1973: 720).

12 Robbins et al. (2009) show the irony involved in law-breakers actually favouring a corrupt system that allows them to break laws, and the benefits of such a regime.

13 The relationship between sociality and the breakdown of normative authority leading to farmers' suicides on a large scale in India is brought by Vasavi 1999.

14 Forest committees can refer to a range of local or village-level user groups that have been set up in India as a result of several state-sponsored programmes and legislations, as well as international agency (e.g. World Bank) sponsored resource conservation and management programmes.

15 I wish to thank Soma Kishore Parthasarathy whose ongoing work attempts to redress this gap. She shows (in her work on southern Rajasthan) that even where policy-makers are sensitive to the need to regenerate and redesign access to the commons, a strong gender focus is missing to the detriment of women who constitute the most heavily dependent group on the commons for food, income and nutrition security.

16 For a discussion of diverse attempts to 'commonise' the public and privately owned resources in an urban context, and the law-breaking involved in these, see Parthasarathy 2011.

17 I thank Mr Rambhau Patil, a long-term and veteran fishworkers' activist for these insights. See also Parthasarathy 2011 for a more environmental understanding of the 'urban', and Karmarkar 2012, for a study of endangered fishing livelihoods in the context of globalisation.

18 The Samata judgment refers to a judgment of the Supreme Court of India on a petition filed by Samata – a NGO fighting against land alienation among adivasi populations in the coastal region of Andhra Pradesh. The judgment is regarded as path-setting, as it declared null and void all land-transfers for private mining in the forested areas that fall under the Fifth Schedule of the Indian constitution. Further it cancelled all mining leases granted by the government in Scheduled Areas. The judgment also urged the state to involve tribal cooperatives in mining activities while complying with the

Forest Conservation Act and the Environment Protection Act, in association with Gram Sabhas under the provisions of the Panchayat (Extension to Scheduled Areas) Act. In addition the judgment made it mandatory to set aside 20 per cent of the net profits from mining activities for providing educational, health and infrastructure facilities in those tribal areas where mining is carried out.

19 The Mullaperiyar dam is a century-old masonry dam on the Periyar river in Kerala but controlled and operated by the state of Tamil Nadu. The controversy is about the safety of the dam, raising its level and the fairness of the lease agreement. The people of Kerala wish to decommission the existing dam and construct a new one in the interests of safety, while the state of Tamil Nadu is worried about agricultural losses due to decreased supply of irrigation water following from a possible reduction in the dam height or in the interregnum of decommissioning and re-construction.

20 The narrowness can be described in instrumental terms, i.e. the use of a resource, or in sectoral terms, to refer to a particular resource such as water or forests.

References

Adams, W.A. (2012) 'I made a promise to a lady: critical legal pluralism as improvised law in Buffy the Vampire Slayer', *Critical Studies in Improvisation/Études critiques en improvisation*, vol. 6, no. 1, www.criticalimprov.com/article/view/1083/1707.

Agrawal, A. (1999) *Greener Pastures: Politics, Markets and Community Among a Migrant Pastoral People*, Durham, NC: Duke University Press.

Agrawal, A. and C.C. Gibson (1999) 'Enchantment and disenchantment: the role of community in natural resource conservation', *World Development*, vol. 27, no. 4, pp. 629–649.

Appadurai, A. (2006) 'Is homo hierarchicus?', in R.S. Khare (ed.) *Caste, Hierarchy, and Individualism: Indian Critiques of Louis Dumont's Contributions*, Oxford: Oxford University Press, pp. 177–191.

Baerlocher, B. and P. Burger (2010) 'Ecological regimes: towards a conceptual integration of biophysical environment into social theory', in Matthias Gross and Harald Heinrichs (eds) *Environmental Sociology: European Perspectives and Interdisciplinary Challenges*, Springer, Netherlands, pp. 79–93.

Bavinck, M. (2001) 'Caste panchayats and the regulation of fisheries along Tamil Nadu's Coromandel coast', *Economic and Political Weekly*, vol. 36, no. 13, pp. 1088–1094.

Bavinck, M. (2013) 'Governance, poverty and social justice in the coastal fisheries of India', in Nicky Pouw and I.S.A. Baud (eds) *Local Governance and Poverty in Developing Nations*, vol. 31, Routledge, pp. 115–136.

Baviskar, A. (2001) 'Forest management as political practice: Indian experiences with the accommodation of multiple interests', *International Journal of Agricultural Resources, Governance and Ecology*, vol. 1, no. 3, pp. 243–263.

Baviskar, A. et al. (2011) 'A plan for resolving Mullaperiyar conflict', *Economic and Political Weekly*, vol. 46, no. 51, pp. 4–5.

Bourdieu, P. (1998) *Practical Reason: On the Theory of Action*, Palo Alto, CA: Stanford University Press.

Brara, R. (2006) *Shifting Landscapes: The Making and Remaking of Village Commons in India*, New Delhi: Oxford University Press.

Bromley, D.W. and M.M. Cernea (1989) *The Management of Common Property Natural Resources: Some Conceptual and Operational Fallacies*, World Bank Discussion Papers 57, Washington, DC: World Bank Publications.

Chouhan, H.A. (2012) 'Coastal zone management and fishing community in Mumbai', M.Phil. dissertation, Indian Institute of Technology, Bombay.

Chouhan, H.A. and D. Parthasarathy (2013) 'CRZ rules, urbanisation and livelihoods in the margins in globalizing Mumbai: impact on the fishing community', paper presented at the National Seminar on Development, Identity and Politics: Identities of the Marginalised in Contemporary India.

Cleaver, F. (1998) 'Incentives and informal institutions: gender and the management of water', *Agriculture and Human Values*, vol. 15, pp. 347–360.

Das, D. (2007) 'Cultural politics, identity crisis and private capitalism in coal mines of Meghalaya, Northeast India', Artisanal and Small-Scale Mining in Asia-Pacific Case Study Series, Case Study No. 16. Artisanal and Small-Scale Mining (ASM) in Asia-Pacific Portal, www.asmasiapacific.org/download_file.php?uid=100.

Das, V. (2006) 'The anthropological discourse on India', in R.S. Khare (ed.) *Caste, Hierarchy, and Individualism: Indian Critiques of Louis Dumont's Contributions*, Oxford: Oxford University Press, pp. 192–205.

Eberhard, C. and N. Gupta (2005) 'Legal pluralism in India : an introduction', *Indian Socio-Legal Journal*, vol. XXXI, pp. 1–10.

Ghai, D. (1993) 'Foreword', in J. Friedmann and H. Rangan (eds) *In Defense of Livelihood: Comparative Studies on Environmental Action*, Sterling, VA: Kumarian Press, pp. vii–viii.

Grove, R., V. Damodaran and S. Sangwan (1998) *Nature and the Orient: The Environmental History of South and South-East Asia*, Oxford: Oxford University Press.

Guha, R. (1999) *Elementary Aspects of Peasant Insurgency in Colonial India*, Durham, NC: Duke University Press.

Guha, R. (2000) *The Unquiet Woods: Ecological Change and Peasant Resistance in the Himalaya*, Berkeley, CA: University of California Press.

Guha, R. and M. Gadgil (1989) 'State forestry and social conflict in British India', *Past & Present*, vol. 123, no. 1, pp. 141–177.

Guha, R. and M. Gadgil (1992) *This Fissured Land: An Ecological History of India*, Oxford: Oxford University Press.

Guha, R. and M. Gadgil (1995) *Ecology and Equity: The Use and Abuse of Nature in Contemporary India*, London: Routledge.

Gunder, M. (2003) 'Passionate planning for the others' desire: an agonistic response to the dark side of planning', *Progress in Planning*, vol. 60, no. 3, pp. 235–319.

Harris, M. (1965) 'The myth of the sacred cow', in Anthony Leeds and Andrew P. Vayda (eds) *Man, Culture and Animals*, Washington DC: American Association for the Advancement of Science, pp. 217–228.

Jewitt, S. (1995) 'Europe's "Others"? Forestry policy and practices in colonial and postcolonial India', *Environment and Planning D: Society and Space*, vol. 13, no. 1, pp. 67–90.

Jodha, N.S. (1985) 'Population growth and the decline of common property resources in Rajasthan', *Population and Development Review*, vol. 11, no. 2, pp. 247–264.

Jodha, N.S. (2001) *Life on the Edge: Sustaining Agriculture and Community Resources in Fragile Environments*, Oxford: Oxford University Press.

Johnson, C. (2004) 'Uncommon ground: the "poverty of history" in common property discourse', *Development and Change*, vol. 35, no. 3, pp. 407–434.

Karmarkar, D. (2012) *Fishy Spaces: Globalisation and Livelihood of Indigenous Fisherman: A Case of Mumbai*, Saarbrücken: Lambert Academic Publishing.

Kleinhans, M.M. and R.A. Macdonald (1997) 'What is critical legal pluralism,' *Canadian Journal of Law & Society*, vol. 12, pp. 25–63.

Kumar, D. (1990) 'The evolution of colonial science in India: natural history and the East India Company', in J.M. MacKenzie (ed.) *Imperialism and the Natural World*, Manchester: Manchester University Press, pp. 51–66.

Kurien, J. (1991) *Running the Commons and Responses of the Commoners: Coastal Over-fishing and Fishermen's Actions in Kerala State, India*, Geneva: United Nations Research Institute for Social Development (UNRISD).

Lahiri-Dutt, K. (ed.) (2006) *Fluid Bonds: Views on Gender and Water*, Kolkata: Stree Publishers.

Macdonald, R.A. (1998) 'Critical legal pluralism as a construction of normativity and the emergence of law', in A. Lajoie et al. (eds) *Théories et émergence du droit: Pluralisme surdetérmination et effectivité*, Montreal: Editions Themis, pp. 12–23.

Meinzen-Dick, R. and A. Knox (1999) 'Collective action, property rights, and devolution of natural resource management: A conceptual framework', Workshop on Collective Action, Property Rights, and Devolution of Natural Resource, Puerto Azul, Philippines, June: https://library.conservation.org/Published%20Documents/2009/1999%20Meinzen.%20Collective%20action%20property%20rights%20_%20devolution%20of%20natural%20resource%20mgmt.pdf.

Merry, S.E. (1988) 'Legal pluralism', *Law and Society Review*, vol. 22, no. 5, pp. 869–896.

Moore, S. F. (1973) 'Law and social change: the semi-autonomous social field as an appropriate subject of study', *Law and Society Review*, vol. 7, pp. 719–746.

Mosse, D. (1997) 'Ecological zones and the culture of collective action: the history and social organisation of a tank irrigation system in Tamil Nadu', *South Indian Studies*, vol. 3, no. 1, pp. 1–88.

Mosse, D. (2003) *The Rule of Water: Statecraft, Ecology and Collective Action in South India*, Oxford: Oxford University Press.

North, D. C. (1989) 'Institutions and economic growth: an historical introduction', *World Development*, vol. 17, no. 9, pp. 1319–1332.

Ostrom, E. (1990) *Governing the Commons: The Evolution of Institutions for Collective Action*, Cambridge: Cambridge University Press.

Padmaja, R. (2012) 'Mapping the social network architecture of rural communities: gender and technological innovations in the semi-arid tropics of India', PhD dissertation, Indian Institute of Technology, Bombay.

Parthasarathy, D. (2003) 'Law, property rights, and social exclusion: a capabilities and entitlements approach to legal pluralism', in R. Pradhan (ed.) Proceedings of the XIIIth International Congress of the Commission on Folk Law and Legal Pluralism, 7–10 April 2002, Chiang Mai, Thailand.

Parthasarathy, D. (2007) 'Land laws, minerals, and development: a case for legislative innovations', in C. Eberhard (ed.), *Law, Land Use and the Environment: Afro-Indian Dialogues*, Pondichery: IFP, pp. 67–92.

Parthasarathy, D. (2011) 'Hunters, gatherers, and foragers in a metropolis: commonizing the private and public in Mumbai', *Economic and Political Weekly*, vol. 46, no. 50, pp. 54–63.

Pathak, N., E. Taraporewala, M. Wani, A. Bose and A. Kothari (2003) 'Towards self-rule and forest conservation in Mendha-Lekha Village, Gadchiroli'. http://cmsdata.iucn.org/downloads/mendha_india_report_icca_grassroots_discussions.pdf.

Piper, T. (2010) 'The Improvisational Flavour of Law, the Legal Taste of Improvisation', *Critical Studies in Improvisation/Études critiques en improvisation*, vol. 6, no. 1. https://journal.lib.uoguelph.ca/index.php/csieci/article/viewArticle/1191/1725.

Rai, S.P. (2007) 'Livestock-environment interaction in watersheds: a case study of Kohane watershed project in Maharashtra', M.Phil. dissertation, Indian Institute of Technology, Bombay.

Rangarajan, M. (1996) *Fencing the Forest: Conservation and Ecological Change in India's Central Provinces: 1860–1914*, Oxford: Oxford University Press.

Robbins, P. et al. (2009) 'Conservation as it is: Illicit resource use in a wildlife reserve in India', *Human Ecology*, vol. 37, no. 5, pp. 559–575.

Sathyapalan, J. and M. Gopinath Reddy (2010) *Recognition of Forest Rights and Livelihoods of the Tribal Communities – A Study of Western Ghats Region, Kerala State*, Hyderabad, Andhra Pradesh: CESS Monograph/RULNR Monograph, Centre for Economic and Social Studies.

Sivaramakrishnan, K. (1995) 'Colonialism and forestry in India: imagining the past in present politics', *Comparative Studies in Society and History*, vol. 37, no. 1, pp. 3–40.

Sivaramakrishnan, K. (2008) 'Science, environment and empire history: comparative perspectives from forests in colonial India', *Environment and History*, vol. 14, no. 1, pp. 41–65.

Sousa Santos, B. de (1995) 'Three metaphors for a new conception of law: the Frontier, the Baroque, and the South', *Law and Society Review*, vol. 29, pp. 569–584.

Sundar, N. (2000) 'Unpacking the "joint" in joint forest management', *Development and Change*, vol. 31, no. 1, pp. 255–279.

Sundar, N. (2011) 'The rule of law and citizenship in central India: post-colonial dilemmas', *Citizenship Studies*, vol. 15, no. 3/4, pp. 419–432.

Tamanaha, B.Z. (2000) 'An non-essentialist version of legal pluralism', *Journal of Law and Society*, vol. 27, no. 2, pp. 296–321.

Vasavi, A.R. (1999) *Harbingers of Rain: Land and Life in South India*, Oxford: Oxford University Press.

Von Oppen, M. and K.V. Subba Rao (1980) *Tank Irrigation in Semi-arid Tropical India. Part I: Historical Development and Spatial Distribution*, Patancheru: ICRISAT Progress Report No. 5.

Walling, W.A. (2011) 'Land, politics and conflict: political ecology of a village in Nagaland', PhD dissertation, Indian Institute of Technology, Bombay.

Warhaft, S. (2001) 'No parking at the bunder: fisher people and survival in capitalist Mumbai', *South Asia: Journal of South Asian Studies*, vol. 24, no. 2, pp. 213–223.

Washbrook, D. (1981) 'Law, state and agrarian society in colonial India', *Modern Asian Society*, vol. 15, no. 3, pp. 649–721.

3 The Godavarman judgment

Erasing the plurality of land use in Gudalur, Nilgiris[1]

Ajit Menon

Introduction

In 1995 T.N. Godavarman Thirumulpad, a member of the Nilambur Kovilagam family, filed a writ petition in the Supreme Court in the hope of preventing further deforestation in the Gudalur region of the Nilgiris, Tamil Nadu.[2] In his petition, T.N. Godavarman Thirumulpad alluded to a pristine forested past of the Gudalur region under his family's control and bemoaned the destruction of the forests thereafter. One year later, on 12 December 1996, the Supreme Court reacted by passing interim orders that instructed all state governments to stop tree felling and the conversion of forests to non-forests without proper application of the Forest Conservation Act (FCA). The Tamil Nadu government, in addition, was instructed to stop all tree felling on janmam lands in Gudalur, lands that historically belonged to the Nilambur Kovilagam and other janmis.[3] Forests, the Supreme Court pronounced, should be understood in the dictionary sense of the word.[4]

The Supreme Court went further. It directed state governments to set up committees to assess the extent of lands that were not legally classified as forests but fell in the dictionary meaning and to oversee the compliance with the FCA. Most states, including Tamil Nadu, formed state-level empowered committees. In 2002, the Central Empowered Committee (CEC) was established. The CEC's main purpose was to adjudicate on matters of law and make recommendations to the Supreme Court. A Special Investigation Team (SIT) was also established by the Supreme Court in 2000 to check illegal movement of forest produce.

In this chapter I aim to locate the Godavarman judgment[5] within the wider political economy of conservation, analyse the normative position of the judgment in terms of land use and see what its impact has been on small farmers[6] in Gudalur, the area from which the writ petition originated. My engagement with legal pluralism, the subject of this volume, is in terms of what I call the 'plurality of desirable land uses'. I am less interested in the multiple legal domains that legal pluralism scholars argue exist than in the multiple normative visions of land use promoted at different points of time in varied combinations of the statutory and customary.[7] I suggest that the Supreme Court's judgment and its understanding of conservation privileged a 'more forest is better' approach, in the process erasing the complex history of land use in the region and the state's role in promoting such land use.

There are multiple dimensions to my analysis. First, I briefly locate Gudalur and highlight the competing imaginations of what Gudalur 'should be'. Second, I try to situate the Supreme Court's Godavarman judgment within the wider contours of public interest litigation (PIL)[8] in India, paying attention to the Supreme Court's defence of conservation and the particular form of conservation that the Court privileged. Third, I question the inherent assumptions of the Supreme Court interim judgment in terms of attributability vis-à-vis forest degradation by looking at the history of state priorities during the colonial and post-colonial periods and illustrating how the state was complicit in the transformation of the forested landscape into a wooded plantation economy. Fourth, I highlight how the judgment has reinforced the labelling of small farmers as encroachers, no longer treating them as 'necessary labour'.[9] The chapter is therefore both an attempt to understand the judgment and a normative critique of it in terms of the privileging of forests as the preferred land use.

Imagining Gudalur

The broad region of Gudalur, comprising Gudalur and Pandalur taluks, is situated in the lower Nilgiris and is adjacent to Wayanad district of Kerala, which lies to the west. According to the 2011 census, the population of the two taluks was 231,073. From a heavily forested area in the mid-nineteenth century, gradually Gudalur was converted into a plantation economy, first coffee plantations and later tea. The bulk of Gudalur's inhabitants migrated to the region in the latter half of the nineteenth and twentieth centuries because of the perceived availability of land or to work on large plantations. In-migration to the region was encouraged by state policies that were aimed at revenue generation and the production of food. Gudalur today is comprised mostly of small-scale tea estates and large corporate estates. More than 90 per cent of all landholdings are categorized as small.

The downside of such in-migration was that adivasis (tribals) who resided in this area were increasingly marginalized. Adivasis engaged mostly in shifting cultivation and collection of forest produce and did not have 'formal' property rights to their land. Hence, it was easy for migrants to claim land as settled agriculture was uncommon. Some migrants were able to obtain formal title to land while others encroached upon large estate lands (Menon et al. 2013).

Gudalur is also an important 'conservation corridor'. Its forests are rich in biodiversity, encompass a number of elephant corridors and are important catchment areas for rivers. Gudalur is part of the Nilgiris Biosphere and contained within it is the Mudumalai Tiger Reserve (earlier Mudumalai National Park and Wildlife Sanctuary). A number of legislations have also been passed that are specific to Gudalur and other parts of the Nilgiris, namely The Tamil Nadu Preservation of Private Forest Act, 1949 and The Tamil Nadu Hill Areas (Preservation of Trees) Act, 1955.

These competing socio-economic and conservation priorities signal different imaginations of what Gudalur should look like. They also suggest the possibility of conflict over competing priorities and trade-offs between different priorities.

It is with this background in mind that the Supreme Court's Godavarman judgment should be examined and an analysis undertaken with regard to the 'forest question' in Gudalur.

The Godavarman judgment: a political economy and conceptual reflection

In an interview to *Down to Earth* magazine in 2002, T.N. Godavarman Thirumulpad explained why he filed a PIL in the Supreme Court against the Union of India in 1995:

> I was travelling through Gudalur and saw large areas of forests being felled and timber logs stacked up for sale. These forests at one time belonged to my family, the Nilambur Kovilagam. The ecological history of the Nilgiris has always been closely linked to the history of the Nilambur Kovilagam .... The trees were being felled in violation of various legislations and rules.

His contention was, in other words, that his family had protected these forests in the past but that these very same forests had been subsequently degraded despite the existence of legislation aimed at protecting them. His appeal to the Court was that these violations should be stopped.

The Supreme Court took T.N. Godavarman's contentions seriously. Besides passing general orders that restricted felling of trees and non-forest use of forest land throughout the country, the Court passed specific directives for Tamil Nadu and Gudalur. These included the following:

1 A complete ban on felling of trees in all 'forest areas' except:

   a Trees which have been planted and grown, and are not of spontaneous growth, and;
   b In areas which were not forests earlier but were cleared for any reason.

2 Order to the state government to constitute a committee within four weeks of the judgment to identify all 'forests'.
3 Concession to tribals who are part of the social forestry programme in respect of patta (private) lands, to continue to grow and cut according to the Government Scheme provided that they grow and cut trees in accordance with the law applicable.
4 Permission to plantations to cut planted trees in the plantations so long as they have been identified by Tamil Nadu Tea Plantation Corporation Limited (TANTEA)[10] and is done under the supervision of the statutory committee constituted by the State Government.
5 Permission to plantations to cut fuel wood trees outside of forest areas if approved by TANTEA in their report.[11] Eucalyptus and wattle trees can also be felled in these areas as permitted by the statutory committee.

6 Trees in 'forest areas' identified by the State Government and are not in active use by plantation cannot be felled and there can be no expansion of plantations so as to lead to encroachment.
7 Trees that are already cut before the interim orders of the Court dated can be removed but not those in janmam areas. This is a one-time measure.
8 Felling of trees in Janmam Lands is subject to the Civil Appeal Nos. 367 to 375 of 1977 of C.A. Nos. 1344-45 of 1976. After orders are passed, this aspect may be re-examined.[12]

Of most relevance to the Gudalur area were the restrictions placed on felling of trees in plantations and in janmam lands. Gudalur is predominantly a tea plantation economy, approximately 45 per cent janmam and 55 per cent non-janmam.[13] While the judgment allowed farmers and estate owners to cut plantation trees in non-janmam areas, it specified that such cutting was limited to the trees identified by TANTEA and to areas within plantations that were not considered forests. In janmam areas, tree felling was completely prohibited subject to the outcome of litigation that was ongoing against the Janmam Estate (Abolition and Conversion into Ryotwari) Act of 1969 (hereafter the Janmam Abolition Act). The consequences of the order will be examined in a later section. For now, I try to understand how the judgment came about and the conceptual parameters of the judgment in terms of conservation and land use.

The 1996 interim judgment was one of many interventions by the Supreme Court in response to 'environmental' PILs. The Court had from the early 1980s increasingly allowed third-party litigation so as to protect what was perceived of as public interest in domains as varied as the environment, child labour and prisoners' rights (Sahu 2008: 377). The Court increasingly took the position that the executive was not adequately upholding laws and even fundamental rights, hence the need for its intervention. The Court, moreover, in trying to ensure that environmental laws were implemented and that polluters pay for the damage they cause in relation to the environment, proceeded on the assumption that doing so would ensure a better quality of life for its citizens (Sahu 2008: 390).

Whether this has been the case in general and in the particular case of the Godavarman judgment requires a more detailed enquiry. Has the Supreme Court first of all always ruled in favour of environmental conservation concerns? When it has, what form has environmental conservation taken? And for which public has conservation been good, a question of utmost importance when one recognizes that the public is itself segmented? With regard to the first question posed, a number of scholars (Bhushan 2004; Menon 2007; Sahu 2008) have argued that the Supreme Court has not always taken a uniform position in favour of environmental conservation. Though it is difficult to generalize about judgments, the indication is that environmental conservation has often in the past taken a back seat when it has conflicted with large development projects justified in the name of 'national development'.[14] As Bhushan has argued (2004), this is likely to have been the case in the 1990s and early 2000s with the opening up of the economy and a renewed focus on economic growth. Environmental conservation, however, has taken precedence in cases that appear to be driven by more middle-class concerns such as environmental pollution and the preservation of 'natural' landscapes for tourism or wildlife protection. The Godavarman case is an example of the latter, a so-called pristine hill environment in danger of being denuded of its forested landscape. In other words, there is some evidence to suggest that Supreme Court judgments have themselves had a hierarchy of conservation priorities in relation to development and the form it takes. What I argue later is that while the Godavarman judgment might well have been aimed at protecting public forests, it had a detrimental impact on some local livelihoods.

There are a number of more case specific factors that also contributed to this particular judgment. First, the Godavarman judgment had its own local historical context. Forest protection (including protection of private forests and trees) became very much part of the state agenda in the mid- twentieth century. The first law enacted was the Madras (later Tamil Nadu) Preservation of Private Forests Act of 1949 that aimed at preventing the destruction of private forests and restricting forest privileges granted by janmis to their lessees. This was followed by the Madras (later Tamil Nadu) Private Forests (Assumption of Management) Act of 1961 that went further and empowered the state to take over private forests and manage them for a period of time (Section 3). As these acts were not successful in preventing the conversion of forest lands into estates, the Janmam Abolition Act, an act aimed primarily to introduce ryotwari settlement[15] in janmam estates and undertake agrarian reform by bestowing lands on farmers, was used as a means to claim back undeveloped forest land[16] (see later section). The Godavarman judgment was, therefore, very much in line with earlier legislative attempts by the executive to assume and manage private forests.

Second, one must remember that Gudalur is part of the Nilgiri Biosphere, an international biosphere reserve constituted by UNESCO in 1986. It is an ecologically important landscape in terms of wildlife, biodiversity and watershed management. The writ petition by T.N. Godavarman Thirumulpad was, therefore, likely to catch the imagination of the public at large and the courts as well. The continued reluctance and/or hesitancy of the courts and the government to come up with a solution that could result in 'forests' being converted to non-forest land is also because the wider Western Ghats has been proposed as a UNESCO World Heritage Site. The Wildlife Protection Amendment Act of 2006, that provides for tiger reserves as a legal category, and the consequent creation of Mudumalai Tiger Reserve have reinforced the region's location at the centre of environmental conservation.

Finally, the Supreme Court was some distance from the 'scene of the crime'. To what extent the Court engaged with local actors in passing the judgment is not clear. The indication, however, is that the judgment was based more on these wider supra-local conservation discourses than a detailed analysis of the relationship between forests, plantations and livelihoods, or wider normative concerns about competing land use possibilities in Gudalur. A case could have been made, for example, that adivasis depended on forests more and hence the need to preserve them. However, the interim judgment only mentions adivasi rights in terms of their rights to private lands within social forestry schemes. Even when the Supreme Court established the CEC, it was primarily to undertake investigations regarding matters of law at the request of the Supreme Court.

From a land use point of view, the Supreme Court's judgment appeared to be premised on the belief that more forests are better for society. Equally important questions such as 'for whom are more forests better?' or 'what type of forests are better for whom?' were not debated. This assumption, as Fairhead and Leach (1996) in the context of central Africa have argued, is not only problematic factually but also potentially detrimental to local livelihoods. Equally important, as Rosencranz and Lele (2008) have highlighted, is that the distinction between forests (defined in a dictionary sense) and non-forests undermines fluid and varied land use practices in the country that transgress dictionary-defined or property rights-based classifications of forests. Put another way, the boundary between forest and non-forest lands is not always clear when small farmers collect fuelwood, graze their cattle or even practise agriculture. Farmers cultivate forests lands and collect fuelwood on private lands (not only forests). While the judgment defined forests according to a dictionary definition, this was done so as to facilitate the Forest Department's takeover of these lands. Moreover, it is important to note that even non-forest lands were wooded landscapes. Developed plantations of tea require shade trees. Finally, small-scale farmers, who comprise a significant percentage of the population, have large areas under home gardens – often as much as 400 trees per hectare.[17]

The other problematic assumption of the judgment was that forests are best managed by the Forest Department. The Supreme Court, while reprimanding the bureaucracy for not adequately implementing the FCA, continued to put its faith in that same bureaucracy by insisting that the FCA be more judiciously implemented and that too in dictionary-defined forests. The Court, in other words, privileged the state's role in implementing the FCA as a means to curb deforestation. In the next section, I question the Court's decision through a historical look at land use transformation in Gudalur.

State–janmi[18] dynamics and the transformation of the forested landscape

There is little disagreement that large areas of Gudalur's moist deciduous and evergreen forests have been converted into plantations. What requires more scrutiny, however, are the reasons behind land use change and the state's role in it. This history is important not only to pinpoint attributability for 'forest degradation' but also to question the Court's remedy, namely more robust implementation of law as a means to prevent further degradation.

Gudalur's land use history is complex and different from other areas that fell under the Madras Presidency. First, unlike in most other areas where the colonial state took full territorial control of land, in Gudalur approximately 45 per cent of the 72,000 hectares remained under the control of janmis.[19] It is in these areas that forests were first cleared for plantations. Ironically, given the writ petition by

T.N. Godavarman Thirumulpad, it was his family the Nilambur Kovilagam that leased out much of their land to British planters to grow coffee and later tea.[20] The first lease was given in 1845 to J.H. Ouchterlony. The Nilambur Kovilagam was to lease out approximately 20,000 hectares of land to estates out of which large private or corporate estates accounted for 16,000 hectares and smaller estates 4,000. Ouchterlony estate, now named Manjushree estate, was the largest area leased by the Kovilagam family in Gudalur. Even in non-janmam areas, the colonial state was to follow suit by escheating large parts of land and selling them under the Madras Wasteland Rules, 1863.

The promotion of the plantation economy by the colonial regime was primarily aimed at raising revenue. Whereas in janmam lands, the janmi charged janmabhogam and the colonial state an assessment on cultivated land, in non-janmam areas the government claimed both the janmabhogam and assessment. In the latter, wasteland was sold under the Waste Land Rules, for between 8 annas and Rs 2 per acre (for forest land). A coffee tax of Rs 2 was levied under the Waste Land Rules on all land cultivated with coffee, be it janmi or government escheated land. In order to encourage the planting of coffee this tax was only payable after the third year of planting giving planters the incentive to put more land under plantation crops.[21] A regularized system of revenue assessment, therefore, slowly emerged in Gudalur. R. Cockerell, the Commissioner of Nilgiris, in a letter written to the Acting Secretary of the Board of Revenue in 1875, implored that rules governing land use should be that of a business policy and that a forest should not be reserved 'merely because it is picturesque'.[22] The settlement of Gudalur in the 1870s and 1880s by the colonial state was a means by which the colonial administration ascertained the extent of land cultivated so as to maximize its revenue.[23] Revenue settlement, notwithstanding, the British continued to accept the proprietorship of janmis. As I (and my co-authors) have argued in another paper (Menon et al. 2013), the janmam areas of Gudalur were a zone of accommodation where the British felt their economic interests were best served through janmi proprietorship of land. This was the case because the costs of monitoring the cultivation of large tracts of land would have been very high. By allowing the janmis to retain ownership of land and to collect assessment from the janmis directly lowered the transaction costs of the British while ensuring revenue. Gudalur was, therefore, a mosaic of land tenure systems – each playing its role in the colonial state's drive to increase revenue.

Even in the post-colonial period, the state supported the growth of the plantation economy albeit for different reasons at times. The Grow More Food Campaign between the 1940s and 1960s resulted in in-migration and the further conversion of land, not only for plantation crops but also paddy (rice). Problems of citizenship in erstwhile Ceylon led to the repatriation of almost half a million Tamils from the estates of Ceylon as a result of the signing of the Shastri-Srimavo Pact between India and Ceylon in 1969. Much of this labour ended up in Gudalur as Gudalur had a similar climate to the hill regions of Ceylon. The Tamil Nadu government started TANTEA, mostly in non-janmam areas, so as to absorb labour. Repatriates were also recruited by large estates in erstwhile janmam areas such as Manjushree.[24]

The state provided financial incentives to private estates to absorb repatriates.[25] TANTEA plantations created between 1968 and 1980 comprised about 2,500 hectares and importantly were created by clearfelling of forests.

The colonial state had also promoted other land uses in the late nineteenth century as a way to raise revenue. Gold was discovered in forested areas both on government and private lands in the 1880s though this was only in the Devala and Pandalur regions of Gudalur. Auriferous quartz was seen to be a lucrative source of income. The colonial state's main strategy was to promote private capital in mining and then claim a royalty on gold.[26] The colonial government deputed staff from the Geological Survey to help identify gold-rich areas. Post and telegraph offices, hotels, bungalows and even a racecourse were established in Pandalur to entice private companies to invest in the area (Francis 1908: 17). In janmam areas, the colonial government claimed a percentage of the spoils. In non-janmam areas, the government could do the same or even retain the right to mine lands itself.[27] Although the gold-mining industry did not last for long in the Gudalur region given the limited and poor quality of gold found in the region, while it did last it signalled the colonial government's pre-occupation with raising revenue and its willingness to exploit forested areas.

The colonial state also saw Gudalur as an important source of timber in the late nineteenth century. Mudumalai was under the control of the Nilambur Kovilagam but was leased out to the Forest Department from 1858 onwards, first for a period of five years, to reduce dependence for timber on other hill areas such as the Annamalais and other colonial outposts such as Burma.[28] In 1863, the lease was extended for 99 more years for Rs 3,500 per year.[29] The government was allowed to plant trees but had to pay a stump fee of Rs 1 per felled tree to the Nilambur Kovilagam.[30] The Forest Department, however, had no right to minor forest produce. This was leased out to private individuals. Under Clause 11 of the agreement, the Nilambur Kovilagam also had the right to collect minor forest produce.

Although the Forest Department articulated forest conservation concerns, it was mainly to ensure the sustainable supply of timber. Concerns were particularly expressed that kumri (shifting) cultivation and forest fires would impact sustainable timber yield. In the 1870s, the Commissioner of the Nilgiris expressed this forthrightly by saying that the government must manage Mudumalai better as the supply of teak was dwindling and most of the first-class teak trees had already been cut.[31] J.S. Gamble, Conservator in Charge of the Northern Division of the Nilgiris, ten years later, while expressing hope that young trees of teak (*Tectona grandis*), vengai (*Pterocarpus marsupium*) and puvam (*Schleichera trijuga*) amongst others would mature, acknowledged that no systematic working was taking place.[32] Similarly, while the Nilambur Kovilagam at times included restrictions on tree cutting in leases with tenants, these were progressively diluted over time (Krishnan 2009: 286).

Even when the colonial administration annulled the lease with the Nilambur Kovilagam, reserved the area under Section 26 of the Forest Act in 1889 and drew up working plans (Joseph 1978: 7),[33] the indication is that further denudation of Mudumalai took place. Improvement felling was the strategy adopted by the Forest Department in the late nineteenth and early twentieth centuries. It was stopped in 1910 with the implementation of Cox's Working Plan, though in practice it continued till 1920. Around this time, improvement felling was replaced by clearfelling. The Forest Department's inspection notes of 1926 admit that the working of the forests had led to the removal of 'a great deal more teak than ought to have been removed'.[34]

It is also doubtful whether the constitution of Mudumalai as a reserved forest in 1927 and parts of it into a wildlife sanctuary in 1940 had positive conservancy effects at least in the short-run. This was the case because Mudumalai continued to be imagined in different ways at different points of time and by different colonial administrators. It was one thing to believe that maximizing timber supply and conservancy were mutually realizable, but entirely a different thing to reconcile agriculture and forest protection. People lived in and practised agriculture within Mudumalai. And in the 1940s when the Grow More Food campaign assumed importance because of the Second World War, there were colonial administrators who felt that agriculture should be promoted. Lasrado, the Conservator of Forests in Ootacamund, in fact, expressed concern that Mudumalai was the wrong place for a wildlife sanctuary and that neigbouring Segur would in fact be more suitable given the paddy lands within Mudumalai.[35]

Coffee planting, gold mining and timber procurement shaped the nature of the forested landscape in Gudalur in the second half of the nineteenth century and first half of the twentieth century. Both the colonial state and the Nilambur Kovilagam, in promoting these activities, were primarily interested in maximizing their revenue or in the former's case providing the necessary resources to service the colonial economy. Forests were resource sites that needed to be exploited, both physically and financially, opened up and civilized (Philip 2004). The Nilambur Kovilagam and the colonial state were mutually implicated in this.

The other point highlighted is that while concerns about conservation were regularly raised within the colonial bureaucracy and by the Nilambur Kovilagam family, these conservation concerns were often determined by resource needs or were diluted in actual practice. For example, on the one hand, the scientific workings of Mudumalai's timber reserves were for the most part meant to ensure long-term timber supply. On the other hand, restrictions on tree cutting in janmi plantations became less stringent over time, allowing for the increased expansion of tea. This is not to say that there were no dissenting voices especially within the colonial bureaucracy. The Forest Department, and specific officers in particular, were quite vocal about the need to prevent the rich forests of the region from being felled. More often than not, however, forest protection played second fiddle to resource demands.

From the Janmam Abolition Act to the Godavarman judgment[36]

In the mid-twentieth century, priorities appeared to partly change. In non-janmam areas, the Forest Department had already reserved small tracts of forests under the Madras Forest Act, 1882.[37] In janmam areas, however, it was only in the 1940s that the state took action through protective legislation (also applicable to non-janmam areas). The first law enacted was the Madras Preservation of Private Forests Act of 1949 and was aimed at preventing the destruction of private forests[38] and restricting forest privileges granted by janmis to their lessees (Krishnan 2009: 286). The state obtained power to restrict sale of land (Section 3-1) and restrict the cutting of trees (Section 3-2). However, this Act was not successful, due to the state's limited ability to police private forests. As a result, the Madras[39] Private Forests (Assumption of Management) Act of 1961 was passed. The state under this Act was allowed to take over private forests and manage them for a limited period of time. It served more than 130 notices on farmers/estates in Gudalur. This Act too was met by resistance by farmers and challenged in court by estate owners and hence remained largely ineffectual.

The Janmam Abolition Act, 1969, had the most significant impact on the land situation in the janmam parts of Gudalur. The Act, while intended to introduce ryotwari settlement in janmam estates and institutionalize a system of agrarian reform (Krishnan 2009: 289), became a means by which the state staked claim to undeveloped forest lands in private estates. Sections 8, 9 and 10 conferred rights of ownership on cultivators. Section 8 lands were lands cultivated by janmis. Section 9 lands were lands cultivated by tenants and Section 10 were leased estate lands that had been encroached upon and cultivated for at least 3 years prior to the passing of the Act. Only about 3,500 hectares of land were distributed to cultivators under these sections, less than 10 per cent of the total landholdings of the Nilambur Kovilagam. Almost 17,000 hectares were designated as Section 17 or leased lands and a little more than 5,000 hectares as Section 53 or forest lands (GoTN 1969: 5–11; PUCL 2002).

Section 17 proved to be both the most controversial and telling in terms of its immediate implications. The government retained the right to either extend leases or cancel them on Section 17 land. The government, in other words, decided how Section 17 lands could be used. Lands within Section 17 plantations were categorized as either 'developed' or 'undeveloped'. Developed lands comprised of lands planted with tea whereas undeveloped lands were deemed by the state to be forests. Government was to retain control over undeveloped land. Under Section 11 of the Act, no patta could be granted for lands within estates that contained forests, tank beds, drainage channels and irrigation channels, threshing floors, cattle stands, rivers, streams and other poramboke.[40] According to 'official data' at the time of the Act, out of the approximately 17,000 hectares of Section 17 estate area, 13,500 hectares were 'undeveloped' or forest.

The potentially contradictory aims of the Act from the state's perspective, namely to settle land, implement agrarian reform and claim undeveloped lands as forests, resulted in a struggle in the courts in the 30 or so years after the Act was enacted. First, estates challenged the Act in the Madras High Court on the ground that the settlement process in the late nineteenth century had conferred ryotwari tenure, hence making it non permissible for the government to stake its claim to land in the form of a zamindari-type abolition act. The second contention raised by petitioners in the Supreme Court, after the first challenge was rejected,[41] was that forests were not part of an estate unless they were used for agriculture and hence the state could not lay claim on them through a legislation aimed at zamindari abolition. Finally, the petitioners also argued that the state's intent to claim forests went against the spirit of a legislation aimed at agrarian reform.[42] Each of these contentions, in different ways, was meant to highlight that the Act was more about state usurpation of land for forest protection than for agrarian reform.[43]

The post-enactment period of the Janmam Abolition Act (after 1974) witnessed the complex and contradictory priorities of state line departments. Although the courts, for the most part, passed judgments in favour of the Act and the state's claim to forest lands within plantations, the state bureaucracy continued to encourage the growth of the plantation economy (Krishnan 2009). Large-scale in-migration took place to Gudalur region in the 1970s and 1980s from neighbouring Kerala and erstwhile Ceylon via the plains of Tamil Nadu. In-migrants settled in both janmam and non-janmam areas. The growth of plantations and plantation labour led to land grabbing by estate laborers who sought long-term security in land. Land grabbing was facilitated by large estate owners who saw in encroachers a pool of casual labour who did not need to be protected as permanent labour had to be according to the Plantation Labour Act of 1951. Land grabbing by small farmers, though primarily for livelihood purposes, resulted in the dispossession of adivasis who were to a large extent alienated from their lands and consequently compelled to work in plantations.

The 1996 petition was, therefore, an attempt by the Nilambur Kovilagam to ensure that the Court instructed the government to prioritize forest conservation. The Godavarman interim judgment, to recall what was stated earlier, had specific directives for Tamil Nadu that appeared to be even stricter than the general instructions. The Court ordered a complete ban on tree felling in forest areas. This included an order preventing felling in forested (undeveloped) areas of janmam estates, further encroachment and even the removal of felled trees from janmam lands. Clearly the Court was taking cognizance of the Janmam Abolition Act and acting upon the belief that the intent of the Act to preserve undeveloped forest land was sound.

Has the interim judgment been effective from a conservation point of view? At one level, the 1996 interim order appears to have been ineffective at stopping further conversion of lands into estates. In the previous section, it was pointed out that even in the late 1990s, encroachment continued. On 28 April 2003, the CEC submitted a report in which it issued contempt notices to 642 persons/estate owners responsible for felling of trees. Subsequent to that, it submitted a supplementary report after a field visit to Gudalur that highlighted continued encroachment, ineffectiveness of top forest officials and victimization of sincere government staff (CEC 2003).

At another level, however, the state has at particular junctures evicted farmers from their land. This occurred more after the 1996 Godavarman judgment.

Krishnan (2009) argues that such evictions were relatively insignificant compared to the extent of land grabbing and regularization of encroachments due to the legal ambiguity prevalent in Gudalur as a result of ongoing court cases. While that might be the case, I suggest that the legal ambiguity he speaks of had detrimental impacts on farmers in other ways. This is because, as he himself highlights, the dominant discourse perceived of local migrants and farmers as anti-conservation and the forest problem in Gudalur as one of encroachments, land grabbing and deforestation (Krishnan 2004: 21). The most significant adverse impact, from the perspective of estate owners and small farmers, was from the restrictions on tree felling and transport. These restrictions have meant that it has become legally almost impossible for farmers to use the trees on their land. While farmers do still grow trees on their land, they make a distinction between *kaattu marangal* (forest trees) and *sondha idathu marangal* (own land trees). Forest trees include venthekku (*Lagestroemia lanceolata*), senthuram,[44] vattakanni of two types (*Kydia calycina* and *Clerodendrum viscosum*), rosewood (*Dalgerbia latifolia*) and also ainy (*Artocarpus hirsute*), jack (*Artocarpus integrifolia*), naval (*Eugenia sp.*), thani (*Terminalia bellirica*), mani (*Trema orientalis*) and lavanga (*Cinnamomum zeylanicus*). Private lands still have such trees, but farmers are reluctant to plant them as they are a sign of encroachment. Rather, farmers grow own land trees, such as arecanut (*Areca catechu*), silver oak (*Grevillea robusta*) or konna (*Cassia fistula*). These trees provide fruits, branches, leaves and shade but are not as economically valuable as forest trees.[45]

The government has also curtailed the developmental bureaucracy in particular parts of Gudalur. This is most notable in areas such as O'Valley, in the southeast of Gudalur taluk, where all lands are Section 17. Farmers in O'Valley have ration cards but other developmental activity is restricted. The District Collector passed an order on 30 January 2006[46] cancelling all schemes and public works in reserved forests and Section 17 lands on the ground that Section 17 lands are 'forest lands'. Farmers complain about their inability to get loans and the lack of investment in the area. A check post was established on the road to O'Valley in order to intercept illegal timber products. Forest Department staff also uprooted several acres of coffee, tea and spices.[47] Moreover, farmers say that despite the order being cancelled in November 2007,[48] the government polices farmers and treats them as encroachers. Although O'Valley only comprises about one-tenth of the wider Gudalur area, there are restrictions in other janmam areas too although perhaps to a lesser extent.

It is important to make the distinction between livelihood encroachment and speculative encroachment, the latter implying the buying of land for longer term investment purposes. The interim orders do not distinguish between the two. By 1996, a large number of small-scale farmers had converted Section 17 lands into primarily tea estates. Many of them had come to Gudalur as a result of pro-active state policies. Should these migrants be treated in the same way as speculative encroachers? Both the PUCL report of 2002 and the CEC report of 2003 distinguish between small-scale encroachment and large-scale encroachment, a distinction that is similar to that of livelihood and speculative. According to the

PUCL (2002) report, those engaged in the former, namely small farmers, were often falsely promised land and the necessary papers by local government officials, while the latter were 'land grabbers' able through political contacts and financial means to acquire legitimate papers. On the ground, the reality appears to be more complex with the line between small encroachers and land grabbers being more fluid. Nonetheless, there is a distinction. Moreover, more rigid enforcement of laws adversely affects farmers' current livelihoods. In other words, while the Godavarman judgment might not have stopped encroachment, it does appear to have had an impact on the livelihoods of existing encroachers.

While the land situation in Gudalur appeared suspended in limbo, the Supreme Court in 2005 issued orders in the Godavarman case. The 2005 judgment makes interesting reading. While the three-judge bench reiterated the importance of forests for conservation and the need to be circumspect in converting forest for non-forest purposes, it also recognized the importance of development. In other words the Court, on the one hand, spoke about the need to be precautionary in terms of land use changes away from forests. However, on the other hand, it spoke about payments for forest conversion based on net present value[49] to support compensatory afforestation, i.e. afforestation in lieu of the area converted to non-forest use.[50] If one was to interpret the Court's judgment in a broad sense, farmer claims to undeveloped land could be recognized as long as it was compensated for through state afforestation initiatives.

In practice, compensatory afforestation has not applied to small-farmer claims on land but rather to larger industrial projects only. As I argued earlier, there appears to be a hierarchy of priorities with regard to conservation and development. The case of small-farmer livelihood claims to land in Gudalur appears to be less of a priority, i.e. these forests are not to be converted to non-forest land. Despite the fact that many of these so-called forest lands are already converted to agriculture, the government holds on to the claim that these are dictionary-defined forests and hence should be under the control of the Forest Department.

In 2006, the Ministry of Environment and Forests sought to once again define forest, highlighting the need to come up with an ecologically sound and socially desirable definition. The definition eventually decided upon was that forest was to be an 'an area notified as forest in any Act or recorded as forests in any Government record'. While all areas that had trees, scrub, grassland, wetland, water bodies or any other forests (including unclassified state forests on community-owned lands) could be notified as forest, it was not to include man-made plantations, fruit orchards or agroforestry tree crops on private or community lands. Small tea estates would appear to be 'man-made plantations'. The question is whether the government in power is willing to take the time to distinguish between genuine cases of small farmers seeking title to land they cultivate and speculative interests attempting to make monetary gains by investing in land. From a normative point of view, as Lele (2007) has suggested, it is necessary to examine the importance of particular land uses to different actors and prioritize them. This remains a profoundly political decision.

Conclusion

In this chapter I have analysed and critiqued the normative underpinnings of the Godavarman judgment by both taking a historical look at land use change in Gudalur and the consequences of the judgment on small farmers there. My purpose has been twofold: to trace the environmental history of the area and to comment on the judgment in terms of preferred land use. Underlying both the writ petition and the judgment was an implicit assumption that more forests were preferable and that the state was best equipped to protect the forests. However, the environmental history of the region suggests that the state, along with the Nilambur Kovilagam and other janmis, was responsible for the transformation of the landscape because it prioritized revenue generation. State interests no doubt changed over time, but conservation was just one of many interests. Hence, when the Supreme Court passed the Godavarman judgment restricting non-forest use in dictionary-defined forests, the status of small farmers, who had been central to the state's efforts at transforming the landscape to a wooded plantation economy, as encroachers was reinforced, especially in janmam areas. Legally ostracized, along with larger estates, small-farmer livelihoods have become more precarious because of restrictions placed on harvesting of trees and access to developmental funds. Even in non-janmam areas, the letter of the law with regard to private forest and tree protection acts has become more stringent.

It is also important to note that the Supreme Court's judgment undermined the plural nature of land use and the fluid boundary between forests and non-forests. Using a dictionary definition of forest allowed the Forest Department to stake claim to all forests or undeveloped lands regardless of proprietorship. These 'forests' often had multiple non-forest land uses that were effectively curtailed by the court order. The impact of this judgment, moreover, has gone well beyond the boundaries of Gudalur. A Forest Bench of the Supreme Court now sits in judgement over land use and land use changes in dictionary-defined forests throughout the country.

Having said that, the Supreme Court in its 2005 order allows for the conversion of forests, advocating compensatory afforestation as a form of redress. Is there then not a case to be made for allowing conversions of lands so as to recognize claims made by small farmers? This would also be in the spirit of earlier government orders that were aimed at regularizing anomalies vis-à-vis encroachments and disputed claims to land.[51] One challenge would be to decide upon who are legitimate claimants, the same challenge that has ostensibly stalled the implementation of the Scheduled Tribes and Other Traditional Forest Dwellers (Recognition Forest Rights) Act, 2006. Another challenge would be deciding whether a market-based approach to forest conversion such as net present value[52] is an appropriate manner in which to make decisions about land use changes and if so what the state's role would be in regulating this market.

The bigger point that I have tried to make in this chapter is that the conflict over the forested landscape is increasingly about the plurality of normative visions that underlie decisions about land use. This is the case because the political economy of economic growth and conservation often result in the state acquiring land ostensibly for the greater common good. The Godavarman judgment was justified in the name of one such greater common good, namely conservation; however, the costs of conservation have been significant in terms of social costs especially for small farmers.

Notes

1 An earlier version of this chapter was presented at the 'Conference on Legal Pluralism in Natural Resource Management', organized by Asian Initiative on Legal Pluralism and supported by the Commission on Legal Pluralism, at Amrita University, Coimbatore on 31 March 2012. My thanks are due to the participants there for their useful remarks. I would also like to thank Sharachchandra Lele for detailed comments that have strengthened the chapter. Finally, I would like to thank all those farmers in Gudalur who gave me their time, and the staff of the Tamil Nadu State Archives, Chennai, for assisting me in finding records pertaining to Gudalur's history.

2 A different version related to the Supreme Court case told to me by Sharachchandra Lele is that T.N. Godavarman Thirumulpad (sometimes spelt Tirumulpad) first filed a case in the Madras High Court and that the timber lobby appealed the verdict. Subsequently, a case was filed in the Supreme Court from which T.N. Godavarman Thirumulpad actually backed out. However, the highest court continued the case *suo moto*.

3 In Malayalam, *janmi* implies birth or birth right and hence hereditary ownership. The janmam system of land tenure has existed from the pre-colonial times in Travancore and Malabar. The Malabar Tenancy Act of 1930 defines a janmi as 'a person entitled to the absolute proprietorship of land' (Section 3 of the Act). About 45 per cent of Gudalur was historically under the control of janmis as opposed to directly under British rule.

4 The *Oxford English Dictionary* defines forest as 'a large area covered chiefly with trees and undergrowth'. Such a definition is open to interpretation and can potentially include all wooded areas regardless of proprietorship.

5 When I speak of the Godavarman judgment in this chapter, I am most often referring to the 1996 interim order of the Supreme Court unless I specify otherwise. This order has effectively become a final order given the fact that the courts have not agreed to settle Section 17 land (leased land) and give property rights to cultivators of this land.

6 The term small farmer is used to describe farmers who have small holdings (less than 2 hectares) and who may also be employed within large estates. According to data from 2005–2006, small holdings comprise well over 90 per cent of total holdings in both Gudalur and Pandalur taluks, the two taluks that comprise the region known as Gudalur. (The data were obtained from the Statistics Department, Ootacamund and is part of the Tamil Nadu Agricultural Census.)

7 I choose to juxtapose statutory with customary land use and not statutory law with customary law so as not to enter into the debate about whether customary land use practices are sanctioned within something called customary law. Many legal pluralism scholars insist not only on the presence of rules but also an organizing authority to enforce these rules. Elsewhere I have argued that such a definition of law might result in underplaying conflicts between statutory law and customary practice (Menon 2005). However, as my purpose is to focus on the impact of the Godavarman judgment on existing land use practices, I do not enter that debate here.

8 A PIL is a litigation aimed at protecting 'public' interest. Under Article 32 of the Constitution, PILs can be filed to seek remedy for enforcement of fundamental rights. PILs can be filed by concerned individuals, institutions or non-governmental organizations. PILs can also be introduced by the courts *suo moto*. I will argue that public interest is a

contested notion, and that PILs can benefit some members of the public while alienating other members.

9 Encroachment in Gudalur is a complex problem. Large estate owners have extended their plantations significantly over the last few decades. Small farmers and estate labourers have also grabbed land. It is my argument that the state, in its segmented form, was aware of this encroachment but often allowed it because of its own political and economic compulsions. It is also my argument that many small farmers though supported by state policy eventually became encroachers when the state focused more on conservation.

10 TANTEA was started in 1968 by the government of Tamil Nadu as a means to rehabilitate Sri Lankan repatriates by providing them employment in tea estates. TANTEA was managed by the Forest Department until 1976 when it was brought under corporate management.

11 I have been unable to get hold of the TANTEA report. Based on the Godavarman verdict and writings about the verdict, one can presume that the report had details of trees that could be felled outside of forests.

12 A number of civil appeals were filed against the Janmam Estate (Abolition and Conversion into Ryotwari) Act of 1969. The Civil Appeal Nos. 367–375 refer to appeals filed by Manjushree Plantations Ltd and others against the State of Tamil Nadu. See Dutta and Yadav (2011: 64–74) for more details about the 1996 Interim Order and its legal history.

13 Revenue comprised two components: the janmabhogam and the assessment. The former was a tax on the land and the latter on cultivation, normally based on the 'quality' of the land as opposed to actual produce. Large parts of present-day Gudalur came under the jurisdiction of janmis who had absolute proprietorship over the land. Janmis collected janmabhogam (or land tax) from the cultivators whereas the British collected an assessment on produce from the cultivators. Non-janman lands were directly under the control of the British and hence they collected janmabhogam.

14 It is no doubt risky to generalize about national development taking precedence over environmental conservation. However, it can be argued that development projects seen to generate large supra-local benefits such as dams have tended to be viewed favourably by the courts – though there is a glimmer of hope that this might change with the advent of pro-marginalized people legislation such as the Scheduled Tribes and Other Forest Dwellers (Rights to Forest) Act, 2006.

15 The ryotwari system was one in which the British collected revenue directly from the cultivators of the land.

16 Plantations comprised both cultivated land under plantation crops and undeveloped forestland that was not converted to plantation crops.

17 This number was obtained in the course of doing fieldwork in the region between 2009 and 2011.

18 Janmi is used instead of janmam as reference is being made to the relationship between the state and landlords.

19 The British accommodated those janmis who did not oppose their conquest of the Southeast Wayanad from Tipu Sultan. In that sense, customary forms of land tenure were recognized by the British.

20 The indication is that prior to the mid- nineteenth century Gudalur was a much more forested area. J.H. Wilkes (cited from Muthiah 1993: 31–32) wrote that 'the whole of it was then an unbroken sheet of forest' and that 'when Ouchterlony first came to the valley it was uninhabited' barring wild elephants and 'Kurumba Dacoits'.

21 Tamil Nadu Archives (TNA), Board of Revenue Proceedings 1878, No. 729 dated 18 March, pp. 2293–2295.

22 TNA. Letter No. 66 dated 6 July 1875, Board of Revenue Proceedings 1875, Forest No. 162, No. 2,210 dated 7 August.

23 Prior to settlement, the British were not aware of the actual extent of cultivated land. As revenue assessment was collected directly from tenants and not from the janmis, it was possible that some tenants were not paying assessment.

24 Jagdish 1998: 86.
25 TNA. G.O. 1919, Miscellaneous Series, Revenue Department, dated 10 September 1969.
26 TNA, Board of Revenue, No. 501, dated 25 March 1881, pp. 1573–1577.
27 TNA, Board of Revenue, No. 1729, dated 13 August 1881.
28 TNA, Board of Revenue Proceedings 1878, No. 220, dated 25 January.
29 TNA, Board of Revenue Proceedings 1876, Forest No. 72, Board No. 2044, dated 11 August.
30 TNA, Board of Revenue Proceedings 1885, No. 271/Forest 54, dated 27 January.
31 TNA, Board of Revenue Proceedings 1885, No. 271/Forest 54, dated 27 January.
32 Working in forestry terms implies 'scientific' felling of trees according to particular principles. Usually, particular blocks were worked (or felled) at a given point of time, followed by working of other blocks.
33 The Board of Revenue passed a resolution sanctioning the notification of Mudumalai as reserved land in 1886. See TNA, Board of Revenue, Forest No. 212, dated 21 April 1886.
34 TNA, Chief Conservator of Forests, Press No. 97, dated 4 May 1926.
35 TNA, Chief Conservator of Forests, Miscellaneous 147/54, dated 10 April 1954.
36 This section depends significantly on the work of Krishnan (2004, 2009).
37 Forests were reserved in Cherangode.
38 Private forests were defined as forests located in estates as per the Madras Estates Land Act, 1908, and other forests outside of estates exceeding two hectares.
39 This act was renamed Tamil Nadu Private Forests (Assumption of Management) Act in 1969 when the state of Madras was renamed Tamil Nadu in 1968 (Tamil Nadu Adaptation of Laws Order, 1969).
40 'Poramboke land' means the land that is the property of the government and that is not assessed and hence outside the revenue accounts.
41 The petitioners also appealed against the High Court judgment that pronounced that the settlement process was not an act of conferring ryotwari tenure on the janmis.
42 A much more detailed analysis of the legal challenges to the Janmam Abolition Act can be found in Krishnan (2009).
43 The legal challenges to the Act highlighted the contested nature of land use in Gudalur.
44 The scientific name of this species could not be identified.
45 Menon et al. 2013.
46 Ooty vide no. RC.A5. No. 2992/2006, dated 30 January 2006.
47 *The Hindu*, dated 23 January 2007[0].
48 The Nilgiris MP expressed his regret regarding 'forest rules standing in the way of implementing development schemes in O'Valley' (*The Hindu*, dated 17 February 2007). He insisted that the 'state's foremost duty is to serve people' and asked for the sanction of public schemes.
49 Net present value in this case refers to the loss of value of forest resources to stakeholders at the time of forest conversion.
50 The Court set up a committee headed by Kanchan Chopra, a leading environmental economist. The Chopra Committee report made several suggestions regarding the methodology of calculating net present value, the need for different valuations for different types of forests and the constitution of three different funds (Central, State and Local) so as to compensate stakeholders at different levels. None of these recommendations was taken up (Lele 2007).
51 In 1990, the Ministry of Environment and Forests issued six government orders, the most significant one being with regard to the recognition of rights to forest land 'encroached' upon before the FCA was passed in 1980. However, little action has been taken with regard to this government order.

52 Net present value refers to the current value of an environmental resource keeping mind its value over time.

References

Bhushan, P. (2004) 'Supreme Court and PIL: Changing Perspective under Liberalisation', *Economic and Political Weekly*, 1 May, pp. 1770–1774.

CEC (2003) *Supplementary Report 5 in C.C.P. 193 of 2001 Regarding Violation of The Honorable Supreme Court's Orders in Respect of the Janmam Lands, Nilgiris, Tamil Nadu*. New Delhi: CEC.

Dutta, R. and B. Yadav (2011) *Supreme Court on Forest Conservation* (third edition), New Delhi: Universal Law Publishing Co.

Fairhead, J. and M. Leach (1996) *Misreading the African Landscape: Society and Ecology in a Forest-Savanna Mosaic*, Cambridge: Cambridge University Press.

Francis, W. (1908) *The Nilgiris – Madras District Gazetteer*, Madras: Madras Government Press.

GoTN (Government of Tamil Nadu) (1969) *The Tamil Nadu Gudalur Janmam Estates (Abolition and Conversion into Ryotwari) Act, 1969*, Madras: GoTN Law Department.

Jagdish, P. (1998) *Working Plan for Gudalur Forest Division*, Chennai: Tamil Nadu Forest Department.

Joseph, J.S. (1978) *Tamil Nadu Forest Department Management Plan for Mudumalai Wildlife Sanctuary 1978–1887*, Chennai: Tamil Nadu Forest Department.

Krishnan, S. (2004) *Deforestation and Conflict in the Nilgiri Wynaad: a Sociological Study of Protest, Resistance and Legal Dispute*, PhD thesis, University of Madras.

Krishnan, S. (2009) 'Of Land, Legislation and Litigation: Forest Leases, Agrarian Reform, Legal Ambiguity and Landscape Anomaly in the Nilgiris, 1969–2007', *Conservation and Society*, vol. 7, no. 4, pp. 283–298.

Lele, S. (2007) 'A "Defining" Moment for Forests?' *Economic and Political Weekly*, 23 June, pp. 2379–2383.

Menon, A. (2005) 'Where Are the Forests? Legal Pluralism and Land Use Change in the Kolli Hills', *Indian Socio-Legal Journal*, vol. 31 (special issue on legal pluralism), pp. 11–26.

Menon, A. (2007) 'Engaging with the Law on Adivasi Rights', *Economic and Political Weekly*, vol. 42, no. 24, June 16, pp. 2239–2242.

Menon, A., C. Hinnewinkel and S. Guillerme (2013) 'Denuded Forests, Wooded Estates: Statemaking in a Janmam Area of Gudalur, Tamil Nadu', *Indian Economic Social History Review*, vol. 50, no. 4, pp. 449–471.

Muthiah, S. (1993) *A Planting Century – The First Hundred Years of the United Planters' Association of Southern India – 1893–1993*, Madras: Affiliated East-West Press Private Ltd.

Philip, K. (2004) *Civilizing Natures – Race, Resources and Modernity in Colonial South India*, New Brunswick, NJ: Rutgers University Press.

PUCL (People's Union for Civil Liberties) (2002) *Fact Finding Report into the Land Situation in Gudalur Taluka, Nilgiris District*, available online at www.pucl.org.

Rosencranz, A. and S. Lele (2008) 'Supreme Court and India's Forests', *Economic and Political Weekly*, 2 February, pp. 11–14.

Sahu, G. (2008) 'Implications of Indian Supreme Court's Innovations for Environmental Jurisprudence', *Law, Environment and Development (LEAD) Journal*, vol. 4, no. 1, pp. 377–393.

4 Unearthing the roots of statutory forest law

Iron smelting and the state in pre- and early-colonial India[1]

Sashi Sivramkrishna and Amalendu Jyotishi

'The consumption of charcoal for smelting of iron has been the chief cause of the great destruction of our ancient woods.'

(Holland and Hunt 1853: 44)

Introduction

Across the world, charcoal production for iron smelting has been considered responsible for destroying large tracts of medieval forests, sometimes of entire regions (Sivramkrishna 2009). Did iron smelting also cause such devastation in pre-colonial India? Could this have been one of the earliest reasons for the East India Company to intervene with statutory laws to preserve, conserve and manage forests? Unfortunately, answers to these questions are not unequivocal; however, in attempting to find them we articulate a fundamental change in the relationship between the state and smelter that developed during early colonial rule. From one of *mutual interdependence* in pre-colonial India, the relationship between the colonial state and smelter turned into one of *competition*. It is in this transformation that we locate the origins of statutory forest laws in India through which the colonial state sought to legitimise their claim over forest resources. This, at the same time, fundamentally altered the environment of the smelter; both physically as well as the economic/social/political context in which they had to survive.

To appreciate the argument put forth in this chapter, we need to first recognise the importance of charcoal-iron smelting in pre-colonial India – its scale and geographical scope, and the critical service it provided to the state. This is possible only with a conscious inclusion of military history into the narrative. Indian environmental history has, however, failed to do so, characterising medieval India as an agrarian economy organised through self-sufficient village communities that were 'in approximate equilibrium with their environment, dominated by local production for local use' (Gadgil and Guha 1993: 39).

Such harmonious societies 'have only moderate levels of impact in transforming landscapes' (Gadgil and Guha 1993: 39), deforestation occurring only on account of extending the boundaries of cultivation. Smelters were marginalised to a small subset of this naive economy whose limited role was to supply implements for agriculture as well as material for utensils and other household products. This worldview completely overlooks the massive quantities of iron and steel required by the state for weaponry. It is in the latter role that smelters were able to forge a direct relationship with the state, acquiring independent access to forests for procuring ore and timber for manufacture of charcoal. Smelters, often belonging to specific tribal communities and castes, to a significant extent remained outside or were perhaps excluded from the precincts of village economy both physically and with respect to customary village norms including those governing use of village–forest resources (Elwin 1942; Percy 1864).

By the third decade of the nineteenth century, the East India Company was consolidating its political power over India and with it a fundamental transformation of the economy and society was underway. Most pertinently, the decline of independent feudal states and the war economy terminated the mutual interdependence that had existed for centuries between the smelter and state. The only remaining market for iron smelters was agricultural implementations, building materials and household wares. In order to survive, some strengthened or built a closer relationship with the village economy (Campbell 1894; Thurston and Rangachari 1909). With the expansion of settled agriculture, the market for iron and steel implements actually thrived throughout the nineteenth century. There even existed a preference for implements made from traditional indigenous iron and steel over imported products (Baden-Powell 1868; Elwin 1942; Iyer 1899). There were others, however, who failed to integrate with 'mainstream' village societies, either choosing or perhaps forced into isolation.

In either case, the dependence of these communities on forests continued. It is here that their confrontation with the (colonial) state as competitor began. Not only did the East India Company, unlike its predecessors, stop procurement of iron and steel for weapons from traditional smelters but it also sought new avenues for increasing revenues and profits from trade of Indian products. Iron and steel was considered as having great potential and archival records from the early decades of the nineteenth century reveal that it was concern over destruction of tree cover for charcoal production that induced the Company to assert control over forests, denying smelters of their unfettered access to its resources (see, for instance, Rice 1897). The demand for these resources intensified as the colonial state extended its domain to other sectors including commercial agriculture, plantations, tea production (which needed large quantities of charcoal for drying), railway transport and communication. Traditional iron and steel smelting did not die soon; it continued to exist in many parts of the country well into the twentieth century (Elwin 1942; Roy 2009; Saravanan 1998; Sivramkrishna 2009). The focus of this chapter, however, is to trace the roots of statutory forest law in early-colonial history.

Weapon manufacture in pre- and early-colonial India

'Iron and steel, although not cast-iron, appear to have been known to the Hindus beyond the reach of all record ... the inventions of both iron and steel were made in India at several independent points of time' (Crawfurd 1864: 316). The corrosion- and rust-resistant iron pillars at Delhi, Dhar and Kodachadri dated anywhere between 1,000 and 2,000 years old, are testimony to India's metallurgical achievements. Given its rich deposits of ore, iron and steel were also extensively smelted across the length and breadth of the country, from Kachchh in the west through the Central Provinces into Assam and the Khasi Hills in northeastern India, from Beypore on the southwestern coast, across the Deccan plateau and through the Narmada Valley, into Kumaon and Garhwal in Himachal (Bharadwaj 1982; Elwin 1942; Percy 1864; Trevor 1858) and even further north. In the valley of Kashmir, Sir Walter Lawrence (1895: 62–63) recorded that 'iron has been discovered and worked in several places in the valley, and there are extensive workings of iron ore in the neighbourhood of Sof'.[2]

While the indispensable role of iron and steel in hunting and agriculture has been recognised, it is in warfare that the function of these metals has been disregarded by Indian environmental history. And it is to this particular aspect that we draw attention. The Iron Age commenced in India some three thousand years ago, *c.*1000 BC and even the Indian epic *Mahabharata* makes reference to iron weaponry. There are references in 'the Rig-Veda of chariots armed with iron weapons, of coats-of-mail, arms and tools of various kinds, and of bright-edged hatchets' (Royle 1852: 163). By the time of Alexander's expansion *c.*300 BC we have evidence of steel making in India; Porus having gifted him some 30 pounds of it. Archaeologists have also found evidence of pre-historic weaponry including swords, daggers, tridents, spears, arrows, spades and rods in southern India dating to *c.*250 BC (Mahmud 1988: 20). Excavations from Gujarat revealed that *c.* fourth century BC case-hardened iron had been developed for weapons and implements including arrow-heads, spear-heads, daggers, knives, parallel-sided swords, leaf-shaped spear-heads, barbed arrow-heads, chisels, etc. (Hegde 1996: 358).

More precise and reliable information is available on the use of iron and steel for weaponry in medieval times. While the size of armies ran into tens of thousands during the Mughal period, the use of heavy cannons and war elephants was also widespread. Cannons weighing close to 50 tons, in brass and/or iron were deployed across India; the ones at Ahmednagar, Bijapur and Thanjavur being some of the more well-known of them. Irvine's (1903) graphic account of heavy guns being drawn by up to 500 oxen and four elephants leaves us awe struck by the size and weight of Mughal artillery. The cast-iron balls for such cannons weighed between two to three tons each (Allen 1856: 150). Irfan Habib (1980: 16) summarises the primary place held by artillery in technological development during the medieval period.

In several ways artillery represented the highest achievements of industrial technology during the sixteenth and seventeenth centuries. While the manufacture of cannons was then the real 'heavy industry', on the handgun were lavished all the fruits of the increasing mechanical sophistication attained during that period.

Indian iron cannons were usually made of wrought-iron rings welded together into a barrel. To overcome the limitations in this technology, the Mughal Court in 1666 even ordered the Dutch and English to recruit engineers for the manufacture of cannons (ibid.: 20). European engineers were employed in state-run *kharkhanas* and *topkhanas* manufacturing heavy and light artillery (Singh 2006: 351). Another important component in the armies of feudal states was elephants, which numbered from several hundred to several thousands. Akbar (r. 1556–1605) alone is said to have had more than 6,000, many of them armoured and some even carried light cannons or large muskets. The armour was made of steel plates covered with leather or cloth (Nossov 2008: 12, 14).

Apart from this heavy artillery, medieval Indian armies used a variety of metallic weapons including swords, shields, spears and javelins, arrows and daggers. Verrier Elwin (1942: xxiv) quotes the French gem merchant, Tavernier, who travelled India in the seventeenth century on the steel industry in the 'Kingdom of Golconda':

> [T]hey carry a broad sword like the Swiss, with which they both cut and thrust, and they suspend it from a belt. The barrels of their muskets are stronger than ours, and the iron is better and purer. This makes them not liable to burst. As for the cavalry, they have bow and arrow, shield and mace, with helmet and a coat of mail.

Indian steel, called *wootz*, was considered legendary and much has been written about it; the Arab, Edrisi, summarises its eminence (cited in Elwin 1942: xxiii): 'the Hindus excel in the manufacture of iron. They have also workshops wherein are forged the most famous sabres in the world. It is impossible to find anything to surpass the edge that you get from Indian steel.'

While the scientific and metallurgical ingenuity of Indian arms and ammunition manufacture in ancient and medieval times has justifiably been portrayed with admiration, the environmental implication of this activity has not received similar attention. In fact, a reading of Irvine's (1903) classic work on the Mughal army made us wonder how Indian environmental history could fail to consider the role of metallurgy and armament production in their studies.

Iron smelting: scale and the environmental implications

Metallurgical history is replete with accounts of iron smelting from across India. To John Percy (1864: 254) 'the large accumulations of slag which occur in various localities in India' was evidence of extensive production of iron through the ages. Verrier Elwin (1942: 239) in his classic work on the iron-smelting tribe, the Agaria, asserts that, although no precise figures can be given, 'iron-smelting was at one time a widespread industry in India, and there is hardly a district away from the great alluvial tracts of the Indus, Ganges and Brahmaputra, in which slag-heaps are not found'. According to one estimate, annual production in pre-colonial India c.1800 was around 200,000 tons (Agarwal n.d.).

Even as the smelting industry was in decline towards the close of the nineteenth century, there were more than a hundred furnaces operating in the Malabar; in

North Arcot there was smelting being carried out in 86 villages (Elwin 1942: 240). Elwin also refers to many other centres of iron smelting including Madura, Salem, Tiruchirappali, across erstwhile Mysore and Deccan plateau, in Nellore, the Kappatgud Hills in Dharwar, Belgaum, Ratnagiri, Rewa Kantha, Kaira and Ahmedabad, Kathiawar and Kachchh, Bengal, Bihar and the Central Provinces, Assam and the Naga Hills. Using data from several sources including Buchanan (1807) and Rice (1897), Sivramkrishna (2009) mapped out the iron smelting locations in the Maidan[3] region of the present state of Karnataka and also found large heaps of slag and crucibles during his visits to some of these sites. According to Bharadwaj (1982: 223), 'during the eighteenth century there were thousands of furnaces working in various parts of India and each were producing near ½ to 3 tons of iron per annum' although there were some of 'unusual capacity' operating in Birbhum c.1852. Large furnaces were also found in the Central Provinces; Tendukera on the Narmada was a town 'entirely engaged in iron making' in the mid-nineteenth century (Trevor 1858: 15).

The essence of the iron-making process has remained the same over millennia. The ore, either mined or collected from sand, is melted and the oxygen in it burnt out. In traditional iron making the fuel that performed this dual operation was charcoal.[4] Charcoal burns at elevated temperatures of about 1,100 degrees Celsius, high enough to reduce the oxides in the ore. Such temperatures cannot be achieved by burning dry wood, thereby making charcoal an essential raw material in the smelting process.[5]

Traditional iron making in India used about 16 kilograms of charcoal for a kilogram of iron[6] and to produce a kilogram of charcoal requires 4 to 7 kilograms of wet wood. Therefore, to produce a kilogram of refined iron would need about 60 to 100 times its own weight in wet wood. A more graphic estimation is that production of '2500 tons of refined wrought iron, 140,000 tons of wood were required which could be obtained from 437 square miles[7] of heavily wooded land' (Biswas 2007: 280). Cleghorn (1864), quoting a report of 1856 studying the iron mines of the Western Himalayas, states that native smelters used 28 trees to produce 1 ton of crude iron. Even more charcoal was needed as fuel to soften and transform refined semi-products into their final forms. If steel were to be produced from smelted iron, further melting and forging operations required even greater quantities of charcoal.

Anthropology of iron smelting

The objective of this section is to draw out pointers from the literature that establish the mutual interdependence between smelters and state and the independence of smelters from the agrarian village economy. These relationships were influenced by one important technological element: without transport networks, smelting had to be located close to the ore as well as timber for charcoal production. This often meant that iron smelting was carried out in dense and remote forest tracts, spatially distant from the agrarian village economy. As Elwin (1942: 13) reports, the 'movements' of the Agaria, an iron-smelting tribe, 'were controlled by two chief factors a supply of ore and a forest of *sarai* trees, from which charcoal suitable for use in the furnaces can best be made'. They were a 'very unsettled people, leaving a place as soon as the neighbouring jungle fails to satisfy their requirements' (ibid.: 52).[8]

Extending east from Nagpur, northwards towards Ranchi, the Agaria were considered as one of the most significant iron-smelting tribes in India: 'a people absorbed in their craft and their material; they seem to have little life apart from the roar of the bellows and the dang of hammer upon iron' (ibid.: xxvii). Although Elwin's observations related to the mid-twentieth century, they do indicate the 'separateness' of the Agaria from caste Hindus (ibid.): '[W]e can see the entire social process at work in Raipur. A group of Gond takes to iron-smelting. Despised by their brethren they become a separate group under the name of Agaria.' The iron-smelting tribes were distinct from caste Hindu blacksmiths; distinct not only occupationally but also socially. For instance (ibid.):

> [T]he Mirzapur Agaria confine themselves almost entirely to mining and smelting iron. He does no blacksmith's work: all he does is to smelt the iron and work it up into rough ingots, which are afterwards converted into axe-heads and agricultural implements by the Lohar, who is admittedly a recent immigrant into the hill country and utterly repudiates any connection with the iron-smelter of the jungles.

Like elsewhere in the world, from Africa to Europe, iron smelters were both reviled and feared. In India, the Agaria were despised socially but at the same time considered to possess supernatural powers: 'If a Hindu touches an Agaria bellows, he is penalised. The Agaria house is usually apart, away from the rest of the village' (ibid.: 133). There is little in Elwin's work that tells us of the life of the smelters in medieval India; however, in spite of it being situated in a period when this tribe were drawn closer to village communities on account of their dependence on the market for agricultural implements (which too was in decay by this time), the sense of separateness and isolation of the Agaria from village communities is stark and indisputable.

Wandering blacksmiths

The work by John Percy (1864: 261) on early modern metallurgy, carried out almost a century before Elwin's, describes a similar first-hand account of iron smelters in Bengal:

> The village of Kunkerai ... like all such villages is inhabited exclusively by the iron smelters, and is distinguished from the agricultural villages by the filth, poverty, and degraded condition of the inhabitants. The iron smelters of Orissa, as I believe, generally in Bengal form a class apart from the agricultural inhabitants, belonging, indeed, to the isolated aboriginal tribes which, under varying names, are found in all the hilly tracts of the peninsula ...

> In Orissa there are several of such tribes, differing in their relative degrees of civilisation: the iron smelters of Talcheer and the neighbouring districts belong to the large tribe of the Kols or Coles. They are to a certain extent nomadic in their habits, remaining in one spot only as long as plentiful supplies of ore and wood are obtainable in the immediate vicinity ... The heavy rains and increasing jungles soon obliterate the remnants of the deserted village, with the exception of the large accumulations of slags, which remain for centuries, monuments of an unprogressed art. Such lumps of slag are frequently found in the jungly districts, where no iron manufacture has been carried on within the memory of the inhabitants.

There are other references that reinforce the point that iron smelters had a distinct existence from agrarian village communities: Balfour refers to 'the *Taremook* or wandering blacksmith' also called by different names in different parts of the country; *Ghisari* in *Dekhani* (Deccan), *Lohar* by the *Mahratta* and *Bail-Kumbar* by the *Kanarese* (Elwin 1942: 67). In their study of Orissa, Stirling and Peggs (1846: 9) mention that in the wilder tracts the necessaries of life are not attainable, and frequently subsistence of any sort is only procurable with the utmost difficulty. Many of the natives (here) are iron smelters and charcoal burners.

The fact of iron smelters in India being distinct from the agrarian economy had percolated even to more popular writing. In a book on the varieties of trees found in forests, the author (Taylor 1845: 72) incongruously mentions:

> In India there is a particular caste, or rank, of the natives, who live entirely in the woods, and gain their subsistence by burning charcoal. The other inhabitants, however, who are very particular in such matters, never have any personal dealings with them; though, in an indirect way, they purchase their commodities.

In the same vein, *The Penny Magazine* (1842: 435) reported:

> In India charcoal is manufactured by a particular caste, who dwell entirely in the woods, and have neither intermarriage nor intercourse with the Hindoo inhabitants of the open country. They bring down their loads of charcoal to particular spots, whence it is carried away by the latter people, who deposit rice, clothing and iron tools – a payment settled by custom.

In an archived volume of the *Scientific American* (1921) we discovered an interesting passage that once again pointed to the separateness of Indian smelters from the agrarian community:

> In Lower Bengal, in which portion of our Indian empire there are entire villages exclusively inhabited by iron smelters ... There are whole tribes in India who have no other occupation than iron smelting. They, of course, sink no shafts and open no mines, and are not permanent in any place. They

simply remain in one place so long as plentiful supplies of ore and wood are obtainable in the immediate vicinity. In many cases the villages formerly inhabited by them have passed out of existence, but the waste, or rather wasted products, of their operations remain.

Colonial records, although a majority of them are from the latter part of East India Company rule or the early years of British Raj when the military apparatus of many native states had already been disbanded, indicate the close relationship between the smelter and the state for production of weapons. Dobbs (1908: 5; emphasis added) draws an interesting link of a nomadic community of blacksmiths in Bundelkhand to their 'military' past:

> At certain seasons [they] migrate from Rajputana … wander about from place to place with their families, goods, and chattels, and forged ploughshares for a fee. According to community lore, they had left Chittore when that city fell to the Mughals, vowing never to return until Chittore was liberated *with the swords that they would themselves make and sell to the prospective liberators.*

Baden-Powell in his handbook of the economic products of Punjab (1868: 1) begins with iron ore:

> In the hills due north of Peshawur, is the source of the Bajaur iron, which is of fine quality, and is used in the manufacture of the gun barrels of Kuhat and Jammu, and not a little also, it may be presumed, in the formation of steel for the blades of the Bukhara and Peshawur.

In Mandi, he finds:

> The iron produced by this rough industry is paid for by the Raja [of Mandi], at the rate of one rupee per *pucka* maund. The natives only work these mines, so lucrative to their master, and so unproductive to themselves.
>
> (ibid.: 3)

In the hill states of Shimla, a passage from the work of a Mr Marcadieu (ibid.: 4) once again points to the direct ownership of mines by the local Raja:

> Passing from the Kot Khai district to Jubal you arrive at Cheel … and in the possession of the Raja of Rampur … ten small smelting furnaces work irregularly for the Raja's profit, and produce small quantities of iron, mostly consumed in the Raja's territories.
>
> (ibid.: 7)

Finally, while describing some indigenous varieties of steel, we find clear references to former times when the output of this industry was used for weaponry (ibid.):

> Guleri comes from Gwalior in Hindustan, it is a tenacious metal and used for wire drawing, gun barrels, &c. ... Faulad or steel, used to be imported from Hindustan for the manufacture of armour, shields, &c., ... at the present day when the manufacture of such armour is not carried on ... The *bajauri* from Bajaur, north of Peshawur, is not much exported to the Central Plain districts, though it was formerly used for gun making.

Hugh Cleghorn (1864: 85), first Commissioner for the Conservancy of Forests and later Inspector-General of Forests, in his report on the forests of the Western Himalayas provided an interesting first-hand account of his journeys through the hills and valleys among which one comment markedly substantiates our argument. On the mountainous tracts from the Sutlej to the Ravi, iron was found in great abundance: 'under the Sikh rule, this iron was extensively used for gun barrels'.

In a study of iron and steel smelting in West Bengal, Sanyal (1968: 103) reported that iron and steel smelted by tribes was of high quality, tough, soft and malleable all at the same time. This even prompted two Englishmen, Messrs Farquhar and Motte,

> to establish their factory in Birbhum in 1779 to produce shot and shells, cannon, etc. In fact in their application to the government they stated that for this quality of softness Birbhum iron was eminently suitable for almost every work in cast iron particularly for the fabrication of cannon.

Bharadwaj (1982: 223–224) informs that in the fifteenth century Assam was considered 'the seat of iron smelting' where 'cannons and small arms were the chief products of this industry'. Here 'smelting of iron has always been a chief branch of industry amongst the hill-tribes' (Royal Geographic Society 1856: 393).

Unlimited demand

Apart from tribes, there are references to a section of smelters and refiners, particularly in Bengal, who were Hindus and even Muslims. Large furnaces (*kotsal*) were located close to *aurangs* (markets) from where ore was procured and converted into *kutcha* (crude) iron. This was further converted into *pucka* (refined) iron in *kamarsals* where *lohars*, *kamars* and other caste Hindus were employed. Larger furnaces, sometimes 80 or 90 of them located close to an *aurang*, employing 7,000 to 8,000 people, used Muslim artisans to produce the *kutcha* iron and caste Hindus to refine this to *pucka* iron. This would be then be used for making 'garrisons, gun carriages, shots, shells, artilleries' (Singh 2006: 356).

These large iron works were often under the control of the urban and rural aristocracy such as the 'Choudhuries of Ganpur' (Sanyal 1968: 105) who had 'an unlimited demand for military hardware' (Singh 2006: 356) including arms and ammunition, knives, swords, daggers (Sanyal 1968: 105). However, what is more striking is that socially these caste Hindus and Muslims employed in the large furnaces and refineries were not tied to the village economy. Singh (2006: 354) categorically states that 'the work group were no longer familial but a group of free craftsmen, generally of the artisan caste, sometimes headed by a master craftsmen'. The output from these industries was not particularly for local consumption: 'the iron is frequently sent for sale to considerable distances from the places of manufacture' (Percy 1864: 258).

The separateness of iron smelting from the agricultural economy is evident when we understand, in contrast, the role and position of the village blacksmith, the *lohar*. The blacksmith would be supplied with raw material procured from smelters to produce agricultural implements for which he would receive a fixed share in proportion to the number of ploughs owned by each household in kind. The *lohar* was also expected to repair agricultural implements free of charge (Singh 2006: 355). This 'interdependence and reciprocity in economic exchange served to maintain the cohesiveness of the village community' (Vani 2002: 21).

In southern India too, remnants of traditional iron smelting can be found across different landscapes, from the coastal belt over the Western Ghats and across the Deccan plateau. The name Mangalore is believed by some to be from the word *mikala* or charcoal, which used to be made on the banks of the river Netravati, the wood obviously collected from nearby forests. The *Canara* (formerly referred to as Kanara) *District Gazetteer* reports that iron was formerly manufactured in different parts of the Sahyadris (the Western Ghats) although by 1882 there was no ore smelted here (Enthoven 1883: 262). There is also reference to smelting being carried out by the 'Hill Tribes of the Ghats' (Percy 1864: 257).

Across the plains of the Deccan plateau (Maidan), it seems more likely that iron smelting was carried out by caste Hindus. In the iron-rich Sandur ranges in the present state of Karnataka, blacksmiths were of the *kammara* caste. But here too their separateness from the village community is apparent (Thurston and Rangachari 1909: 141; emphasis added):

> They have a temple of their own, dedicated to Kali, in the village, where the worship is conducted by one of themselves. The name of *Baita Kammara*, means *outside* blacksmiths, is applied to Kamsala blacksmiths, who occupy a lowly position, and work in the open air or outside a village.

There are other scattered references from southern India that indicate a nomadic form of life adopted by iron smelters. In 1822 at Nersa, Belgaum district, 'iron was worked by a wandering tribe who came yearly in the fair season from Goa or the Savantvadi state … the villagers were wholly unacquainted with the nature of the process by which the metal had been extracted' (Campbell 1894: 53fn). Another report mentions that 'furnaces could be carted from place to place' (Agarwal n.d.).

Under the Vijayanagar Empire, which ruled over southern India between the fourteenth and sixteenth centuries, permission for cutting down trees for charcoal and for digging ore was regulated with a yearly fee called *hommal gutta*, which was proportioned to the quantity of iron made in the district (Rice 1897: 1.477). This system may have continued into the nineteenth century. The system was neither a fully commercial one nor 'communal'; it had elements of both. The ironsmith, probably of the prosperous and once wealthy Salahuva Vakkalu mining caste, extracted ore as well as traded iron to towns and directly to the state for the military (Elwin 1942: 240). At the same time the smelters were also linked to workers and the village through a system of reciprocity. They would exchange some produce with farmers in return for which they received allowances of grains and sometimes land for cultivation at low rents. The smelter-blacksmith would also sell for cash some of the output to village people for non-agricultural purposes such as construction of houses (Campbell 1894: 233).

The *Gydda Cavila*, or what Buchanan (1807: 1.391) refers to as 'keeper of forests' or 'renter of forests', would take forests on rent by paying a certain sum of money to the government and thereon grant permission to various stakeholders for the right to collect forest produce for a fee. In Madhugiri, the share 'to the keeper of the forest, for permission to make charcoal' was 100 Fanams out of a total cost of 276 Fanams, i.e. more than 36 per cent of the cost (not including labour costs). In Doray Guda, where ore was collected, the payment 'to the renter of mines and woods' was 130 Fanams, or 30 per cent of the total expenses (excluding labour costs). Though a steep fee was charged, strict control and monitoring of forest resources hardly seemed to be a concern of the *Gydda Cavila*. This is made clear in a remark by Buchanan: '[T]he renter has no occasion to come near the mine. He knows the men that get a supply of ore, and each pays yearly a certain sum, and takes as much ore as he pleases' (1807: 2.18, 2.40).

Implements of war

Pre-colonial south India was also rife with war. Just as an indication, in erstwhile Mysore alone, the three decades between 1767 and 1799 saw four major wars fought between the British East India Company and the erstwhile State of Mysore then under the rule of Hyder Ali and later his son, Tipu Sultan. These Anglo-Mysore wars employed tens of thousands of soldiers. Apart from conventional arms such as swords, daggers, armours and helmets, guns, muskets, cannons and even rockets were used by Tipu Sultan's army. *The Mysore Gazetteer* reports that within the old fortifications at Ramnagaram iron was worked into 'implements of war' (Rao 1929: 231). Where did all the feedstock for weapons come from? Buchanan (1807: 1.173, 1.180) makes explicit reference to the Sultan having purchased iron from smelters of the Maidan giving them 'great employment; as he made his shot of this iron, by hammering'. He reiterates:

> According to the iron-smelters' own account, the Sultan gave them a high price for their iron, and by his great demand afforded them constant employment. It is probable, however, that he compelled them to work much harder than they were inclined to do.

In his Revenue Regulations, Tipu Sultan ordered a doubling of iron foundries: 'If there are ten iron foundries in your district, you are, by encouragement, to increase them to double the number' (Parthasarathi 2008: 10). The intermittent wars and battles in Mysore would have created enormous needs for iron and steel, a 'boom' for iron smelters of the Maidan.

We conclude from these observations made at various points of time and place that it is inappropriate to simply subsume iron smelters under the agrarian village economy. In fact what seems to clearly emerge here is that customary norms actually sustained the separateness of smelters from the village economy. In parts of India this was also reinforced by the technological necessity of smelters to be nomadic and in proximity to forests for ore and timber. Although excluded from the village economy, there was a mutual interdependence between smelters and the state arising from the production of weaponry.

One contemporary source (Rao n.d.) succinctly captures the close relationship between them:

> The nomadic wanderers, Vanjaras tribe of Rajput origin came into the Sikh fold quite early during travels of Guru Nanak Dev. For their livelihood, the Vanjaras had been trading in all types of human consumables along with weaponries for rulers of the time by traveling in big caravans from one corner of the country to another. The Sikligars among the Vanjaras were excellent iron smiths capable of manufacturing all types of weapons. Few of their families from Marwad first came into contact with Guru Hargobind for the first time (1595–1644), when they offered services for weapon manufacturing and recruitment as Sikh soldiers. The Vanjaras still consider Sri Hazoor Sahib as their highest place of worship.

Customary norms, inextricably linked to the caste system and tribal communities in so far as India is concerned, have often been viewed as providing rules for the allocation of natural resources among competing stakeholders in society. There is a critical presumption here that may easily be overlooked – the existence of chronic scarcity of such resources in the first place that makes rationing and allocation necessary. More than natural resources, medieval India in reality faced a persistent scarcity of labour. Bose (1993: 17), for instance, while discussing Bengal at the time of the Great Famine of 1770, explicitly states that labour scarcity was not merely an outcome of famine, the famine actually occurred in the context of a 'relative deficit of labour'. From the Midnapur District Records he noted that Chittagong District, which escaped the famine, had a mere quarter of its land cultivated in 1761 on account of 'labour scarcity' (ibid.).

More pertinent to us, however, are the hill districts of India where iron smelting was more extensively practised. From Assam, Bonsall (1860: 446; emphasis added) reported that in 1841 'the country was almost entirely covered with a dense jungle, and *with such a sparse population*, that it became necessary to procure several thousands of coolies from China and Bengal'. Similarly, from Dehradun Thornton (1858: 485) found that in the hill districts the 'evils of uncertain seasons, an inconceivably sparse population, poverty of soil, distance of markets' prevailed. Further south, towards the Satpura hill ranges and north of the river Tapti, a region where iron smelting was widespread, large continuous tracts of jungle that were 'either uninhabited or contain a sparse population, chiefly of Bheels (tribes)' were reported (Select Committee 1858: 79).

Such labour scarcity would have necessitated allocation of occupations and strict adherence to it, without inter-occupational mobility. Furthermore, in a resource-abundant economy, the independent smelters may not have come into conflict with village communities and the destruction of forests observed by officers of the East India Company in the early 1800s (as we will see later in this chapter) may have merely been a localised phenomenon and of little consequence to the rest of the economy. Instead, in a resource-abundant but labour-scarce war economy, customary norms to 'separate' smelters[9] would have been more important than rationing of forest resources between village communities and smelters. In other words, these norms acted as a 'marker of autonomy from the plains more than a mechanism to set forth rules and regulations for land use' (Menon 2006: 11).

Modernised iron manufacture and deforestation

The East India Company in the early phase of colonial expansion was ardently interested in exploring new prospects for commerce and revenue, for which many extensive surveys were conducted. Among several possibilities, India's abundant resources for iron and steel production received their attention. The Company was keen to exploit these resources using modern industrial production techniques and technology that had already been adopted in Europe and England (Littell 1845: 382–383):

> We have heard that some of the superabundant wealth of this country is likely to be appropriated to the development of a vast field of enterprise in the south of India. Some of the provinces in that part of the country abound in iron ores of various kinds, of the richest and purest descriptions ... a small association of gentlemen in India engaged in the prosecution of it, some years ago, and by their labours and at their cost, results of unexampled value have been established ... With the improvements now in the course of introduction at their works in India, there is now no doubt that iron may be made there, and sold at very large profit, for the consumption of the whole of the markets of Asia, so as to supersede foreign importations; and that it can be disposed of in this country [England], at a great profit, to replace the produce of Sweden and Russia, for conversion into steel, and for use in all purposes where a superior quality of iron is required.

But here they encountered traditional Indian smelters as competitors for the same resources. It is around this period that we find a proliferation of reports on the wasteful nature of traditional Indian iron-smelting methods. Deforestation on account of charcoal smelting was *widely reported from all across India* with calls for putting an immediate stop to this activity. Statutory forest laws were seen as the solution to ensure that their objective is met: a virtual monopoly over natural resources including both iron ore as well as timber for charcoal production. The traditional Indian smelter not only confronted a competitor but also a competitor possessing complete regulatory powers.

Archival sources clearly show concerns over destruction of forests by smelters and the need for preservation and conservation. Below are some of the remarks we have extracted from archival sources pertaining to different parts of India.

The Central Provinces (Hughes 1851: 8):

> There are few large trees at present; the demand for charcoal to supply the wants of the numerous iron-furnaces and refineries leading to a great destruction of timber. The only locality where wasteful cutting is not allowed is on Maudih hill; and the timber is yearly improving; the yield, however, will never be great enough to form a permanent supply for any great smelting works.

Kunjamullay Hills of Salem (King and Foote 1865: 384–385):

> The jungles of Salem district are being thinned, and in many places ruined, by the careless and wasteful way in which wood is cut down for wasteful purposes; more still, perhaps, by the miserable native method of making charcoal … the Forest Conservancy Department have as yet had little power in materially diminishing this evil.

Malabar, Kerala (Gibson 1857: 5):

> I may here, in passing, allude to the importance of keeping up a source of supply for both these products in Malabar, seeing that the charcoal used in the extensive Ironworks at Beypore has risen in price … in the course of time the cost of chief smelting material – charcoal – will be so great as to preclude the works being carried on to a profit.

The Deccan plateau (Maidan) (Rice 1897: 1.477; emphasis added):

> The third and by no means the least harmful was the practice of iron smelting … The wasteful methods employed led to an enormous consumption of fuel and a corresponding denudation of jungles in the Maidan and regions bordering on the Malnad abounding in iron ore. The late General Dobbs, then Superintendent of the Tumkur District, thus graphically describes in 1854–1855 the damages wrought to tree vegetation by iron smelters: 'The district generally is very bare of trees. The jungles were however extensive when I first assumed charge in 1835, but these are disappearing fast under the axe of the iron and steel manufacturers. When I first visited the

> beautiful range of hills running between Chiknayakanahalli and Hagalwadi, they were clothed in trees from top to bottom; not a tree now remains except a few unfit for burning. In the immediate neighbourhood of Tumkur (Davaraidrug Hills) where three-fourths of the wooding has disappeared. I stopped the progress of destruction by prohibiting iron forges altogether … no one who has not witnessed the process can conceive the destruction made by these forges.' Even greater ruin was caused in the Chitaldrug District from the same cause. Almost barren waste has taken the place of former wooded tracts, and that too in a district with but scanty rainfall. Luckily some forests were preserved by not being easy of access and *they are now most carefully preserved.*

The coastal regions of Canara (Townsend 1859: 189):

> One of the difficult questions connected with forest conservancy is regarding the making of charcoal for iron smelting … Not only is there great waste in the making of charcoal, but there is great waste when made, the charcoal being inferior. The blacksmiths insist upon the wood being either of bamboo or jambay. Europeans make good charcoal from common wood. Engineers and Surveyors should inform the Forest Assistant of cases of destruction of timber with which they meet.

At Kangra (Baden-Powell 1868: 4):[10]

> The obstacles to be contended in attempting to extend the manufacture [of iron] are … the reckless destruction of forests without any measures being adopted for their renewal, the extravagant waste of wood in the manufacture of charcoal and of the ore in the smelting and refining, owing to the rudeness of the furnaces and other appliances … measures are being adopted for the conservation and renewal of the forests.

In general, Indian methods of charcoal making were considered particularly wasteful (Balfour 1862: 76):

> Charcoal so prepared is of little value in reducing iron ore, and the process is wasteful … native iron smelters only employ fuel from one to three inches in diameter; and, to procure this, they take the saplings, or the tops and branches of the largest hardwood trees, allowing the trunks to decay. For, large trees are not adapted for fuel for native smelting, as the cost of splitting them adds greatly to the expense; and, unless the logs are split the inner wood is not carbonised.

Dietrich Brandis (1897: 138), first Inspector General of Forests and the person responsible for setting up the Indian Forest Service as well as formulation of the Forest Act of 1866, also carried the same view:

> In order to produce the large quantities of charcoal required [for production of native iron and steel], wood formerly was cut in an irregular and wasteful manner, without any regard to the regeneration of forests … where however reserved forests have been formed and have been efficiently protected, the position of matters has become completely altered.

Caution must be exercised here before reaching any final conclusion from British reports. The destruction of forests reported may have been only a localised phenomenon that, however, served to justify the preconceived plans of the colonial regime. This can be contended on the basis of reports and statements that speak of abundant forest cover not far from cleared tracts. For instance, in the Kumaon ranges (Selections of the Home Department 1855: 13–14):

> Within a few miles of the mines, undoubtedly, there is not much timber, and I doubt whether there ever was any very great quantity; but Mr. Henwood was evidently unaware of the existence of the extensive and untouched forests of oak and pine which cover the sides of the Doodatolee, Doorga Dee, Byansee, Budhangurh, Bhutkot, and Doonagiree ranges, within five to twelve miles from the mines.

Priorities of the colonial state

Indigenous iron smelting and need for conservation was one side of the coin; as seen above, the colonial administration was simultaneously propagating their own iron and steel industries to exploit forest resources. Iron produced in India would compete with iron imported from England and perhaps even prove to be an alternative source to Swedish and Russian iron being imported into England. While it is true that even in sixteenth- and seventeenth-century medieval India, European technology and manufacturing units did 'create intense competition with indigenous armament proto-industry' (Singh 2006: 352) there is no evidence that the state turned hostile towards their domestic suppliers. The priorities of the colonial state were, however, fundamentally different.

Consider, for instance, the Nerbudda Coal and Iron Company; registered under limited liability with a capital of £250,000 the company was formed with the sanction of the Secretary of State for the working of iron mines at Mopani and Tendukera, where the latter, as we have seen above, was the seat of many traditional iron smelters. The company would further 'receive from the government a concession on the mines upon favourable terms' including nominal rents for the first five years, followed by royalties and carriage of the produce at moderate rates. The directors of the company were, not surprisingly, all British (Bradshaw 1867: 473).

While Talcher in Orissa is well-known for its coalfields today, Thomas Oldham, Superintendent of the Geological Survey of India (1859: 11), provides a comprehensive account of traditional iron smelting that was extensively carried out there, the need for its 'replacement' and conservation of forests. Beginning with a word of praise, Oldham states 'the iron produced in the Talcher District has long been known as of excellent quality and highly priced for its tenacity ... charcoal iron of the best quality' but the tone of his study thereafter turns critical. He criticises the methods used as 'rudest' by castes that are the 'poorest' and 'wretched', exploited by *mahajans* literally as slaves. From here Oldham once again makes a familiar argument: 'the wasteful consumption of fuel often compels them to remove to spots where it is more abundant ... the description is applicable to all jungle districts which I have seen' (ibid.: 12); 'in many districts, however, this timber (*sal*) has been nearly exhausted and other trees are used' (ibid.: 13); 'the ingenuity with which they seem to have adopted a process for obtaining the very smallest possible amount of useful fuel from the greatest amount of timber' (ibid.: 14).

After a complete description of the indigenous methods of charcoal making and smelting, the geologist comes to his proposed solution: first, to develop the industry of this district with 'simpler means adopted for obtaining a better result ... with the experience of other countries to guide in such trials ... with skilled labour and practical experience from Europe or elsewhere' (ibid.: 21); and, second, this valuable material (fuel) must be economised as far as may be possible with 'strict care taken to cut the forest systematically, and to renew its growth steadily and constantly' (ibid.: 29). The kind of plant that would achieve these objectives was to have an annual capacity of 6,000 tons with an investment of £60,000 to £70,000. The iron would 'be manufactured at a cost equal to, if not less than, that at which it is produced in England' (ibid.: 30).

'On the subject of preserving our forests from destruction' (Selections of the Home Department 1855: 10), Capt. Ramsay, Senior Assistant Commissioner of Kumaon to Mr Batten, Commissioner, contends that:

> If the miners cut fuel judiciously, the forests in the vicinity of Semul Khet and Khetsaree would furnish a permanent supply of fuel. If a Company took a lease of the mines, the forest attached to them ought to be under the management and protection of the said Company, but if, hitherto, the mines were worked by a native lessee, it would be hopeless to expect the charcoal-burners to observe any organised system ... [this] is applicable to all parts of the District where iron or copper mines exist.
>
> (ibid.)

In the valley of Giri in the Western Himalayas, Cleghorn (1864: 1, 3) informs us:

> There is a great consumption of wood and charcoal in connection with the iron smelting, for which the locality is famous ... on our way, we passed in two days fifty mules, and nearly a hundred coolies laden with iron ... We ascended the Giri ... elevation 7,500 feet, where iron smelting has long been practiced.

Observing the practices of the local charcoal-burners, Cleghorn (ibid.: 4) supports William Hay, previous superintendent of the Shimla Hill States who

> attempted to initiate conservation rules for charcoal burning, levying a small rate according to the girth of the trees felled. Charcoal makers should cut only in such places as are assigned to them in Government forests … all existing wood will be required for the successful working of the iron mines.

In Bir *taluka*, he supports the report made by a committee that recommended:

> If iron were made on an extensive scale by the native processes … no extent of forest would be sufficient … if measures were not taken to renew the supply by means of plantations, and a proper forest conservancy … and improved methods of manufacture both for charcoal and iron.
>
> (Cleghorn ibid.: 88)

Cleghorn (ibid.: 88) further articulates the need for forest regulation with the appointment of an Assistant Conservator on the Beas to effectively address through 'strict conservancy management', the conflicting interests of various stakeholders. The latter included: 'The enormous indents for railway sleepers … the pressing demands for other public works; the great consumption of fuel for iron manufacture; and the prospective want of wood for tea-boxes in Kangra valley.'

Writing on the industrial resources of India, Montgomery Martin (1868: 161) avers that although it has 'inexhaustible supplies of the richest ores … the want of fuel has always been a great difficulty'. The blame is leveled against the 'people who in India live by charcoal-making have desolated thousands of square miles of forest-land, by wantonly wasteful treatment of the trees, to their own great loss, and to the serious disadvantage of the native iron trade'. This problem arose with the modern plants at Porto Novo as well as the Beerbhoom Iron Works. The proposed solution was similar once again: large-scale plants with a capacity of at least 2,000 tons/week and 'skillful management of forests … over which the proprietor has control' (ibid.: 162).

In a rare article by J.M. Heath (1847: 77), founder of the Porto Novo Iron Works on the southeast Indian coast in the present state of Tamil Nadu, he candidly discusses the priority afforded by the government towards modern iron works:

> With a view to encourage the undertaking I have engaged in, the Court of East India Directors have, in consequence of the earnest recommendation of the Madras Government, granted me certain privileges: such as the power of cutting fuel, and raising ore in Government lands, rent-free, for a certain time.

Saravanan (1998: 130) goes on to point out that at the time of renewal of his licence, Heath was turned by the Collector on account of the fact that 'it would not only interfere with the supply of the country furnaces and other manufacturers'. Moreover, 'very many make their livelihood by burning charcoal and bringing it for sale to the iron smiths, and it was his [the Collector's] duty to protect these livelihoods' (Roy 2009: 595). Heath, as we have seen, was not the only one contemplating investment in India's iron and steel sector; the slow and definite decline in the Company's monopoly powers attracted a number of British entrepreneurs to explore possibilities in this sector.

Praising English efforts at establishing smelting plants in southern India, Littel (1845: 383) appreciates the local Indian government, under the sanction of the East India Company, having 'granted them considerable pecuniary assistance, and has conveyed to them rights and privileges, which, with those obtained from private proprietors of lands, give them complete and exclusive possession of all the materials for iron making in the provinces'. Decades later, Brandis (1897: 139) speaks of the 'repeated attempts made to carry on charcoal iron smelting on a large scale in Salem district' between 1824 and 1867 that failed on account of the lack of 'efficiently protected and regularly managed' forests; he therefore sought the 'efficient protection and good management of a sufficient area of forest in the vicinity of the old Native Iron works[11], so as to enable them to continue their operations'.

Going back several years before British enterprises commenced operations in India, Benjamin Heyne (1814: 226) described traditional techniques of iron smelting in great detail from several locations in the Northern Circars[12] and threw light on the state of mind of the British in exploiting India's iron ore resources; at Ramankapetta, he remarked that 'if the Company were inclined to establish any large iron works, there is no doubt that this place would be eminently worthy of notice'. The concern, however, was availability of fuel (ibid.: 223):

> Were the manufacture of iron to be established here upon a large scale, the greatest difficulty would probably be the introduction of powerful blowing machines in place of these puny bellows. No doubt the East India Company, if it thought proper, might easily establish such a manufactory in different parts of their extensive dominions; and altogether supersede the necessity of the importation of iron from Europe. But I have strong doubts whether the establishment of extensive iron manufactories, in countries destitute of pitcoal, be a prudent measure.

Attributing strategic motive to statutory forest law

Herein lies the earliest basis for statutory forest laws: the interests of the East India Company in securing access over the forest resources once under unfettered access by smelters was now brought under laws for their preservation and conservation although with the right for a rational and scientific exploitation by industry. Sir William Hunter (1886: 522) has tersely presented the basis for the development of statutory forest laws:

> Up to about twenty-five years ago, the destruction of forests by timber-cutters, by charcoal-burners, and above all, by nomadic cultivation,[13] was allowed to go on everywhere unchecked ... But as the pressure of population on the soil became more dense, and the construction of railways increased the demand for fuel, the question of forest conservation forced itself into notice.

In 1844 and 1847 the subject was actively taken up by the governments of Bombay and Madras. In 1864, Dr Brandis was appointed Inspector-General of Forests to the Government of India, and in the following year the first Forest Act passed the Legislature (No. VII of 1865). Indiscriminate timber-cutting was prohibited; the burning of the jungle by the hill tribes was confined within bounds. Forest conservation became a reality in India.

It has been argued that the motive of the British in restricting charcoal burning and shifting cultivation was essentially economic: to preserve trees and ores for the iron industry, teak trees for the railways, to create 'free' labour in hilly regions for construction and plantations, and to widen the tax net. Could these restrictions have served a more strategic interest of the incipient British regime: control over manufacture of weapons?

Gadgil and Guha (1993: 118–119) mention that 'in the early nineteenth century, and following the defeat of the Marathas, the East India Company razed to the ground teak plantations in Ratnagiri nurtured and grown by the legendary Maratha admiral Kanoji Angre'. This has rather spontaneously been attributed to the destructive energy of the British race all over the world. A more reasonable and rational possibility for the destruction of the trees may have been to exercise control over local iron and steel production for weaponry by deterring charcoal making, after all the plantation was raised by a military official.

Evidence of dismantling of forts across India (East India Company 1800: 238) and purposeful destruction of arms and ammunition does support such a possibility. For instance, in 1857, the British government collected several thousands of weapons from the Moplahs of the Malabar and systematically destroyed them at the Beypore plant. Quoting Charles Wood, Krishnan (1954: 71) elaborates:

> These knives were all made out of the native iron from the Indian blast-furnaces, and wonderful material they were. To break them was impossible ... the remarkable quality of the iron, and that it could so beautifully be tempered. These war knives were sent up to the works in native bullock-carts from Calicut, in charge of sepoys, in lots of about 1,000 to 1,500 at a time, until they were all destroyed.

The perceived threat of the British government in the proximity of tribes to defeated feudatories[14] could have meant that control over forests served a strategic, not merely economic purpose; this possibility has hitherto seldom been explored in the study of Indian history and the evidence presented in this chapter is an attempt to begin a debate on this.

Conclusion

Our study puts forth an altered narrative of Indian environmental history by turning the focus on traditional iron smelting rather than the agrarian village economy. The relationship of mutual interdependence that had existed between smelters and the state in pre-colonial medieval India was severed with the advent of colonial rule. But this was only half the story; the colonial state in pursuing its own commercial and military objectives considered the traditional smelter as a competitor for resources and even perhaps a militaristic threat. Although, in some cases, a demand for iron and steel products for agricultural implements and household wares thrived in the colonial economy, the traditional smelters' access to ore and wood for charcoal was no longer unfettered. Smelters had to operate in a new context of resource scarcity and competition with the state, institutionalised through statutory forest laws. This reading of environmental history further provides a basis for understanding what is clearly discernible even today in many mineral-rich forest regions of India: the proximity between tribal communities and the state, although it has turned to one of tension and conflict in asserting rights over mines and forests. Meanwhile, the degree of separateness between tribal communities and the 'mainstream village economy' continues to exist.

Notes

1 This chapter was earlier published with the same title in *Economic and Political Weekly*, vol. 48, no. 5, 2 February 2013.
2 A more detailed exploration from smelting locations across India follows in a later section of the chapter.
3 The flat and open plains of the Deccan plateau.
4 It is not charcoal per se that is the defining element of traditional iron and steel. Even today, large-scale manufacturers of iron and steel in Brazil continue to smelt iron and steel using charcoal rather than coke to reduce the oxides in the ore. The easy availability of wood is the determining factor in this choice. Utilisation of charcoal in iron smelting is, therefore, a necessary, but insufficient, condition in defining traditional iron and steel making.
5 Abraham Darby replaced charcoal with coal in the eighteenth century.
6 The manager of the Company's Porto Novo establishment (on the east coast) reported that they used 13.25 tons of charcoal for every 1 ton of iron produced (King and Foote 1865: 383).
7 This is equal to approximately1,132 square kilometres or approximately twice the area of the Rajiv Gandhi (Nagarhole) National Park.
8 Although beyond the scope of this study, it may be pertinent and interesting to explore the interrelationship between shifting agriculture and charcoal burning for iron smelting. It seems more than a mere coincidence that tribal communities have been associated with both these activities.
9 As we have seen, smelters did sell iron to village blacksmiths. But here too it was an arm's-length arrangement with social segregation. The 'separateness' of smelters would also ensure that the state's supply of weaponry was unaffected by social and economic changes in the village economy.
10 Kangra District was then in the British province of Punjab but is now in the state of Himachal Pradesh.
11 These old Native Iron works refer to the likes of the Porto Novo plant and not to traditional smelting.
12 This region includes some coastal parts of present-day Andhra Pradesh and Orissa.
13 Nomadic or shifting cultivation may have a close relationship to iron smelting and charcoal burning. It makes sense to clear the forests for charcoal and then utilise the cleared land for cultivation. Both the smelter/charcoal-burner and shifting cultivator shared nomadic lifestyles. The possibility that these cultivators were primarily smelters requires further study. The decline of the traditional iron industry may have meant

that some tribes became dependent almost fully on agricultural produce from shifting cultivation.

14 The imposition of the Criminal Tribes Act, 1871, classified the Vanjaras/Sikligars as criminals. The demonisation of their sect compelled them to make a mass migration into jungles in most backward tribal belts to save their lives (Rao n.d.).

References

Agarwal, P. (n.d.) *Did You Know?*, viewed on 24 February 2012 (www.infinityfoundation.com/mandala/t_dy/t_dy_Q15_frameset.htm).

Allen, D.O. (1856) *India Ancient and Modern*, Boston: John P. Jewett & Co.

Baden-Powell, B.H. (1868) *Handbook of the Economic Products of the Punjab*, Roorkee: Thomason Civil Engineering College Press.

Balfour, E. (1862) *The Timber Trees, Timber and Fancy Woods*, Madras: Higginbotham & Co.

Bharadwaj, H.C. (1982) 'Development of Iron and Steel Technology in India during the 18th and 19th Centuries', *Indian Journal of History of Science*, vol. 17, no. 2, pp. 223–233.

Biswas, A.K. (2007) 'Technology in History with Special Reference to Ancient and Medieval India', in Dasguta, J.B. (ed.), *History of Science, Philosophy and Culture in Indian Civilisation, Vol. XV, Part I*, New Delhi: Centre for Studies of Civilisations, pp. 261–289.

Bonsall, S. (1860) 'Tea: Its Culture and Manufacture', in *Report of the Commissioner of Patents for the Year 1860, United States, Dept. of Agriculture*, Washington, DC: Government Printing Office, pp. 446–448.

Bose, S. (1993) *Peasant Labour and Colonial Capital: Rural Bengal since 1770, Volume 3, The New Cambridge History of India*, Cambridge: Cambridge University Press.

Bradshaw, G. (1867) *Railway Manual, Shareholders' Guide and Official Directory for 1867*, Manchester: Henry Blacklock & Company.

Brandis, D. (1897) *Forestry in India: Origins and Early Developments*, Dehra Dun: Natraj Publishers, reprint 1994.

Buchanan, F. (1807) *A Journey from Madras through the Countries of Mysore, Canara, and Malabar*, Volumes 1–3, New Delhi: Asian Educational Services, reprint 1999.

Campbell, J.M. (1894) *Gazetteer of the Bombay Presidency, Vol. XXI, Belgaum*, Bombay: Government Central Press.

Cleghorn, H. (1864) *Report upon the Forests of the Punjab and the Western Himalaya*, Roorkee: Thomason Civil Engineering College.

Crawfurd, J. (1864) 'On the Supposed Stone, Bronze and Iron Ages of Society', *The Anthropological Review*, vol. II, no. VII, pp. 313–318.

Dobbs, W.E.J. (1908) *A Monograph on Iron and Steel Works in the United Provinces and Oudh*, Allahabad: F. Luker, Superintendent, Government Press.

East India Company (1800) *Copies and Extracts of Advices to and From India.*

Elwin, V. (1942) *The Agaria*, London: Oxford University Press.

Enthoven, R.E. (1883) *Kanara District Gazetteer*, Bombay: Central Government Press.

Gadgil, M. and R. Guha (1993) *This Fissured Land: An Ecological History of India*, New Delhi: Oxford University Press.

Gibson, A. (1857) *Forest Reports of the Bombay Presidency for the Years 1849–50–1855–56*, Bombay: Bombay Education Society's Press, Byculla.

Habib, I. (1980) 'The Technology and Economy of Mughal India', *Indian Economic & Social History Review*, vol. 17, no. 1, pp. 1–34.

Heath, J.M. (1847) 'Coal and Iron in India', *The Artisan*, no. IV-Third Series, 1 April.

Hegde, K.T.M. (1996) 'Archaeology and Ecology of the Northern Subcontinent', in Hermann, J. and E. Zurcher (eds), *History of Humanity, Volume III: From the Seventh Century B.C. to the Seventh Century A.D.*, London: UNESCO & Routledge, pp. 356–358.

Heyne, B. (1814) *Tracts, Historical and Statistical, on India*, London: Black, Parry, & Co.

Holland, J. and R. Hunt (1853) *A Treatise on the Progressive Improvement & Present State of the Manufactures in Metal, Vol. I*, London: Longman.

Hughes, W.H. (1851) *The Karanpura Coal-Fields, Memoirs of the Geological Survey of India, Vol. VII, Art. 7*, Calcutta: Government of India.

Hunter, W.W. (1886) *The Indian Empire: Its People, History and Products*, New Delhi: Asian Educational Services, reprint 2005.

Irvine, W. (1903) *The Army of the Indian Moghuls: Its Organisation and Administration*, Delhi: Low Price Publications, reprint 2004.

Iyer, V.S.S. (1899) 'Report on Prospecting Work in Parts of the Chitaldroog and Tumkur District during the Field Season 1896–99', *Mysore Geological Department Records*, vol. II, pp. 105–107.

King, W. and R.B. Foote (1865) 'On the Geological Structure of Parts of the Districts of Salem, Trichinopoly, Tanjore and South Arcot in Madras Presidency', *Geological Survey of India, Memoirs of the Geological Survey of India, IV*.

Krishnan, M.S. (1954) 'Iron Ore, Iron and Steel', *Bulletin of the Geological Survey of India*, Series A: Economic Geology, p. 9.

Lawrence, W.R. (1895) *The Valley of Kashmir*, New Delhi: Asian Educational Services, reprint 2005.

Littell, E. (1845) *Littell's Living Age, Vol. IV*, Boston: T.H. Carter & Company.

Mahmud, S.J. (1988) *Metal Technology in Medieval India*, New Delhi: Daya Publishing House.

Martin, M. (1868) 'The Progress and Present State of British India', *The London Quarterly Review*, no. CCXXVI, April.

Menon, A. (2006) 'Where Are the Forests? Legal Pluralism and Land Use Change in the Kolli Hills', in Eberhard, C. and N. Gupta (eds), *Legal Pluralism in India: Special Issue of the Indian Socio-Legal Journal*, vol. XXXI, no. 148, pp. 11–26.

Nossov, K. (2008) *War Elephants*, Oxford: Osprey Publishing.

Oldham, T. (1859) 'Preliminary Notice on the Coal and Iron of Talcheer, in the Tributary Mehals of Cuttack', in *Geological Survey of India, Memoirs of the Geological Survey of India, Vol. I*, Calcutta: Government of India.

Parthasarathi, P. (2008) 'Iron Smelting in the Indian Subcontinent c.1800', viewed on 12 February 2012 (www.lse.ac.uk/economicHistory/seminars/Epstein%20Memorial%20Conference/PAPER-Parthasarathi.pdf).

Penny Magazine, The (1842) 'Society for the Dissemination of Useful Knowledge', 5 November.

Percy, J. (1864) *Metallurgy: Iron & Steel*, London: John Murray.

Rao, H. (1929) *The Mysore Gazetteer, Vol. 4*, Mysore: Government Press.

Rao, K.A. (n.d.) *The Great Warrior Tribes of Mudiraja*, viewed on 1 March 2012 (http://mudiraja.com/mudiraju_warriortribes.html).

Rice, B.L. (1897) *The Mysore Gazetteer, Part 1 and 2*, Mysore: Government Press.

Roy, T. (2009) 'Did Globalisation Aid Industrial Development in Colonial India? A Study of Knowledge Transfer in the Iron Industry', *Indian Economic & Social History Review*, vol. 46, no. 4, pp. 579–613.

Royal Geographic Society (1856) *A Gazetteer of the World, or Dictionary of Geographical Knowledge, Vol. I*, Edinburgh: A. Fullarton & Co.

Royle, Prof. (1852) 'On the Arts and Manufactures of India, from a Lecture by Prof. Royle', *The American Journal of Science and Arts*, vol. XLI, pp. 160–174.

Sanyal, H. (1968) 'The Indigenous Iron Industry of Birbhum', *Indian Economic Social History Review*, vol. 5, pp. 101–108.

Saravanan, V. (1998) 'Commercialisation of Forests, Environmental Negligence and Alienation Tribal Rights in Madras Presidency: 1792–1882', *Indian Economic & Social History Review*, vol. 35, pp. 125–146.

Scientific American (1921) 'Primitive Iron Manufacture', viewed on 15 February 2012 (http://chestofbooks.com/crafts/scientific-american/sup5/Primitive-Iron-Manufacture.html#ixzz1nH4LPr3M).

Select Committee (1858) *Fourth Report from the Select Committee on Colonization and Settlement (India)*.

Selections of the Home Department (1855) *Selections from the Records of the Government of India: Papers Regarding the Forests and Iron Mines in Kumaon*, Calcutta: Thos. Jones, Calcutta Gazette Office.

Singh, A.K. (2006) *Modern World System and Indian Proto-Industrialisation: Bengal 1650–1800*, New Delhi: Northern Book Centre.

Sivramkrishna, S. (2009) 'Production Cycles and Decline in Traditional Iron Smelting in the Maidan, Southern India, c. 1750–1950: An Environmental History Perspective', *Environment and History*, vol. 15, pp. 163–197.

Stirling, A. and J. Peggs (1846) *Orissa: Its Geography, Statistics, History, Religion and Antiquities*, London: John Snow.

Taylor, J. (1845) *The Forest, or Rambles in the Woodland*, New York: Betts & Anstice.

Thornton, E. (1858) 'The Dehra Doon as a Seat of European Colonisation in India', in *The Calcutta Review*, vol. XXXI, July–December, pp. 485–498.

Thurston, E. and K. Rangachari (1909) *Castes and Tribes of Southern India*, New Delhi: Asian Educational Services, New Delhi, reprint 2001.

Townsend, M. (1859) *The Annals of Indian Administration, Vol. III*, Serampore: J.C. Murray.

Trevor, G. (1858) *India: An Historical Sketch*, London: The Religious Tract Society.

Vani, M.S. (2002) 'Customary Law and Modern Governance of Natural Resources in India – Conflicts, Prospects for Accord and Strategies', in Pradhan, R. (ed.), *Legal Pluralism and Unofficial Law in Social, Economic and Political Development*, Papers of the XIIIth International Congress, 7–10 April, 2002, Chiang Mai, Thailand, ICNEC Kathmandu, Volume I, pp. 409–446.

5 Land, law and resistance

Legal pluralism and tribal conflicts over land alienation in Odisha

Satyapriya Rout[1]

Understanding roots of resistance over nature

Development, in its various *avatars*, has surely been the most powerful influence structuring the social and economic transformation in the non-western world in this century, especially after the Second World War and decolonisation (Sivaramakrishnan and Agrawal 2003). The new face of development, starting from the mid-1980s under a broader framework of neo-liberalism and globalisation, has drawn attention to the other side of this transformation, i.e. its consequences on the environment, and the poor and marginalised who depend upon this environment for their livelihoods. The greater demand for natural resources by the process of development has led to the monopolisation of the resource by the state, and the narrowing down of the natural resource base for the survival of the economically poor and powerless, either by direct transfer of resources away from their basic needs or by destruction of the essential ecological processes that ensure renewability of the life-supporting natural resources (Bandyopadhyay and Shiva 1988; Gadgil and Guha 1992). Within this context of state resource capture, an effort to continue its project of rapid economic growth and deprivation of local communities of these resources, the state has often been successful in using the ideology of development as an effective instrument to legitimise exploitation.

The pattern of development that the state has followed since independence, and more intensively with the neo-liberal agenda of the 1980s and 1990s, has resulted in fundamentally altering two crucial bases of production upon which survival of the majority of economically poor, powerless and marginalised groups depend: land and water (Baviskar 1995). The response of local and tribal communities to this new threat to survival, which is being created by the very process of development, often manifests itself through virulent economic conflicts between the tribal communities, whose resources and livelihoods are now threatened by rapid economic growth agendas, and the state and its allies who are actively pursuing these. Many of the development conflicts that have recently emerged are, in fact, a struggle of tribal and marginalised groups in defence of their traditional rights over land, water, forest and other common resources. In agreement with Baviskar (1995), these conflicts have been contestations between two versions of economy: 'political economy of profit' pursed by the state and its allies, and 'moral economy of need' practised by the tribal and marginalised communities for their survival.

In the context of the discussion above, the present chapter aims at understanding tribal land alienation and attempts of tribal self-governance in the context of tribal resistance to development from a legal pluralistic perspective. Taking the tribal resistance to the Vedanta Alumina Project, in the eastern Indian state of Odisha (previously known as Orissa), as a case in point, the chapter tries to explore and explain the existence and interaction of multiple legal frameworks. The chapter narrates how different versions of state law, and customary law coexist together, and what implications this coexistence of laws has on matters relating to tribal rights to land, forest and other natural resources. In addition to a conceptual analysis of 'legal pluralism' as a perspective, the chapter discusses several state laws and policies related to tribal access and rights to land and local natural resources, as well as existing local customary laws defining property rights over such local resource bases. In conclusion, the chapter highlights the opportunities that the existence of multiple legal orders provides to the tribal communities to struggle and resist in defence of their traditional rights to land.

The empirical work for the research is carried out in two Gram Panchayats, i.e. Lanjigarh Panchayat and Batelima Panchayat of the Lanjigarh block in Kalahandi district, which were hot beds for resistance against the Vedanta Project. We viewed the two panchayats taken for study as socio-political organisations, within which tribal social organisation is embedded, rather than just as political units. A combination of case-study method, group discussion and in-depth interviews was carried out to gather the empirical data for the chapter. To collect the field data, interviews were conducted with the present and past representatives of the two panchayats and other key informants such as local tribal leaders, tribal youth and few tribal women, who had participated actively in the anti-Vedanta struggle. Further, in-depth discussions were also carried out with the members of Civil Society Groups such as *Niyamgiri Surakshya Samiti* and Green Kalahandiat Lanjigarh and Bhawanipatna (the District Headquarters) to gain a wider perspective of the tribal resistance to Vedanta. Besides the primary source, information from various reports, local newspapers and brochures used during the tribal mobilisation was also gathered, which served as the material for the present chapter.

Legal pluralism as a perspective

The point of departure for an understanding of legal pluralism is the acknowledgement of more than one set of available legal systems, and deconstruction of the conventional conceptualisation of law in society (Benda-Beckmann 2002; Griffiths 2002; Tamanaha 2008; Tamanaha et al. 2012). In the conventional conceptualisation, law is viewed as deriving from the notion of sovereignty and the state's monopoly of legitimate use of violence. The legitimate authority of the state as the sole lawmaker is based on the normative notions of internal and external sovereignty, which encompasses the state's authority to exercise exclusive control over the population that inhabits a territory and the wealth and resources that exist within the territory (Beitz 1991; Benda-Beckmann 1997). However, over the last few decades, legal anthropologists have challenged the state's prerogative of law-making as an important form of legitimate power and assertion of its sovereignty, emphasising its non-monolithic characteristics.

To begin with, the state is not a monolithic block having just one set of legal claims. Several institutions of state mechanism often come out with contradictory policies, which are based on different sets of legal regulations and pursue different interests (Benda-Beckmann and Benda-Beckmann 1997: x). Within the single statutory legal system, different federal, provincial and local laws coexist and a multitude of individuals or institutions is involved in creation and maintenance of such legal orders (Griffiths 2011). Individuals, groups or communities at the sub-national level may make, maintain and un-make their own laws of membership and rights over certain resources. These newly created laws may either be re-interpreted versions of state law, or they may be based on different normative orders such as folk, customary and religious legal systems. Further, a single legal repertoire may have different functions in different settings, such as in government offices and community lives, a process that F. and K. von Benda-Beckmann (1991) term 'multi-locality of law'.

Acknowledgement of the existence of multiple legal orders, which exercise control over individual lives, is not exactly a recent phenomenon. Way back in 1913, Ehrlich recognised the existence of an 'untold number of associations in society that exercise coercion much more forcibly than the state' (Ehrlich 1936: 64). From 1970 onwards, legal anthropologists and scholars working on law have increasingly paid attention to the existence of multiple legal orders, and have challenged the centralists' model of single legal field of state law (see Chiba 1986; Griffiths 1986; Hooker 1975; Moore 1978). One of the important characteristics of legal pluralism is that instead of viewing law as a static phenomenon, it conceptualises law as a dynamic force, one that can be modified and negotiated to suit into situations concerned (Hellum et al. 2010).

Legal anthropologists analytically distinguish between the existence of law as 'normative repertoires' derived mostly from the state's legitimate authority and the existence of law in the social spheres (see Forsyth 2007; Shah 2005). Legal repertoires just 'hang in the air', unless and until the 'when' and 'where' of their evolution into a social factor is concretised (Spiertz 2000: 183). It is the social sphere, or 'social field' as Moore (1973) phrases it, which makes the abstractions of legal repertoires a set of social facts or concrete laws. This examines the distinction between law as study of rules and the actual behaviour of practising those rules. Relationships between rules and behaviour can only be studied by looking into real-life situations in different times and spaces. As Geertz (1983) puts it, law is the distinctive manner of 'imagining the real'.

Early scholars of legal pluralism conceptualised it as 'the accommodation of a variety of bodies of law, i.e. customary, religious and state law within national legal systems, applicable under specific conditions to different ethnic, religious and racial groups' (Spiertz 2000: 179). Such a version of legal pluralism reflects the attempt of colonial governments to legitimise western colonial rules of domination and subordination in the colonies, while at the same time recognising some of the traditional legal practices of indigenous people and creating separate socio-economic and legal spheres for them. However, such accommodation of local traditional legal orders has always remained subservient to dominant state (colonial) law during the period of colonisation, as well as the subsequent periods of state formation. The increasing and active presence of the state in the domains of social life of people in the name of sovereignty after decolonisation, led the legal anthropologists to come out with a different version of legal pluralism, which moved beyond the mere dichotomy of 'formal state law' versus 'local customary law'. In addition to customary law, the most common types of non-state legal orders that are identified by recent scholars are religious-based legal systems, such as Shari'ah court in Nigeria (Oba 2004) and adat court in West Sumatra (Benda-Beckmann and Benda-Beckmann 2006b). Further, Santos (2002: 90) mentions about 'suprastate, global legal orders coexisting in the world system with both state and infra-state legal orders'. Recent legal pluralism scholars such as Sousa Santos (2006) and Twining (2003) also discuss the coexistence of transnational legal systems such as international law and European community law with local and national legal systems. Legal pluralism as it is understood today, therefore, refers to coexistence of multiple legal systems pertaining to one and the same domain of social life (Benda-Beckmann 1983). Instead of focusing on the dualistic opposition of state (formal) versus non-state law (customary/local), legal pluralism started focusing on the tensions and contradictions within and between interacting repertoires of law (Shariff 2008).

Any attempt to study the actual social significance of law should not limit its scope to the state centric formal legal repertoires, rather it should view state law as a part of the multiplicity of normative repertoires of society (Rout 2005). Legal pluralism should therefore include in its framework all instances where other non-state, officially non-legal institutions, create and maintain normative orders. In situations where more than one set of legal order exists, as is the case in most social domains, conflicting claims are legitimised and rationalised by taking resort to any one of the legal repertoires available to people from a set of normative orders. Which of the specific legal orders one choses to justify his/her claims is not known in advance, since 'which specific repertoire, in which specific case, people will orient themselves to, will mostly be a matter of expediency, of local knowledge, perceived contexts of interaction, and power relations' (Spiertz 2000: 191). K. von Benda-Beckmann (1981, 1984) calls this process of using different normative repertoires in different contexts to support and rationalise one's claim 'forum shopping'. It has been well known in natural resource management how local power relations affect the process of resource use and management, with those having access to power and government agencies being capable of influencing the state policies in their favour, besides being powerful in the local context to claim a greater share of the resource.

To summarise the argument, legal pluralism holds the notion that any social domain is capable of generating and enforcing normative repertoires and it is thus possible to have several sets of laws. Besides formal state law designed by state legislature and enforced by government agencies, these may include: religious laws consisting of both written and unwritten religious doctrines and practices; local customary laws expressing people's own values; project or donor laws, including regulations associated with particular developmental projects; organisational laws, which are made by user groups; and a range of local norms and practices (Meinzen-Dick and Pradhan 2002). Such coexistence of multiple legal orders or normative repertoires within a single social domain is called legal pluralism.

Tribal right to land, statutory law and the state in Odisha

The term 'Scheduled Tribe' denotes a constitutional category in independent India, which is closely linked with administrative and political considerations. Prior to independence, the colonial administrators identified the tribal communities using a variety of names. It was with the 1901 Census that tribal communities were identified as those who practised animism, and not until subsequent censuses that animism was replaced by tribal religion (Xaxa 1999). There was also a discussion about the terminology in the Constituent Assembly Debates during the process of framing of the Indian Constitution. While some of the tribal representatives in the Assembly favoured the use of the term '*Adivasi*', literally meaning 'the original inhabitants'; the term 'Scheduled Tribe' was accepted by the framers of the Indian Constitution, with the justification that 'the term *Adivasi* is a general term, which has no specific legal *de jure* connotation, where as "Scheduled Tribe" has a fixed meaning because it enumerates the tribes' (Ambagudia 2011: 34). Since then, the term 'Scheduled Tribe' (hereafter ST) is mainly used as a mark of identification and differentiation. That is, to identify a group of people who are distinct in terms of geographical isolation, simple technology and conditions of leaving, general backwardness and practice of animism, physical features, tribal language, custom, social organisation and so on (Xaxa 1999). STs constitute nearly 22.21 per cent of the total population of the state of Odisha in India. There are 62 tribal communities residing in the state, out of which 13 have been recognised as Primitive Tribal Groups (PTGs). Nearly half of the Odisha's area (44.7 per cent) is under Schedule V of the Indian Constitution, which is a predominantly tribal population. STs and Scheduled Castes (SCs) constitute 68 per cent and 20 per cent respectively of the total population in this area (Census of India 2011).

Tribal rights, law and the colonial state

During the pre-British period, tribal areas of Odisha were comparatively autonomous with high degrees of political and economic independence (Padel 1995). The British period witnessed an increased incursion of state and administration in tribal areas, with the need for revenue being the most important motivation behind administrative control. The British land settlement and land revenue system introduced a monetary economy to the tribal areas, which led to large-scale indebtedness of the tribal communities. The new rulers of the land preferred to settle land with non-tribal people, who could pay the revenue and carry out settled cultivation.

This practice resulted in replacement of tribal intermediary tenure holders by non-tribal tenure holders in many tribal areas (Kumar and Choudhary 2005).

Besides revenue from land, the desire to monopolise revenue from the forest, mostly from the sale of timber, led the British as well as the rulers from the erstwhile princely states to reserve and notify more and more areas as forests under various laws and rules. This subsequently restricted tribal access to and use of these resources. Demarcation and notification of large tracts of forest as reserve lands and protected lands under the Forest Policies of the colonial administration imposed restrictions on shifting cultivation and communal ownership by tribal people over these lands. The enactment of Madras Forest Act, 1885 and Indian Forest Act, 1927, for example, restricted tribal access to land and forest, and consolidated the power of the colonial state over the tribal territories. Summarising the issue of tribal dispossession during colonial India, Kumar and Chaudhary (2005) mention that tribal communities faced loss of land on two accounts in the pre-independence era. First, the lowlands held under private ownership by the tribal community members were lost due to the influx of non-tribal people into the region, non-recognition of rights, indebtedness and the inability on the part of tribal members to pay land taxes (Kumar and Chaudhary 2005). Second, the shifting cultivation forest lands, held under customary rights and clan or lineage territories, were lost due to notification of these lands as reserved lands (see Sivaramkrishna and Jyotishi 2013).

Despite the colonial state's attempt to usurp tribal land, the British administration recognised that the tribal communities needed to be dealt through a separate administrative setup than the rest of the country, and thus, categorised tribal dominated areas as 'excluded' and 'partially excluded' areas. During the pre-independence period, three specific Acts were passed, which made provisions for safeguarding interests of tribal people and establishing separate administrative setups for tribal-dominated areas, which mostly corresponds to the present-day Schedule V areas. One of these Acts was the Scheduled Districts Act, 1874, which entrusted the governor of the state with special powers to conduct administration within Scheduled Areas. The colonial administration also passed certain legislations to protect and safeguard the interests of tribal people. The Agency Tracts Interest and Land Transfer Act, 1917, which was enacted to protect the tribal communities from outside money-lenders, prohibited the transfer of land from a tribal to non-tribal peoples, except with a written consent by the district collector (Rao 1998). Further, the Government of India Act of 1935 prohibited application of any federal or provincial legislature to the excluded or partially excluded areas, unless the Governor by public notification so directs.

Tribal rights and the state law in post-independence India

Post-independent India witnessed a paradoxical coexistence of contradicting legal provisions with respect to tribal rights to land and self-governance. In the period following independence, the law served as an important instrument of the state to recognise and protect tribal peoples' rights to land and forest, as well as to restrict and limit such rights on other occasions by imposing the state's hegemony over the tribal communities. It is, therefore, worth unpacking the twin faces of law: as facilitator of the tribal right to land and self-governance and as impeder of the realisation of such rights.

Legal frameworks facilitating tribal rights

When India achieved independence, Jawaharlal Nehru's *Panchsheel* principle provided a vision for respecting the uniqueness of tribal communities and their customary claims to land. Such a vision of tribal administration finds a reflection in the Constitution of India, where several provisions were adopted to protect tribal rights to land. Article 39 of the Directive Principles of State Policy directs the state to distribute ownership and control of the material resources of the community for the common good of society. Under Article 46, the state is obliged to ensure the educational and economic interests of the weaker sections, especially those of the SCs and STs. Besides, tribal people are also given various forms of reservation by Articles 320, 332 and 334 of the Constitution (Mohanty 2001). Perhaps Article 244 best captures Nehru's vision of tribal administration, argues for respect of ST culture, tradition and customs, and makes provision for autonomous functioning of the Scheduled Areas. The section of the Constitution that pertains to disadvantaged populations – the so-called Fifth Schedule – allows the president to declare areas as 'Scheduled', and the governor the power by public notification to not apply acts of Parliament or modify them in accordance with the needs of ST communities. Most importantly, the Fifth Schedule permits the governor to prohibit the transfer of land by or amongst STs as well as regulate allotment of land to non-STs and the working of money-lenders (Menon 2007: 2240).

Soon after independence, the government of Odisha promulgated several legal measures that had both facilitating and constraining effects on tribal rights to land and forest. The Acts enacted for development and welfare of the STs can be further divided into two categories: (1) promotional measures undertaken to allot land to SCs and STs on priority basis; and (2) protective measures undertaken for controlling land alienation, especially from tribal to non-tribal people (Murdia 1975).[2] In order to protect tribal interests, prevent alienation of tribal land to non-tribal peoples and to ensure their self-governance, several laws and policies were enacted in different periods of time. In this section we cite three important legislations that were specifically designed to protect tribal interests and customary rights in forests and matters of self-governance.

THE ODISHA SCHEDULED AREAS TRANSFER OF IMMOVABLE PROPERTY (BY SCHEDULED TRIBES) ACT, 1956

The Odisha Scheduled Areas Transfer of Immovable Property (by Scheduled Tribes) Act was made applicable to the Scheduled Areas in 1956, replacing the existing laws, which provided for protection of tribal land in these areas. As of now, in the Scheduled Areas of Odisha, the transfer of private land from STs and SCs to non-scheduled groups is regulated by this Odisha Scheduled Areas Transfer of Immovable Property Regulation (OSATIP Regulation), 1956. This piece of legislation stated that any transfer of property by a member of a ST shall be null and void unless it is made to another member of a ST or with the prior consent of the competent authority (Section 3 (1), OSATIP Regulation, 1956). However, the OSATIP Regulation, 1956, proved to be insufficient to protect tribal rights. This was in large part because the law permitted the transfer of *patta* land from tribal to non-tribal people after obtaining permission from mandatory authorities. In such transactions, however, manipulation was high and innocent tribal people often lost their land in dubious transfers (Ambagudia 2010).[3]

Further aggravating the situation for the STs, the OSATIP Regulation of 1956 was amended in 1997 to allow land acquisition from tribal areas by non-tribal communities, wherein a clause was inserted that no ST shall be allowed to transfer land if after such a transfer the total land owned by ST will be reduced to less than one standard acre (see Kumar and Chaudhary 2005). Due to severe criticisms from several quarters, however, the Government of Odisha amended the OSATIP Regulation in 2002, and made the Act much more stringent. Some of the salient features of the OSATIP Regulation, 2002 are as follows:

- Any transfer of property by a member of ST in the Scheduled Areas to a non-tribal is not permitted.
- No tribal can transfer land to even another tribal, if the total land remaining after the transfer is less than two acres of irrigated land or five acres of unirrigated land.
- Persons in fraudulent possession of tribal land shall be liable to a fine of up to Rs. 5,000 and two years of rigorous imprisonment.

PANCHAYAT EXTENSION TO SCHEDULED AREAS ACT, 1997

Another piece of legal and policy framework, enacted after independence to uphold the unique identity of the tribal people and the tribal right to land, forest and self-governance, is the Panchayat Extension to Scheduled Areas (PESA) Act, 1997. The PESA Act has extended the provisions of the Part IX of the Indian Constitution relating to Panchayat Raj to Scheduled Areas throughout country with necessary exceptions and modifications. It also directed the states, which have areas designated under Schedule V of the Constitution, to make state-specific Acts on the basis of the PESA Act within one year of the implementation of the Act. To be specific, the PESA Act has provided that the Gram Sabha[4] or Panchayats at the appropriate level shall have the following powers:

1 to be consulted on matters of land acquisition and resettlement;
2 grant prospecting licence for mining lease for minor minerals and concessions for such activities;
3 planning and management of minor water bodies;
4 power to enforce prohibition or to regulate or restrict the sale and consumption of any intoxicant;

5 ownership of minor forest produces;
6 power to prevent alienation of land and to restore any unlawfully alienated land;
7 power to manage village markets;
8 power to exercise control over money lending to scheduled tribes;
9 power to exercise controls over institutions and functionaries in all social sectors;
10 power to control local plans and resources.

The Act stressed that the state-specific legislations can endow panchayats with powers and authority as may be necessary to enable them to function as institutions of self-government. It also warned the state legislatures to contain safeguards to ensure that panchayats at the higher level do not assume the powers and authority of any panchayats at the lower level or the Gram Sabha. In December 1997, almost after a year of implementation of the central Act, the state of Odisha amended the Odisha Gram Panchayat Act of 1964. In consonance with the central PESA Act, three different Acts were passed in the state legislative assembly, i.e. the Odisha Gram Panchayat (Amendment) Act of 1997, the Odisha Panchayat Samiti (Amendment) Act of 1997, and the Odisha Zilla Parishad (Amendment) Act of 1997.

THE SCHEDULED TRIBES AND OTHER TRADITIONAL FOREST DWELLERS (RECOGNITION OF FOREST RIGHTS) ACT, 2006

One of the most important pieces of legislation designed to protect tribal rights to land and forest is The Scheduled Tribes and Other Traditional Forest Dwellers (Recognition of Forest Rights) Act (FRA), 2006. The Act recognises 13 different rights that are central to the lives and livelihoods of tribal people and other traditional forest dwellers across the country. These rights include rights to land under occupation as well as customary land, ownership of minor forest produce, rights to water bodies, grazing areas, habitat of PTGs, conversion of all types of forest villages/settlements to revenue villages, the right and power to protect, conserve and manage community forest resources, etc. All of these rights had been illegally and unjustly denied during the classification of lands as government forests (both before and after independence). The Act also provides safeguards against arbitrary eviction or relocation of tribal people and other forest dwellers living in/dependent on protected areas. Finally, in its most significant and radical step, the law statutorily empowered Gram Sabhas to protect and manage their surrounding forests for sustainable use and for preserving their cultural and natural heritage.

Legal frameworks impeding tribal rights

Although both the central and the state Government have enacted several laws and policy frameworks to uphold tribal rights to land and self-governance during the post-independence period, the state's concern for environmental preservation and capitalist development have stood in the way of realisation of tribal rights by denying such rights in most occasions. With the intention of preserving the pristine natural landscape from any human intervention and promoting capitalist development, the Indian state has rearranged the natural landscape, restricting the rights of tribes to access and use specific geographical territories. As Vandergeest and Peluso (1995: 386) mentioned 'all modern states divide their territories into complex and overlapping political and economic zones, rearrange people and resources within these units, and create regulations delineating how and by whom these zones can be used'. Such a process of rearranging territories and imposing restrictions of access and use of these areas has been carried out both by the colonial and the independent state in India with the twin interests of environmental protection and capitalist development in mind. This process of territorialisation has led to the usurpation of land and forest from the tribal communities (Menon 2007). The attempts to scientifically manage the forests in India have led to promulgation of several Acts during both the colonial and post-independence period, which curtailed the traditional and customary rights of tribes over these lands. During the colonial era, two specific forest legislations were enacted that were applicable to Odisha, The Madras Forest Act, 1882 and the Indian Forest Act, 1927. The Madras Forest Act, 1882 was in force in the districts of Ganjam, Koraput, Baliguda and some areas of Kandhamal district, whereas the Indian Forest Act, 1927 was applicable to the rest of the state. Both of these Acts denoted large tracts of forest as 'reserved', regardless of prior claims based upon traditional and customary rights on these lands.

The state of Odisha enacted the Odisha Forest Act, 1972, which divided the total forest area into three categories, namely Reserved Forests, Village Forests and Protected Forests. Chapter II of the Act was devoted to the Reserved Forests, according to which the state Government was conferred with the power to declare any land as Reserved Forest, in lands which were the property of Government or over which the Government had property rights. Once declared as Reserved Forest, the Government enjoyed monopoly rights on not only the physical area of the forest, but also on the trees and other forest produce therein. Entering into the forest area that was declared as reserved, for grazing cattle and/or using any forest produce, was also regarded as an offence, punishable under Section 27 of the Act.

Additionally, there are several other environmental legislations, such as the Forest Conservation Act, 1980, the Wildlife Protection Act, 1972, and the Mines and the Mineral Act, 2011, which further impeded tribal rights to land and forest, and increased state control in the name of protecting environment.

Perhaps the most crucial law responsible for land alienation and dilution of tribal rights to land is the Land Acquisition Act, 1894, and its amended version of 1984. Menon (2007) mentioned that an estimated 10 million tribal people have been displaced due to developmental programmes that have made use of the Land Acquisition Act in the name of the greater common good. This Act has given the state the sovereign power to assert its eminent domain to acquire any private or government land for the public purpose.

Another factor responsible for the curtailing of tribal rights to land and self-governance in Odisha is the misinterpretation and faulty implementation of some of the laws, originally designed to protect such rights. For example, even though the Odisha Panchayati Raj Amendment Act of 1997 tried to retain the provision of the PESA Act, on many counts it did not respect the spirit of the Central Act. In its attempts to manoeuvre with the Central Act, the Odisha Amendment Acts of 1997 have modified certain provisions of the PESA Act, and have undermined the basic essence of the Act, which is to ensure self-governance in the tribal areas.

It may be summarised that several legislations approached the question of tribal rights to land, forest and other natural resources differently. While in some cases, they received recognition by the state's law-making agencies, they were regarded as secondary in others. Having gained a perspective of the available legal frameworks and their varied implications for realising tribal rights over natural resources, the following section depicts the case study of tribal resistance over Vedanta Alumina in the state of Odisha, and describes the implications that these legislations may have for tribal communities' rights to land and forest.

Tribal customary law, land and resistance against Vedanta in Lanjigarh

Vedanta's inroad into Lanjigarh[5]

Vedanta Alumina's entry into Odisha dates back to April 1997, when the state-owned Odisha Mining Corporation signed a Memorandum of Understanding (MoU) with Sterlite India, an associate of Vedanta, to extend the right to mine bauxite in the Niyamgiri Hills of Lanjigarh in the Kalahandi district of Odisha. However, during July 1997, the Supreme Court of India challenged mining on protected forest land in the Scheduled Areas of Andhra Pradesh in its infamous Samata Judgment. The Supreme Court of India held that the provisions of Schedule V also applied to the transfer of private or government land in the Scheduled Areas to non-tribal people. The Court ordered the establishment of a committee, comprised of senior government officials at the state level, to consider the feasibility of permitting the industry to carry on mining operations and, if necessary, to place it before a Cabinet sub-committee to take appropriate action. Such an act of judicial activism protecting tribal interests resulted in halting Sterlite India's mining initiative in Kalahandi's Lanjigarh.

In July 2002, after almost five years, the Government of Odisha announced that the decision of the Supreme Court in the Samata case in Andhra Pradesh was not relevant to Odisha, and that the state's existing laws were sufficient enough to protect the tribal communities, thereby proceeding with the Vedanta refinery-mining project. In June 2002, the district collector's office of Kalahandi wrote a letter to affected landowners of the 12 villages of the Lanjigarh area. The letter declared that the District Administration intended to acquire 391 hectares of private land and 628 hectares of common village land for Vedanta's refinery factory at Lanjigarh. In June 2003, Vedanta Resources signed an MoU with the state Government of Odisha for construction of a refinery for aluminium production, a power plant and related mining developments at Lanjigharh in Kalahandi district of Odisha. As per the MoU, Sterlite Industries Limited, an associate of Vedanta Resources, was to set up a refinery with a capacity of 1 million tons per annum for processing aluminium for export. Subsequently, on 5 October 2004, the Odisha Mining Corporation signed a new agreement with Vedanta Alumina for an 'integrated project' including the Lanjigarh refinery, the Niyamgiri bauxite mine, another bauxite mine at Karlapet or elsewhere in the state, and an aluminium smelter in northern Odisha. Vedanta Aluminium subsequently started construction of the Lanjigarh refinery and certain aspects of the mining project, although it had yet to obtain the required regulatory clearances. In 2006, Vedanta Aluminium completed the construction of the refinery and commenced the trial operation using bauxite brought from Korba in the neighbouring state of Chattishgarh, and from other states. The refinery became fully operational in 2007. The Vedanta refinery at Lanjigarh is now located in a 750-hectare complex, with the land acquired from 12 villages from the Lanjigarh block of Kalahandi.

Although Vedanta Alumina was successful in establishing its refinery at Lanjigarh, it had to face several hurdles for its proposed bauxite mining project in the nearby Niyamgiri Hills. In 2004, three writ petitions were filed at the Odisha High Court in Cuttack and in the Supreme Court of India, challenging the proposed mining lease on the grounds that it violated India's constitutional provisions under Schedule V, the Supreme Court's order on the Samata case, and the country's environmental and forest conservation laws.[6] Considering the large-scale opposition to the mining project from various sources, the Supreme Court of India appointed a Central Empowered Committee (CEC) to investigate the matter further. In September 2005, the CEC disallowed mining at Niyamgiri, and stated that the use of an ecologically sensitive area such as the Niyamgiri Hills should not be permitted for mining. Further, it recommended that 'the Supreme Court may consider revoking the environmental clearance dated 22nd September, 2004 granted by the MoEF [Ministry of Environment and Forests] for setting up of the Alumina Refinery Plant by M/s Vedanta, directing them to stop further work on the project'.[7] The Supreme Court's interim order in November 2007 stayed the mining project at Niyamgiri. However, Sterlite Industries (India) Ltd. came out with a revised proposal to which the Supreme Court of India in its August 2008 order granted clearance with certain conditions related to the sustainable development of local communities, protection of the environment and conservation of the wildlife (see Sahu 2012).[8] As a follow up to the Supreme Court August 2008 order, the Government of India and Government of Odisha gave clearance to the diversification of 660.749 hectares of forest land for the mining project in December 2008 and September 2009 respectively.

The Forest Advisory Committee of the MoEF undertook a site inspection of the proposed mining lease area in Lanjigarh of Kalahandi district of Odisha in January–February 2010, and observed several violations of environmental laws, of which the most severe was the case of non-compliance with the FRA, 2006. This led the MoEF to constitute a four-member committee headed by Dr N.C. Saxena, a retired Indian Administrative Service official and member of the National Advisory Council, to examine the proposal submitted by the Odisha Mining Corporation Ltd for diversion of 660.749 hectares of forest land for the Lanjigarh bauxite mines in the Kalahandi and Rayagada districts of Odisha. The committee was given the mandate to investigate the status of the implementation of the FRA, 2006, and the potential impact on cultural and social lives of the *Dongria Kondh* tribe, the biodiversity, wildlife and the ecology of the land. The Saxena Committee found serious violations of FRA of 2006, Forests Conservation Act of 1980, Environmental Protection Act of 2006, and PESA Act of 1997. It reported that

> [a]llowing mining in the area by depriving Primitive Tribal Groups (PTGs) of their rights over the proposed mining site in order to benefit a private company would shake the faith of tribal people in the laws of the land, which may have serious consequences for the security and well being of the entire country.
>
> (Saxena et al. 2010: 9)[9]

Finally, the Supreme Court in its most recent order dated 18 April, 2013 ruled out the mining proposal by Vedanta, and stated that Vedanta has to get clearance from a village assembly, or Gram Sabha (see previous note 4), in each affected village, which will consider the cultural and religious rights of the tribes and forest dwellers living in Rayagada and Kalahandi districts of Odisha. The order stated that '*Gram Sabha* can also examine whether the proposed mining area Niyamgiri, 10 km away from the peak, would in any way affect the abode of *Niyam Raja*.' It further added, 'needless to say, if the bauxite mining project, in any way, affects their religious rights, especially their right to worship their deity, that right has to be preserved and protected'.[10]

The April 2013 judgment of the Supreme Court of India, which is now being discussed as 'the country's first environmental referendum' (Bera 2013), interpreted rights and powers of the tribal and forest dwellers based on two important legal texts, i.e. the FRA of 2006 and the customary and religious rights (sacred rights) provided to the tribal people under the specific provisions for STs in the Constitution (Mahapatra 2013). With regard to the FRA, the Supreme Court stated: '[The] Forest Rights Act has been enacted conferring powers on the Gram Sabha constituted under the Act to protect the community resources, individual rights, cultural and religious rights.' On sacred rights provided to tribal people under specific provisions for STs in the Constitution, the court said:

> Religious freedom guaranteed to STs and the Tribal Forest Dwellers (TDFs) under Article 25 and 26 of the Constitution is intended to be a guide to a community of life and social demands. The above mentioned Articles guarantee them the right to practice and propagate not only matters of faith or belief, but all those rituals and observations, which are regarded as integral part of their religion. Their right to worship the deity Niyam-Raja has, therefore, to be protected and preserved.

Following the Supreme Court order, the Odisha Government prepared a list of 12 villages (five in Kalahandi and seven in Rayagada) likely to be affected by the proposed mining, and issued notices to the collectors of the districts of Kalahandi and Rayagada to hold Gram Sabha meetings between 18 July 2013 and 19 August 2013.[11] In these meetings, all the 12 Gram Sabhas unanimously rejected proposed mining activities by Vedanta, and stressed that the Niyamgiri Hills, spanning 250 kilometres, is the abode of their supreme deity and ancestral kin *Niyama Raja*, who is the protector and preserver of Niyamgiri.[12] Following the decisions by the Gram Sabhas, the MoEF, Government of India finally rejected mining activities by Vedanta on 9 January 2014.

The tribal resistance against Vedanta

Vedanta Alumina's operation in Odisha has witnessed severe protests from local tribes, members of civil society groups and activists since the beginning of land acquisition for construction of the refinery at Lanjigarh in 2002 and the subsequent proposals for mining Niyamgiri Hills for procuring bauxite. Samantara (2006) identifies four key issues with respect to the anti-Vedanta struggle in Lanjigarh: (1) violation of environmental laws and forest conservation laws; (2) violation of the provisions for protection of tribal and under Schedule V of Indian Constitution; (3) negative environmental impacts of bauxite mining and alumina refinery; and (4) continuation of the project against the desire and interests of the local people including the tribal communities. From the very beginning the local tribes, mostly the *Dongria Kondh*, the *Kutia Kondh* and the *Jharnia Kondh* have opposed the proposals of mining and the issue of land acquisition under the banner of a '*Niyamgiri Surakshya Samiti*', a local organisation established to save the Niyamgiri Hills from the mining company. Two more organisations of concerned citizens, civil society groups and activists, i.e. *Kalahandi Sachetan Manch* and Green Kalahandi were set up in Bhawanipatna, the district headquarters of the Kalahandi district to join the local tribes in their struggle against Vedanta. The tribal resistance against Vedanta has witnessed several forms of protest as well as atrocities, by the state and the company, against the tribal communities to suppress their voice. Several strategies, including threats to life, violent attacks by goons and sudden attacks of tribal leaders, were adopted to mute the tribal voices. In one such incident in April 2003, a protest march of merely 350 tribal people, including women and children, was attacked and shattered by private goons sent by the company (Sahu 2012). There was also the alleged murder of Sukru Majhi, a *Kondh* leader on 27 March 2003, while returning to his home from Lanjigarh town.[13] Since then, Lanjigarh's resistance to Vedanta has been an ongoing struggle against violation of tribal customary rights over land and forest.

Tribal customary law and rights over land and forest in Lanjigarh

The Lanjigarh area is primarily inhabited by the *Kondh* tribe and other SCs. The 2001 Census data reveals that the STs and SCs comprise almost three-fourths of the total population, 49 and 24 per cent of the total population respectively. The *Kondhs* of Lanjigarh are mainly divided into three categories: *Kutia Kondh*, *Jharnia Kondh* and *Dongria Kondh*, based upon their settlement. The *Kutia Kondh* live in the foothills of Niyamgiri and the plains, and mostly conduct settled agriculture, and in some cases shifting cultivation. The *Jharnia Kondh* are settled near the springs of Niyamgiri Hills. The *Dongria Kondh* are settled inside the Niyamgiri Hills, the proposed site for Vedanta's mining operations, and are mostly engaged in horticultural activities and shifting cultivation. The *Dongria Kondh*, numbering roughly 7,500, is a unique PTG, and can be compared with the endangered *Jarawas* of Andamans (Samantara 2006).

The Niyamgiri Hills, whose top is to be mined by Vedanta for the extraction of bauxite, has a special place in tribal customary law in Lanjigarh. As per the tribal law, it is considered the most sacred entity for the *Kondhs* of Lanjigarh. The oral history of *Dongrias'* narrates that it was *Niyam Raja* who first established law and order in the tribal land. The tribal people believe that *Niyam Raja* was sent by the supreme creator of this world to maintain law and order situation in the tribal land. The *Niyam Raja* got married to a tribal woman, and established his kingdom in the area inhabited by tribal people of the region. He made the hill as his abode, and reigned over the land with peace and prosperity. The Niyamgiri Hill got its name from King *Niyam Raja*, whose spirit is still believed to be residing in the mountain. Even today, the *Kondhs* worship the *Niyam Raja*, a deity, believed by them to be living in the top of the Niyamgiri Hills. The entire area inhabited by the *Kondhs* is thought to be the kingdom belonging to the *Niyam Raja*. It is believed this deity provides the water that sustains all plant, animal and human life in the vicinity. In addition to worshiping the Niyamgiri Hills (the Forest), the tribes of the locality also worship *Dharni Penu* or the mother earth (the Land). The tribal people worship the Hills (the Forest) and the earth (the Land) at this place of worship and often offer animal sacrifices. On all occasions, the *Dongrias* commence their worship rituals with an offering to their prime deity – the *Niyam Raja*. The Niyamgiri Hills form a biologically rich and diverse habitat, which the tribes in the region rely on for food, fuel wood, forest produces, timber and medicinal plants. Almost all tribal people in the region associate Niyamgiri Hills with their life and livelihood. The streams flowing from the hills form the source of water for them. The tribal people grow crops in the hills. They also earn a livelihood by selling forest produces procured from the Niyamgiri Hills at nearby Lanjigarh market.

As per the customary law of the *Dongrias*, the top of the Niyamgiri Hills is referred to as the '*Kaman Jungle*', which they consider their most sacred place. The local tribal law completely prohibits cutting trees from the top location of the hill, and the local tribes believe that the destruction of forests from this hilltop, which is the abode of the tribal deity, is a loss of their cultural identity, integrity and above all tribal sovereignty enjoyed in the reign of *Niyam Raja*. Therefore, the hilltop is protected by the tribes with their customary laws sanctioned through religious and cultural beliefs. They believe that it is the *Niyam Raja* himself who loves the trees and animals, and, therefore, the tribal people do not hunt or cut trees from this hilltop. It is the same for the forest area, which is very much sacred for the local tribes, and is associated with their life, existence and livelihood, which is to be mined by the Vedanta now. For the local tribes, digging the hilltop is an assault on their basic values of existence in this earth, the murder of their cultural integrity with the hills and an attack on their tribal identity and sovereignty. The case materials that we gathered from the Lanjigarh area suffice the above claims.

During the fieldwork, we were informed the following by Kumuti Majhi, the Convener of the *Niyamgiri Surakshya Samiti* – an organisation established for saving the Niyamgiri Hills. The convener, aged about 55 years, is from Jagannathpur village of Lanjigarh Panchayat, and belongs to *Kutia Kondh* tribe. He possesses the traditional knowledge of several medicinal plants, and can also predict the weather, as well as the future for the local tribal people based upon his knowledge and understanding of the position of planets and stars. Over the past decade, he has assumed a new role, playing a pivotal role in protecting what he calls his '*ma*' and '*mati*' – mother and soil/earth. Since the Vedanta's intrusion into the area, he has spearheaded an organisation called '*Niyamgiri Surakshya Samiti*' to save the Niyamgiri Hills from the clutches of Vedanta. Highlighting the tribal customary law and the importance of Niyamgiri Hills in the tribal life, culture, and value, Kumuti reiterates:

> [W]e are the subjects of the king *Niyam Raja*. *Niyam Raja* reigns this kingdom, and resides in the Niyamgiri Hills. He is our prime deity, supreme creator, and responsible for our very existence in this tribal land. *Niyam Raja* brings us happiness, and provides us everything that is required for human life with his blessings, and has made us who we are today. *Niyam Raja* treats the tribal people like his child, and provides food, water and shelter. Our life, culture, songs, dance and very existence as human being is related to the Niyamgiri Hills. The springs, from which we fetch water comes from the top of the Niyamgiri Hills, and is a blessings of the *Niyam Raja*. Tribal people are self-sufficient here because of the Niyamgiri Hills, which provides food and water to survive, land for cultivation, and herbs and medicinal plants for saving life in cases of illness. Even though the tribal people clear some forest for cultivation, but large trees are never cut from the hill, and especially people here do not touch the top of the hills, since we believe that the hill top is the adobe for the *Niyam Raja*. Now the Vedanta Company wants to mine bauxite from Niyamgiri. This will lead to cutting down of lot of trees from the hill top. Any destruction of trees and the hill is an attack on tribal culture, belief, religion and law. If we don't have Niyamgiri Hill, whom shall we worship? Vedanta and the state are now trying to destruct our identity, cultural practices, and the very essence of life here in this tribal land as a human being.

Similar religious sentiments of *Dongria Kondh* towards Niyamgiri become explicit in Bera (2013), who quotes a tribal women Bejuni, the village priestess of *Dongria Kondh* tribal hamlet in Kesarpadi: 'Your temples are made of bricks and cements, ours are these hills, forests, leaves and streams. If you dig these, we will die with our gods. Like the Brahmans and Kayasthas worship Lord Jagannath, we worship our *Niyamraja*.' The quote echoes the voice of the tribal concerns over development. What we could gather from the discussions is that tribes give a symbolic meaning to the Niyamgiri Hills under their traditional and customary laws, and cannot imagine being a tribal without the Niyamgiri Hills. Life without Niyamgiri will be completely different for the tribes, since they associate their culture to the Niyamgiri Hills. Being tribal is a distinct identity that is essentially related to their culture and cultural practices.

A legal pluralistic understanding of tribal resistance

Legal pluralism as alternative/multiple legal orders

The narration of contradicting legal frameworks with respect to tribal rights to land, forest and self-governance makes it clear that multiple legal orders facilitating and/or constraining tribal rights exist. The tribal people who engage with these alternative legal orders, do so not only as members of an ethnic group, but also as free subjects negotiating power relations. As Chiba (1986) notes, a person living in a number of legal structures is an active agent of the law, who makes a choice between the alternative legal orders available to him/her. A legal pluralistic perspective to the issue of tribal rights to land provides for the availability of multiple legal orders with which the tribes themselves engage. The availability of multiple legal orders with respect to tribal rights to land allows the tribal people to negotiate power relations and adhere to a particular legal order that serves their purpose. It also provides a scope for the tribal communities to present their traditional and customary legal orders as equivalent to other legal orders. In this sense, tribal customary laws need to be understood as an equally important legal order within the broader range of other legal orders either facilitating or impeding tribal rights.

While the tribal communities time and again stressed their traditional rights over *Niyamgiri* based on their customary law, they have also taken recourse to the modern legal framework or the state law to make their point clear. It is pertinent to point out here that when environmental clearance was given to Vedanta based on an interim Supreme Court order in 2008, the *Dongria Kondhs* challenged the project before the National Environmental Appellate Authority.[14] The Supreme Court of India's order on the Vedanta case on 18 April reported that it was the first case of direct challenge of the *Dongria Kondhs* against the project in any court of law.[15] The tribal community challenged the Vedanta Project by raising charges that the full Environmental Impact Assessment Report was not available to public before the public hearing. What is more insightful from a legal pluralistic perspective is the use of multiple legal orders by the tribal community to sustain its claim over *Niyamgiri*, and the cultural and religious rights that they have been afforded. While their resistance against Vedanta was based on their customary, cultural and religious laws, they too resorted to other legal orders available to them to strengthen their claims.

Multiple legal orders and strategies of resistance

The existence of multiple legal orders has influenced the strategies of tribal resistance against Vedanta in Lanjigarh. The customary legal orders' coexistence along with state legal orders creates situations where the tribes are not supposed to be subjected to the state legal order alone. It also gives them a scope for maintaining their independent cultural identity and resistance to any attempt to impose the state legal order on them, which contradicts or violates their own customary legal orders. The tribal people of Lanjigarh adopted their customary legal order and pushed their claims over land and forest, which are preserved in their customary legal order. The broader philosophy of the anti-Vedanta resistance is based upon the notion of tribal rights to land and forest as it is given in the customary legal order, not that of the state legal order. But that does not mean that their strategy of resistance is only confined to their own legal orders. As pointed out in the previous section, tribal resistance against Vedanta has successfully attempted to resort to multiple legal orders available to them to protect their rights over land and forests.

The recourse to the state legal order manifested through the Public Interests Litigations and court cases filed in the Supreme Court of India proves the point that the anti-Vedanta struggle has successfully mobilised formal legal resources, and has deployed specific resources such as scientific and technical inputs, laws and constitutional provisions related to environmental protection to compete with the powerful state and its allies. The Supreme Court of India Judgment in April 2013 elucidates the means by which the anti-Vedanta resistance has used the modern jurisprudence system as an effective tool to protect and preserve the traditional and customary rights of the tribal communities in the Rayagada and Kalahandi districts of Odisha. It is interesting to point out that the tribal resistance in the region has not only made use of both state and non-state legal orders to ascertain claims over nature and natural resources, but also has successfully mobilised formal legal resources to retain the supremacy of their informal/customary institutions over that of the state in matters pertaining to their religion, culture and traditional beliefs. The formal legal mobilisation by the tribal groups has indicated a lack of political will on the part of the Government and insufficient commitment of the state in implementing the existing legal provisions for safeguarding tribal interests in India. We put forth such a claim since the basis for the April 2013 judgment of Supreme Court of India on the Vedanta case was legislation that already existed, but was never taken in the right direction for implementation.[16]

Hierarchy of legal orders

Legal anthropologists often reiterate that, while attempting to sequence different legal orders, the state legal order holds a privileged position of being placed ahead of other legal orders (see Rout 2005). Such sequencing is based on possession of formal legal authority by the state, which makes it distinct from non-state legal orders that are based on customs and traditions. It is, therefore, commonsense that a state legal order will precede the non-state/customary legal orders. However, such a straightforward sequencing would be too simplistic an understanding of the plurality of law. As the case points out, on many occasions states may uphold traditional and customary laws, and make them on par with formal state laws, thereby countering the existence of a fixed sequencing of legal orders.[17] Additionally, when it comes to the hierarchy between state and non-state sources of law, it is interesting to note that in this case there is the existence of a hierarchical notion of different variants of state law, particularly with reference to state laws facilitating tribal rights and impeding them. The state legal orders facilitating tribal rights may only get precedence as long as these laws are deemed to not be in conflict with 'the greater common good', and notions of 'sustainable development' and 'environmental protection' (Menon 2007).

The hierarchical nature of different variants of state law becomes much clearer if we look at the way in which judicial activism has emerged in India, especially with regard to protection of environment as well as rights of the tribal groups. In a recent study of the Supreme Court of India's judgments in environmental cases from 1980 to 2010, Sahu (2014) indicates that the apex court in a majority of cases has upheld the rights of the tribal communities and the claims of the environmental non-governmental organisations (NGOs) against the Government. However, the court's decisions in environmental cases filed against infrastructure projects have gone against these tribal and environmental groups, despite the petitioners making all efforts to prove that state-initiated policies violate statutory acts and constitutional provisions for the protection and improvement of the environment. It proves the point that while on certain occasions issues of tribal rights and environmental concerns have gained priority over issues of industrialisation and economic growth, on others these claims have been toppled over on the grounds of 'greater common good' and 'larger national interests'.

Conclusion

This chapter has examined the tribal resistance to Vedanta in the state of Odisha from a legal pluralistic perspective, and explored the existence and implications of multiple legal orders. Based upon our understanding of the tribal resistance to Vedanta in the present case, and the readings in the discipline of legal anthropology, we may put forth certain concluding observations. To begin with, laws and/or legal orders always exist as plural entities, and an understanding of this plurality is essential in understanding the interactions between different legal orders. As the chapter reveals, the tribal communities who are subject to these plural legal orders are very much aware of it, and thereby switch from one legal order to another to make their claim over the forest resources. It is needless to say that a tribal community's relation with the forest resources is governed by multiple legal orders ranging from traditional, customary and religious laws to formal state laws.

Second, the research highlights the fact that law is never a static phenomenon. It is constantly in the process of making, and subject to negotiations and renegotiations among the parties who are governed by these legal orders. In the natural resource context, as the chapter points out, the communities who claim a resource are always in a process of negotiation with several law-making agencies, including the state, to validate their claim. One of the important factors that has contributed towards this making and shaping of law in the context of natural resources in India is the emerging judicial activism on environmental issues. Over the last few decades, the Supreme Court of India has played a crucial role in redefining environmental law in India, recognising the nexus between tribal rights over nature and environmental protection, and its contribution to protecting and improving the environment.[18] This new and active role of the apex court of the country, and its endeavours to remake and reshape environmental law, has created new dynamism in executive–judiciary relationship. While the legislature and the executive conventionally play a major role in law-making and governance processes, recent developments indicate a more active and significant role on the part of the Indian judiciary in reinterpreting and therefore recreating law. Contrary to its assigned role of interpretation and adjudication of law, the Supreme Court has laid down new principles to protect the environment, reinterpret environmental laws, and created new institutions and structures through a series of illuminating directions and judgments (see Sahu 2008).

Third, in addition to being plural and dynamics, legal orders are also hierarchical in nature. Rather than being a fixed hierarchy, however, legal orders may best be defined as 'floating hierarchies'. The order that maintains precedent over another order hence depends upon the case in hand, the negotiating power of claimants, and broader legal environment (Benda-Beckmann and Benda-Beckmann 2006a). It would therefore be wrong to believe that a fixed hierarchy exists and customary laws always remain subservient to the state laws. Legal orders are instead dynamic and are always in the process of interaction with each other. The making and shaping of alternative legal orders by different contradictory social forces makes our point clear. We may cite here the example of the role of social and protest movements in designing of the PESA Act, 1997, and the FRA, 2006, to substantiate our point about how customary and traditional laws can elevate from the subservient position and are recognised at par with the state laws. Further, the 18 April 2013 order of the Supreme Court of India on the Vedanta case, which asks the state to consult the tribal people and their Gram Sabha to state whether *Dongria Kondhs* have any cultural and religious rights of worshipping *Niyamgiri*, points towards our conceptualisation of 'floating hierarchies' of plural and multiple legal orders.

Notes

1 The author would like to thank Dr Amalendu Jyotishi of Amrita School of Business, Amrita University, Bangalore and Dr Pratyusna Patnaik of National Institute of Rural Development, Hyderabad for their constant encouragement and support to complete the writing of the chapter. The comments and suggestions by Dr Ajit Menon, Madras

Institute for Development Studies, Chennai and Prof. Maarten Bavinck, University of Amsterdam are much appreciated. The financial assistance provided by Swiss Agency for Development Cooperation, Embassy of Switzerland, New Delhi, under its programme 'Local Governance Initiative in South Asia' (LoGIn) for the research is duly acknowledged.

2 Even though SCs can technically speaking also be put under the non-tribal category, on most occasions they are considered on par with STs due to their marginalised status.

3 *Patta* is the legal document provided by the state to claim a private property right over a piece land.

4 Following the seventy-third Amendment to the Indian Constitution, India adopted a three-tier decentralisation structure for devolution of power from the state to the lowest level. These three tiers of local government below the level of provinces in India included: *Zilla Parishad (ZP)* at the district level, *Panchayat Samiti (PS)* at the block or sub-district level, and *Gram Panchayat (GP)* at the village level. GP is constituted as the lowest level of local government formed by either a single village or multiple villages.

5 Part of this section is based upon materials gathered from Amnesty International's (2010) study on Vedanta titled *Don't Mine Us Out of Existence*.

6 Interim Application 1324 and 1474, Writ Petition (Civil) No. 202 of 1995, with Interim Application Nos. 2081–2082 at Writ Petition (Civil) No. 549/2007.

7 For the report of the CEC, see: http://assets.survivalinternational.org/static/files/behindthelies/CEC_report_smaller.pdf (accessed on 19 April 2013).

8 Supreme Court Order, 8 August 2008, on Interim Application No. 2134 of 2007, Writ Petition (Civil) No. 202 of 1995.

9 For the report of the N.C. Saxena Committee, see: www.moef.nic.in/downloads/public-information/Saxena_Vedanta.pdf (accessed on 19 April 2013).

10 Supreme Court Judgment dated 18/04/2013 of the Bench comprising Hon'ble Mr Justice AftabAlam, Hon'ble Mr Justice K.S. Radhakrishan and Hon'ble Mr Justice Rajan Gogoi in Writ Petition (Civil) No. 180 of 2011 Odisha Mining versus MoEF and Others. See: http://supremecourtofindia.nic.in/outtoday/judgments/180.pdf (accessed on 19 April 2013).

11 These 12 villages are: Ejrupa, Phuldumer, Palberi, Kunakadu and Tadijhola in Kalahandi district; and Batudi, Kesarpadi, Serkapadi, Jarapa, Khambesi, Lakhpadar and Lamba of Rayagada district.

12 The first Gram Sabha meeting was held at Serkapadivillae of Rayagada district on 18 July 2013; and the last one at Jerapa village of the same district on 19 August 2013.

13 Personal communication with the tribal leaders during fieldwork. The reason behind Sukru's death is unknown. Tribal people who were said to have witnessed him laying dead in the newly built road to Lanjigarh stated that he was hit by one of the company's trucks while returning to his village alone. Sukru was active in the movement against Vedanta, and was perceived as a threat to the company.

14 Kumuti Majhi and Others versus Ministry of Environment and Forest; Srabbu Sikka and others versus MoEF; R. Sreedhar versus MoEF; Prafulla Samantra versus MoEF and Others, Appeal Nos. 18, 19, 20 and 21 of 2009 of Supreme Court of India.

15 See page 25 of Supreme Court Judgment dated 18/04/2013 of the Bench comprising Hon'ble Mr Justice Aftab Alam, Hon'ble Mr Justice K.S. Radhakrishan and Hon'ble Mr Justice Rajan Gogoi in Writ Petition (Civil) No. 180 of 2011 Odisha Mining versus MoEF and Others. See: http://supremecourtofindia.nic.in/outtoday/judgments/180.pdf (accessed on 19 April 2013).

16 The failure of the implementing agencies of government to discharge their constitutional and statutory duties is much cited as one of the important reasons behind emergence of judicial activism and increasing concerns of the Supreme Court of India in governance arenas (see Baxi 1985).

17 Reference is made here to implementation of several new legislations in the recent years, such as the PESA Act, 1997; the FRA, 2006, and the recent Supreme Court judgments, which have upheld the validity of customary rights of tribal communities.

18 Sahu (2014) identifies three factors that impelled the Supreme Court to play a new role in protecting the environment and upholding the issues raised by tribal communities and environmental NGOs. They are: (1) evolution of Supreme Court from a positivist court to an activist court in the post-emergency period; (2) ideological values and individual preferences of Judges; and (3) active involvement of well-meaning citizens and lawyers who raised environmental issues in the public interest.

References

Ambagudia, J. (2010) 'Tribal Rights, Dispossession and the State in Odisha', *Economic and Political Weekly*, vol. xlv, no. 33, pp. 60–67.

Ambagudia, J. (2011) 'Scheduled Tribes and the Politics of Inclusion in India', *Asian Social Work and Policy Review*, no. 5, pp. 33–43.

Amnesty International (2010) *Don't Mine Us Out of Existence: Bauxite Mining and Refinery Devastate Lives in India*, London: Amnesty International.

Bandyopadhyay, J. and V. Shiva (1988) 'Political Economy of Ecology Movements', *Economic and Political Weekly*, 11 June 1988.

Baviskar, A. (1995) *In the Belly of the River: Tribal Conflicts over Development in the Narmada*, New Delhi: Oxford University Press.

Baxi, U. (1985) 'Environmental Law: Limitations and Potentials for Liberation', in Bandyopadhyay, J. (ed.), *India's Environment: Crisis and Responses*, Dehdradun: Natraj Publishers Pvt. Ltd, pp. 291–309.

Beitz, Ch.R. (1991) 'Sovereignty and Morality in International Affairs', in Held, D. (ed.), *Political Theory Today*, Oxford: Polity Press, pp. 236–254.

Benda-Beckmann, F. von (1983) 'Why Law Does Not Behave: Critical and Constructive Reflections on the Social Scientific Perception of the Social Significance of Law', in *Proceedings of the Folk Law and Legal Pluralism Commission Symposia, Xith International Conference of Anthropological and Ethnological Sciences*, Harold Finkler Compiler, Vol. 1, XIth IUAES Congress, Vancouver, British Columbia, pp. 233–262.

Benda-Beckmann, F. von (1997) 'Citizens, Strangers and Indigenous People: Conceptual Politics and Legal Pluralism', in Kuppe, R. and R. Potz (eds.), *Law and Anthropology: International Yearbook for Legal Anthropology*, Vol. 9, The Hague: Martinus Nijhoff Publishers, pp. 1–43.

Benda-Beckmann, F. von (2002) 'Who's Afraid of Legal Pluralism?', *Journal of Legal Pluralism*, vol. 47, pp. 37–83.

Benda-Beckmann, F. von and K. von Benda-Beckmann (1991) 'Law in Society: From Blind Man's-buff to Multi-local Law', in *Living Law in the Low Countries*. Special issue of *Recht der Werkelijkheid*, Amsterdam: VUGA, pp. 119–139.

Benda-Beckmann, F. von and K. von Benda-Beckmann (1997) 'Natural Resource, Environment and Legal Pluralism: An Introduction', in Kuppe, R. and R. Potz (eds.), *Law and Anthropology: International Yearbook for Legal Anthropology*, Vol. 9, The Hague: Martinus Nijhoff Publishers.

Benda-Beckmann, F. von and K. von Benda-Beckmann (2006a) 'The Dynamics of Change and Continuity in Plural Legal Orders', *Journal of Legal Pluralism*, vols 53 and 54, pp. 1–43.

Benda-Beckmann, F. von and K. von Benda-Beckmann (2006b) 'Changing One Is Changing All: Dynamics in the Adat–Islam–State Triangle', *Journal of Legal Pluralism*, vols 53 and 54, pp. 239–270.

Benda-Beckmann, K. von (1981) 'Forum Shopping and Shopping Forums: Dispute Processing in a Minangkabau Village in West Sumatra', *Journal of Legal Pluralism*, vol. 19, pp. 117–159.

Benda-Beckmann, K. von (1984) *The Broken Strategies to Consensus: Village Justice and State Courts in Manangkabau*, Dordrecht: Foris.

Bera, S. (2013) 'Niyamgiri Answers', *Down To Earth*, 31 August 2013.

Census of India (2011) Government of India.

Chiba, M. (1986) *Asian Indigenous Law in Interaction with Received Law*, London and New York: Kegan Paul International.

Ehrlich, E. (1936) *The Fundamental Principle of Sociology of Law* (translation of *Grundlegung der Soziologie des Rechts*, 1913), Cambridge, MA: Harvard University Press.

Forsyth, M. (2007) 'A Typology of Relationships between State and Non-State Justice Systems', *Journal of Legal Pluralism*, vol. 56, pp. 67–113.

Gadgil, M. and R. Guha (1992) *This Fissured Land: An Ecological History of India*, New Delhi: Oxford University Press.

Geertz, C. (1983) *Local Knowledge*, New York: Basic Books.

Griffiths, A. (2002) 'Legal Pluralism', in Banakar, R. and M. Travers (eds), *An Introduction to Law and Social Theory*, Oxford and Portland: Hart Publishing, pp. 289–310.

Griffiths, A. (2011) 'Pursuing Legal Pluralism: The Power of Paradigm in a Global World', *Journal of Legal Pluralism*, vol. 64, pp. 173–202.

Griffiths, J. (1986) 'What Is Legal Pluralism?', *Journal of Legal Pluralism*, vol. 24, pp. 1–50.

Hellum, A., S.A. Shaheen and A. Griffiths (eds) (2010) *From Transnational Relations to Transnational Laws: Northern European Laws at the Crossroads*, Aldershot: Ashgate.

Hooker, M.B (1975) *Legal Pluralism: An Introduction to Colonial and Neo-Colonial Laws*, Oxford: Clarendon Press.

Kumar, K. and P.R. Chaudhary (2005) *A Socio-Economic and Legal Study of Scheduled Tribe's Land in Odisha*, Washington, DC: The World Bank.

Mahapatra, R. (2013) 'Jerapa Becomes 12th Village to Reject Vedanta', *Down To Earth*, 19 August 2013.

Meinzen-Dick, R.S. and R. Pradhan (2002) 'Legal Pluralism and Dynamic Property Rights', Collective Action and Property Rights (CAPRi) Working Paper, No. 22, Washington DC: IFPRI.

Menon, A. (2007) 'Engaging with the Law on Adivasi Rights', *Economic and Political Weekly*, vol. 421, no. 24, pp. 2239–2242.

Mohanty, B.B. (2001) 'Land Distribution among SCs and STs', *Economic and Political Weekly*, vol. 36, no. 40, pp. 3857–3868.

Moore, S.F. (1973) 'Law and Social Change: The Semi-Autonomous Field as an Appropriate Field of Study', *Law and Society Review*, vol. 70, pp. 719–746.

Moore, S.F. (1978) 'Law and Social Change: The Semi-Autonomous Field as an Appropriate Field of Study', in Moore, S.F. (ed.), *Law as Process: An Anthropological Approach*, London: Routledge and Kegan Paul, pp. 54–81.

Murdia, R. (1975) 'Land Allotment and Land Alienation Policies Programmes for SCs and STs', *Economic and Political Weekly*, vol. 10, no. 32, pp. 1204–1214.

Oba, A.A. (2004) 'Lawyers, Legal Education and the Shari'ah Courts in Nigeria', *Journal of Legal Pluralism*, vol. 49, pp. 113–161.

Padel, F. (1995) *The Sacrifice of Human Being: British Rule and the Kondhs of Odisha*, New Delhi: Oxford University Press.

Rao, P. (1998) 'The Struggle against Land Acquisition', *Economic and Political Weekly*, vol. 33, no. 3, pp. 81–83.

Rout, S. (2005) 'Whose Forest Is It? Customary Rights and Legal Pluralism in Joint Forest Management in Odisha', *Indian Socio-Legal Journal*, vol. 31 (Special issue on Legal Pluralism in India).

Sahu, G. (2008) 'Implications of Indian Supreme Court's Innovations for Environmental Jurisprudence', *Law, Environment and Development (LEAD) Journal*, no. 4/1.

Sahu, G. (2014) 'Why the Underdogs Came Out Ahead: An Analysis of the Supreme Court's Environmental Judgments, 1980–2010', *Economic and Political Weekly*, vol. 49, no. 4, pp. 52–58.

Sahu, M. (2012) 'Industrialisation, Marginalisation and Contemporary People's Movement in Odisha', *South Asian Journal of Socio-Politico Studies*, vol. 13, no. 1.

Samantara, P. (2006) *Niyamgiri Waiting for Justice*, Berhampur, Odisha: Lokshakti Abhiya, Odisha Unit.

Saxena, N.C., S. Parasuraman, P. Kant and A. Baviskar (2010) *Report of the Four Member Committee for Investigation into the Proposal Submitted by the Odisha Mining Company for Bauxite Mining in Niyamgiri*, New Delhi: Ministry of Environment and Forests, Government of India.

Shah, P. (2005) *Legal Pluralism in Conflict: Coping with Cultural Diversity in Law*, London: Glass House Press.

Shariff, F. (2008) 'Power Relations and Legal Pluralism: An Examination of "Strategies of Struggle" among the Santal Adivasi of India and Bangladesh', *Journal of Legal Pluralism*, vol. 57, pp. 1–43.

Sivaramakrishnan, K. and A. Agrawal (2003) 'Regional Modernities in Stories and Practices of Development', in Sivaramakrishnan, K. and A. Agrawal (eds), *Regional Modernities: The Cultural Politics of Development in India*, New Delhi: Oxford University Press, pp. 1–61.

Sivaramkrishna, S. and A. Jyotishi (2013) 'Unearthing the Roots of Colonial Forest Laws: Iron Smelting and the State in Pre- and Early-Colonial India', *Economic and Political Weekly*, vol. 48, no. 5, pp. 39–49.

Sousa Santos, B. de (2002) *Toward a New Legal Common Sense*, London: Butterworths LexisNexis.

Sousa Santos, B. de (2006) 'The Heterogeneous State and Legal Pluralism in Mozambique', *Law and Society Review*, vol. 40, pp. 39–75.

Spiertz, H.L.J. (2000) 'Water Rights and Legal Pluralism: Some Basics of a Legal Anthropological Approach', in Bruns, B.R. and R. Meinzen-Dick (eds), *Negotiating Water Rights*, London: Intermediate Technology Publications, pp. 245–268.

Tamanaha, B.Z. (2008) 'Understanding Legal Pluralism: Past to Present, Local to Global', *Sydney Law Review*, vol. 30, pp. 375–411.

Tamanaha, B.Z., C. Sage and M. Woolcock (eds) (2012) *Legal Pluralism and Development – Scholars and Practitioners in Dialogue*, Cambridge: Cambridge University Press.

Twining, W. (2003) 'A Post-Westphalian Conception of Law', *Law and Society Review*, vol. 37, pp. 199–257.

Vandergeest, P. and N.L. Peluso (1995) 'Territorialisation and State Power in Thailand', *Theory and Society*, vol. 24, no. 3, pp. 385–426.

Xaxa, V. (1999) 'Tribals as Indigenous People of India', *Economic and Political Weekly*, vol. 34, no. 51, pp. 3589–3595.

6 Community rights and statutory laws

Politics of forest in Uttarakhand, Himalayas[1]

Pampa Mukherjee

> Forests are all gone now. There used to be thick growth of Sal and Oak when I came to this village as a young bride. I am seventy years now. In fifty years I have seen everything change. I see more guards and officials now rather than trees. The government is there not to improve our condition but to win elections.
>
> (Rukmini Devi, Bhansali village, Nainital)

Introduction

In many parts of Uttarakhand, one of the newly created Indian hill states, one finds numerous accounts like Rukmini Devi's above. For the rural *pahari*[2] community, the formation of this new political entity[3] has yet to make a substantive difference to their everyday lives and to the state of forests around them. In fact, many of them enumerate incidences of conflict that the villagers have had with the state while asserting their customary claim on forest resources. Few lament that, once a composite entity, the forest is now being fragmented and has been demarcated into diverse property regime types such as reserved and village (*panchayat*) forests. The existence of multiple property regimes and conflicting rules and regulations has made the relationship between the people, state and forest a contested domain.

Given the above context, the present chapter aims to highlight the dominance of statutory laws over local self-governing institutions and how community space is constricted in the name of participatory governance. It argues that, while for both national government and international donor agencies democratic decentralisation has become a major concern, they tend to treat communities as mere beneficiaries rather than as active partners when implementing their programmes at the field level. It also highlights the fact that the introduction of new Joint Forest Management (JFM) in 1996 has overridden the customary claims of communities on forests practised over decades (Poffenberger and Mcgean 1996). Further, it shows how boundaries and fences have become sites of anxiety, creating artificial enclaves and plots, and in the process excluding communities from their rightful access to resources. The chapter, which is based on extensive field research in the Nainital district of Uttarakhand, draws its insights from in-depth interviews with local residents.

The field

Uttarakhand was formed in 2000. Created in the last round of state reorganisation, Uttarakhand is the outcome of *jan andolans* (people's movement) in the region that hastened the pace of political processes towards statehood. In other words, the movement for a separate state[4] was the culmination of earlier social movements that were in a sense instrumental in laying the foundations for the articulation of new mountain state.[5] In fact the famous *chipko* movement[6] spearheaded by the women of the region is one the finest examples of environmental movements in India. Administratively the region has 13 districts.[7]

Agriculture is the predominant economic activity and three-quarters of the land holdings belong to sub-marginal or marginal categories of farmers, with an average of 0.37 hectare of land each. Land distribution is relatively equal, cases of land holdings of over 2 hectares are rare and landlessness is low. The area's agro-pastoral economy remains predominantly subsistence-based, with roughly 50 per cent of rural households, including the rural elite, highly dependent on the village commons and forest lands. Moreover, the level of urbanisation is extremely low in most districts, thus ruling out significant industrial or service activity. As a result, a large portion of the population is dependent on forests for economic sustenance. Lack of employment has led to a high male out-migration in search of employment, which ensures that the women left behind have effectively become managers of the rural household economy.

Forests constitute a significant portion of the land use map of Uttarakhand, covering 60 per cent of the total geographical area – it is the fourth most forested state in India. Forests are a source of livelihood for rural residents and provide resources such as fodder, fuel, green manure and construction timber, all of which are critical to the household economy. In the absence of such resources, effective household incomes would decline substantially. In such a context, the process of determining how forests can be collectively and appropriately managed is vitally important. It is worth mentioning here that the forest in Uttarakhand is managed by different administrative agencies, with three different categories of forest land for this purpose:

1 forests under the Forest Department;
2 *Panchayati* or community forests under *Van Panchayats* (Forest Councils);
3 forests under the Revenue Department.

Of the total forest area two-thirds is under the jurisdiction of the Forest Department. Of the 34,000 sq. km, 30,000 sq. km (88 per cent) is under the jurisdiction of government, and only 4,000 sq. km (12 per cent) is managed by *Van Panchayats* or the Forest Councils.

Though there exist different property regimes in Uttrarakhand – state, common and private – such distinctions are primarily on paper. In fact, Gururani argues that they are quite ambiguous in everyday practice as there may be overlapping of property types (Gururani 2000: 172). Nevertheless, the local residents can clearly identify different forest types in the region under study, which, apart from their local knowledge of the landscape, is also the result of the strong enforcement of boundary rules and regulations by the forest department to demarcate *reserved forests* from community as well as civil/ *soyam* lands, which are under the Revenue Department. *Van Panchayats* have their own set of working rules concerning forest use. They may vary depending upon the local conditions and requirements, and as these rules are collectively evolved, they are binding on all members of the village(s) sharing a forest patch. It is thus apparent that there exist more than one set of rules and codes of property. It is interesting to note that despite having codified and elaborate rules defined through statutory laws for *reserved forests*, there are numerous instances of 'rule violation' as villagers tend not only to access but also extract non-timber forest products such as fuel and fodder from government-owned forest lands. In fact, in their collective memories, the collection of fuel and fodder are their customary rights, and this co-existence of plural laws creates conditions and relations that permit use, access and abstraction of products from the forest in the region.

A village forest may be shared by one or more villages depending upon their proximity to one another and the area of forest demarcated as *Panchayati* forest. Apart from statutory laws defining governance of forests there are also 'deeply embedded cultural, historical and economic claims that allows rules and codes of property to be redefined and reinterpreted outside their narrow legal confines' (Gururani 2000: 176).

Van Panchayats

Van Panchayats are considered unique examples of the decentralised governance of natural resources in Uttarakhand. They were an outcome of conflicts and compromises that followed the settlements and reservations of forests in the hills in the first part of the last century (Ballabh 1993; Agarwal 1999). The first government-approved *Van Panchayat* was formed in Uttar Pradesh hills in 1921 and later a *Van Panchayat Niyamavali (Rules)* was enacted under the section 28 (2) of the Indian Forest Act 1927, which provided broad guidelines for the supervision and management of forests under the control of *Van Panchayats*. According to recent estimates (2012) there are about 12,089 *Van Panchayats* in Uttarakhand. These *Van Panchayats* manage forest areas of 5,449 sq. kms forming about 14 percent of the total area of the state in 11 hill districts (administrative units) in the state of Uttarakhand: Chamoli, Pauri, Tehri, Uttarkashi, Dehradun, Rudraprayag, Nainital, Almora, Pithoragarh, Champawat and Bageshwar.[8] It may be observed that *Van Panchayats* are present only in the hill districts. Haridwar and Udhamsingh Nagar districts located in the foothills and *Terai* region do not have any *Van Panchayats*.

It may be mentioned here that community forest managed in accordance with the Van Panchayat Act is a hybrid of state ownership and community responsibility. In managing and controlling community forest use Forest Councils are guided by rules laid down by the Revenue Department and by the technical advice of the Forest Department. In contrast to civil forests, community forests, or *Panchayati* forests as they are popularly known, are not 'open' forests. Access to and use of forests are guided by a set of working rules meticulously designed and implemented by the communities. Four identifiable sets of working rules exist relating to use, monitoring, sanctions and arbitration. Though only notionally or nominally owned by the communities, community forests are in a very real sense common property with an identifiable user group, have finite subtractive benefits and are susceptible to degradation when used beyond a sustainable limit. However what is more important is that the local users consider them as their collective property and in a real sense they are not actually divisible. These forests are nevertheless not completely immune from misuse, and their condition varies from poor to very good.

The Forest Council Act prescribes how *Van Panchayats* can be formed and imposes duties on village *Panchayats*. The objective is to protect the forest areas and ensure that forest products are being distributed among the entitled holders in an equitable manner. Kumaun Panchayat Forest Rules[9] enacted under section 28(2) of the Indian Forest Act 1927 provide broad guidelines for the supervision and management of forests under the control of *Van Panchayats*. These Forest Council rules lay down the broad parameters of management practices to be followed by the *Van Panchayats*.

The main functions of *Van Panchayats* are as follows:

1 to develop and protect forests by preventing indiscriminate felling of trees and to fell only those which are marked by the Forest Department and are useful from the point of view of silviculture;
2 to ensure that there is no encroachment on *Van Panchayati* land, and that no rules enacted under the Kumaon and Sodic Land Act of 1948 are violated and that no land is encroached upon for agricultural purposes without prior permission;
3 to construct and fix boundary pillars and to maintain them (Forest Rules 18(c));
4 to carry out the directives of the Sub-Divisional Magistrate in developing and protecting forests (Forest Rules 18(a));
5 to distribute its produce amongst entitled holders in an equitable manner (Forest Rules 18 (e));
6 to close 20 per cent of the area of the forest for grazing every year.

They have the following punitive powers:

1 to levy fines up to Rs. 50 with the prior approval of the Deputy Commissioner (DC) (revised to Rs. 500);
2 to seize intruding cattle and impound them under the Cattle Trespass Act of 1871;
3 to forfeit the weapons of the offender.

They have the following administrative and financial powers:

1 to sell grass, fallen twigs and stone slates to local people;
2 to auction trees up to the value of Rs. 5,000 with the approval of the District Magistrate and Divisional Forest Officer. Auctioning of trees above Rs. 5,000 is done by the Forest Department;
3 to distribute the income realised from resin, timber and fees. This is to be distributed as follows:

   i *zillaparishad*[10] is given 20 per cent for creating and maintaining infrastructure;
   ii *gaonsabha*[11] is given 40 per cent for local development schemes if approved by the Block Development Committee;
   iii the remainder is retained by the Forest Department for maintenance and development of *Panchayat* rules.

On the one hand, the villagers feel that, through the Act, the bureaucracy exercises excessive control over Forest *Panchayats*. Bureaucrats, on the other hand, believe that, in the absence of central control, villagers would clearly fell the entire forest (personal communication with district forest officer, range officers and forest guards in charge of *Van Panchayats* of the study area in the year 2002). Nonetheless, on analysing the rules it becomes quite clear that they, while making the *Panchayats* responsible for proper management of the forests, deny them the necessary powers, which seem rather to be vested in the revenue and forest officials. For instance in section 17 of the 1976 Act it is stated that, before a watchman or any other paid staff is employed by the *Panchayat*, previous approval of the DC is necessary. An offence involving a sum of up to Rs. 50 can be compounded only with the previous approval of the DC. Similarly permission is required if seized property (stolen timber, etc.) is proposed to be sold. Administrative control over the *Panchayat* thus still lies with the DC, and technical control has been given to the Forest Department.

Traditional institutions and contemporary challenges

As has been mentioned above, the formal legal rules that have taken prominence in recent years have eroded the element of trust and cooperation among villagers in the use of land and access to forest resources. In this context the most significant effect is the manner in which the institution of the *Van Panchayat* has been affected. The importance and effectiveness of institutions such as *Van Panchayats* lay in the fact that the 'social boundaries' that they evolved and constructed, and consequently the working rules that they devised to ensure optimal, efficient use of resources, were primarily through people's involvement and general consent. This gave these institutions a certain amount of credibility and legitimacy. However over the years there has been a steady decline of the democratic and participatory space, which these village-level institutions provide to their members. Unfortunately the Forest Department's tendency to monitor the functioning of these institutions through generalised rules and regulations in the name of 'participatory governance' has crippled these institutions, reducing them and the communities to the level of mere implementers or at best non-official managers with no substantial powers. The introduction of JFM in the region in 1997 can be interpreted as an initiative that tends to create artificial boundaries by 'crafting administrative communities for better governance, self sufficiency and cost-management' (Agrawal 2001).

Though the *Van Panchayats* managed to survive these multiple obstacles and challenges to their authority in many villages, they have been faced with two additional crises in the last few years that may have long-term implications i.e. they may either weaken them or bring about their demise as relatively democratic and self-governing forest management institutions. Ironically, these new threats are primarily new initiatives that are being promoted in the name of 'participatory governance' or 'state–people partnership' in managing natural resources. The rapid formation of new *Van Panchayats* under the direction of the Revenue Department and the introduction of 'Village Forest Joint Management' by the Forest Department are two such initiatives and Sarin (2001) points out that in reality they are basically an attempt to transfer more authority to the state at the expense of communities.

New *Van Panchayats*

Until recently *Van Panchayats* were primarily local initiatives, created out of genuine concern of the people to protect their forest, which is both their provider and protector. However, a recent spurt in the creation of *Van Panchayats*, coinciding with the inflow of vast funds in the state for JFM activity, has created new sets of complexity for these self-governing institutions. There has been an increase in the demarcation of remaining civil lands as village forests. For example, in Nainital district there were only 61 *Van Panchayats* at the time of independence, but this number increased to 495 by 1999 (Sarin 2001). The formation of these institutions, which was need-based and demand-driven, has been converted into a supply-driven one. Instead of villagers collectively applying for a village forest, the administration has imposed its decisions, irrespective of whether *Panchayats* are required or not. It also ignores other issues, such as ongoing boundary disputes, and existing community management arrangements.

In the past, a *Van Panchayat* could cover two or more revenue villages. With the coming of a new policy, which requires a separate *Van Panchayat* for every revenue village internal cohesion, cooperation and trust among users have been disrupted. Moreover, some multi-village *Van Panchayats* have been re-organised in an abrupt and authoritative manner without consulting the local villagers, thereby disrupting the internal social adjustments and exacerbating intra- and inter-village conflicts. Traditionally, villagers had developed an effective multi-village governance system that was both democratic and equitable. Reorganisation of *Van Panchayats* has in fact destroyed the traditional culture of resource sharing. According to earlier practices, *Van Panchayats* were formed by taking a number of factors into consideration, one of them being the topography and forest cover, particularly in those cases where the institution was shared by multiple villages. The present abrupt division of Forest Councils allowed neither the forest area nor the species composition to be evenly distributed among the villages, consequently resulting in unequal distribution. Some villages are now left with small forest patches with only Chir pine, while others have all the fodder bearing areas. This again has created bitterness among villages and encouraged conflict rather than catalysing cooperation. The changes have also failed to address any of the major problems plaguing the existing *Van Panchayats* – the lack of effective and easily accessible dispute resolution mechanisms, inter-village inequity in the availability of forest areas, the erosion of *Panchayat* authority, and the limited control over forest-based livelihoods and income. Rather than expanding space for local forest management, the rapid and abrupt formation of *Van Panchayats* seems to have reduced it further. According to a study carried out by the Rural Litigation and Entitlement Kendra (RLEK) in Uttarakhand, the recent increase in government interference has resulted in *Van Panchayats* losing their original character. The interference by the forest department into the functioning of *Van Panchayats* is fast eroding the spirit of forest conservation by the local communities. It is too early to predict the effects that state-driven *Van Panchayat* formation might have on local livelihoods, social relations and forest management practices. The process of their formation, however, gives reason for concern.

Village Forest Joint Management (VFJM)

VFJM, which was introduced by the Forest Department in Uttarakhand in 1997, is not only problematic but also paradoxical. This in large part because VFJM currently strengthens state control by curtailing people's traditional rights rather than expanding democratic space. Unlike JFM in other states, which enables villagers to participate in the management of forest lands under the Forest Department's jurisdiction, the VFJM Rules in Uttarakhand enable the Department to become the dominant partner in the management of *Van Panchayats* and civil forest lands. Moreover, the land brought under VFJM falls under the jurisdiction of *Van Panchayats* or the Revenue Department and not that of the Forest Department. The land is managed in collaboration with *Gram Sabhas*, the democratic institutions of local self-government at the lowest level.

According to VFJM Rules, Village Forest Committees (VFCs) may be formed where there are no *Van Panchayats* and there is an effort to link VFJM with local self-government through *Gram Sabhas*. VFCs are expected to be representative of key local interests, with one seat designated for each of the following: women, scheduled castes/tribes, backward castes and for persons with a particular interest in forests. The effort to link the two institutions – the VFC and the *Gram Sabha* – is reflected in the fact that head of the *Gram Sabha* is also the President of the VFC and one of the forest guards is its member secretary. Additionally, the two officials, the President and the member secretary also jointly hold the committee's account. As *Gram Sabhas*[12] in the hills cover more than one village, it is possible that neither the President nor the secretary of the VFC may be a resident of the village whose forest management institution they head. Whereas linking community forest management institutions with those of local government is highly desirable, the order for constituting VFC is a top-down, mechanical prescription. It says nothing about strengthening participatory governance by the *Gram Sabhas* and VFCs or their respective roles and responsibilities within the local governance structure.

While 'communities' have come to occupy centre stage in most of the discourse on development and participation, they in fact tend to become targets or victims of development projects, whether it is the construction of dams, the creation of parks and protected areas or projects such as JFMs. It is worth pointing out that creation of VFCs emphasising participatory governance of forests was not an outcome of any demand of the people in this hill state, but instead one of the conditionalities of the World Bank's $65m loan given to the Uttar Pradesh Forestry Project for the period 1998–2002 (Sarin 2001). As a necessary fallout of agreements between the state government and the World Bank, JFM received priority in the region, which in fact accounted for 30 per cent of the total budget of the World Bank forestry projects of the state. Ironically enough the Bank's appraisal documents do not state any substantive reason for promoting JFM and neither does it specify any process to ensure participation of different stakeholders in VJFM. In the absence of any knowledge, experience and mechanism available to the Bank to motivate 'participation', the responsibility for framing them rests with the Forest Department with no history or experience of working with *Van Panchayats* or knowledge of how to facilitate 'participatory governance'. Experienced and long-standing *Van Panchayats* with an adequate institutional history along with other civil-society/non-governmental organisations (NGOs) working in the same sector would have been the best alternative but they are distinctively conspicuous by their absence.

Van Panchayats and other community institutions are treated as the objects of attention, rather than active participants in redefining their future destiny. The World Bank project simply assumes the desirability of importing the standard JFM model from other states into Uttarakhand, with all its shortcomings, instead of exporting a strengthened *Van Panchayats* framework to them. In fact, most of the NGOs functioning in this newly formed state demand that Uttarakhand government should not accept World Bank liabilities taken by the Uttar Pradesh government in the name of JFM, eco-development and watershed management.

Though it is too early to see the impacts of VJFM on forest-based livelihoods and forest quality, the content of the VFJM Rules suggests a loss of democratic space for local villagers. Despite claims to empower local forest users, the Rules do much to achieve the opposite, by instituting control over decision-making and thus creating dependence with no control over forest resources. This fact becomes all the more conspicuous if one looks at the formation of committees and selection of villages to be brought under VFJM. Prioritisation and selection of villages for VFJM is done by the Forest Department in accordance with several selection criteria, making it a supply- rather than a demand-driven process. 'Spearhead teams' communicate with and develop microplans for selected villages. These teams consist of one assistant conservator of forest; one ranger or deputy ranger; one forester or forest guard; and two NGO 'social motivators'. Experienced *Van Panchayat* leaders with decades of experience of community forest management have no role as facilitators and technical advisers. Instead they are being motivated to protect forests. The agreement to be signed by the participating villagers refers to them as beneficiaries rather than as equal partners. The discourse, vocabulary and the content of the policy, being highly patronising, encourages hierarchy among stakeholders and managers and thereby reduces the community forests to mere administrative zones (Gururani 2000).

Given the circumstances there is a great apprehension that the taking over of forest management by the Forest Department and its intrusion into the functioning of the *Van Panchayats* will fast erode the spirit of forest conservation by the local communities. It represents another example of the total disregard by the state of traditional, community-run systems of natural resource management in the region.

Discussion

The lamentations and accounts regarding the state of forest in the region such as that of Rukmini Devi in the opening lines of this chapter reveal that while policies and institutions have grown, forests are still vanishing. Through such voices, one can argue that the mere implementation of policies is not sufficient to ensure a truly democratic participatory space. The process has to be need-based and evolved rather than imposed and given. Though democratic decentralisation is frequently initiated as a precondition to participatory development, such participation will merely be passive if the decentralisation process fails to consider the ecological, social, cultural and institutional specificities of a given society. Further participatory governance can have democratic relevance only if 'communities' are brought to the centre stage of decision-making. It will then become necessary to recognise, accept and treat communities as relevant actors rather than mere recipients in using, managing and governing resources. At the same time, it is important to understand the implications of bringing the community back into the development discourse.

Van Panchayats, despite being an excellent example of a state–people partnership that has been relatively successful in managing forest resources in the region, are facing challenges from unrealistic and target-driven policies, which are likely to affect their democratic functioning. There is a need to replicate such institutions in other areas rather than interfering with those, which already exist. Moreover, NGOs need to play more active roles in keeping these institutions alive by bringing the communities to the centre stage of decision-making. In order to strengthen such community-oriented institutions, it is necessary to identify such similar institutions and undertake comparative studies so that any anomalies that may be found can be removed.

Epilogue

More institutional changes have occurred since the early 2000s. Two types of *Van Panchayats* existed in the period before 2005 – one that was carved out of reserved forests and governed by the Indian Forest Act, 1927, and another that was carved out of civil/ *soyam* land and governed by the District Schedule Act, 1931. In 2005, the state government, through the Uttaranchal Panchayati Forest Rules, brought about major changes that substantially altered the nature of these institutions. First, it consolidated these two types of *Van Panchayats* into *Gram-Van* (village forest). Second, local institutions such as *Panchayats* are now given more importance over *Van Panchayats* and the secondary status attributed to *Van Panchayats* has consequently resulted in delayed or deferred decisions in matters relating to local issues. In fact the *Van Panchayats* in the region have started functioning like government bodies. In this context, the 2005 Act is seen as further consolidation of the Forest Department's authority over all types of forests in Uttarakhand (Negi et al. 2012).

Despite the fact that there has been a distinct policy shift towards more participatory development since the 1990s, reflected through constitutional provisions, introduction of recent programmes such as the Mahatma Gandhi National Rural Employment Guarantee Act (MGNREGA) and the Forest Rights Act poses challenges at the institutional domain in realising this shift.[13] Studies have shown that initiatives such as JFM and MNREGA, along with local *Panchayats*, have failed to protect and restore local commons lands, provide access to non-timber forest products, and provide livelihoods. In fact, in many places they have come in conflict with community-led initiatives such as the *Van Panchayats* (Harini et al. 2013). The solution therefore is to move from a piecemeal and exclusive approach towards an all-inclusive, long-term policy and programmatic action that incorporates building capacities of the local communities through appropriate institutional mechanisms.

Notes

1 This is a slightly modified version of the paper published in *Journal of Legal Pluralism*, vol.50, 2004 and the required permission has been received from the journal editor. An epilogue provides an update of events since the earlier publication. The article is based on both official data issued by the state government, Uttarakhand and field work undertaken in 2003 as part of University Grants Commission minor research project on state, NGOs and civil society, Panjab University, Chandigarh.

2 The term *pahari* is a commonly used word for hill people.

3 The creation of the state of Uttarakhand as a new political identity was predicated on the idea of development that was to be need-based, people-centred, indigenous and self-sufficient. The state was thus expected to provide, in the popular imagination, ecologically sound development alternatives that would protect the *jal, jangal* and *jameen* (water, forest and land) of the region (for details see Mukherjee 2012: 201).

4 For details on Uttarakhand movement see Kumar (2000), Mawdsley (2000) and Mukherjee (2011).

5 Some of the movements during the period are the *chipko* movement (1973–1980), Nasha Nahi Rozgar Do (1983–1985), Anti-Tehri Dam movement, Askot–Arakot movement (Kumar 2011).

6 For details on the *chipko* movement, see Guha (1989).
7 Guha (1989).
8 Status as of 31.3.2012, Forest Department, Uttarakhand Forest Statistics 2011–2012, Dehradun physical power. Vishwa Ballabh, 1995 Van Panchayat, Seminar No. 406.
9 The Uttarakhand hills had two administrative divisions, Kumaon and Garhwal. The name 'Kumaon' or 'Kumanchal' has been derived from 'Kurmi', a place near Champawat in Pithoragarh district and 'anchal' meaning area (for details see Atkinson 1886: 238 and 403). This division of Garhwal and Kumaon was based on the principle of administrative convenience and cost-effective management of law. The British came to the Kumaon region in 1815 and their presence in the region since then can be treated as a point of departure for delineating the history of the relationships between agriculture and forests, and the dependence of hill dwellers on forests. Due to the tremendous demand for railway sleepers, they brought most of the forests in Kumaon and nearly 60 per cent of the entire land area under their control, in the process limiting and proscribing customary subsistence rights that villagers possessed (Rawat 2003).
10 The Panchayati Raj Institution in India, which constitutes the local rural governance system, is a three-tier structure at the village, block and district level. *Zilla Parishad* (District Council) is the third tier of the *Panchayat* system at the district level.
11 *Gaonsabha* or *Gram Sabha* literally means a village assembly. A *Gram Sabha* consists of all the adults – i.e. voters (persons above the age of 18 years) – living in the area of a *Gram Panchayat* – the local governance tier at the village level of the Panchayati Raj system. The main functions of *Gram Sabha* are to review the annual accounts of *Panchayat*, and discuss and audit administrative reports of its *Panchayat* and schemes for *Panchayat* works.
12 Depending on the size of population (as a matter of fact, number of voters) a *Gram* is defined under the constitutional law with a specific geographical area, which may consist of a single village or a cluster of adjoining villages. In hilly states such as Uttarakhand, where the number of people in a village is small, a *Gram Sabha* may include more than one village.
13 While these legal initiatives recognise the rights of citizenship in terms of resources or employment, they do so in a segregated and piecemeal manner. For instance, the right to employment (MGNREGA) and forest rights (FRA), rather being combined, are treated as distinct and thus implemented separately leading to conflict of community interests.

References

Agrawal, A. (2001) 'State Formation in Community Spaces? Decentralization of Control over Forests in the Kumaon Himalayas, India', *Journal of Asian Studies*, vol. 60, no. 1, pp. 1–32.

Agrawal, R. (1999) 'Van Panchayats in Uttarakhand: A Case Study', *Economic and Political Weekly*, vol. XXXIV, no. 39, 25 September.

Atkinson, E.T. (1886) *Statistical, Descriptive and Historical Account of the North-Western Provinces of India: Dehra Dun, Garhwal, Tarai, Kumaon, Jaunsar-Bawar*, Vol. 3, Allahabad: District Gazetteers of the United Provinces.

Ballabh, V. (1993) 'Van Panchayats', *Seminar*, vol. 406, pp. 33–35.

Guha, R. (1989) *The Unquiet Woods: Ecological Change and Peasant Resistance in the Himalaya*, New Delhi: Oxford University Press.

Gururani, S. (2000) 'Regimes of Control, Strategies of Access: Politics of Forest Use in Uttarakhand, Himalaya, India', in Agrawal, A. and K. Sivaramakrishnan (eds), *Agrarian Environments: Resources, Representations, and Rule in India*, Durham, NC: Duke University Press, pp. 170–190.

Harini, N. et al. (2013) 'Governing the Commons', Seminar No. 641, www.india-seminar.com/2013/641/641_harini_nagendra_et_al.htm, last accessed on 15 July 2014.

Kumar, A. (2011) *The Making of Small State, Populist Social Mobilisation and the Hindi Press in the Uttarakhand Movement*, New Delhi: Orient BlackSwan.

Kumar, P. (2000) *The Uttarakhand Movement*, New Delhi: Kanishka Publishers.

Mawdsley, E. (2000) 'Redrawing the Body Politic: Federalism, Regionalism and the Creation of New states in India', *Journal of Commonwealth and Comparative Politics*, vol. 40, no. 3, pp. 34–54.

Mukherjee, P. (2011) 'Creation of Region: Politics of Identity and Development in Uttarakhand', in Ashutosh, K. (ed.), *Rethinking State Politics in India: Regions within Region*, New Delhi: Routledge, pp. 107–130.

Mukherjee, P. (2012) 'Globality and Imagined Futures: A Brief History of Uttarakhand's Development Dreams', in Brar, B. and P. Mukherjee (eds), *Facing Globality, Politics of Resistance, Relocation and Reinvention in India*, New Delhi Oxford University Press, pp. 201–233.

Negi, B.S. et al. (2012) 'Administrative and Policy Bottlenecks in Effective Management of Van Panchayats in Uttarakhand, India', *Law, Environment and Development Journal*, www.lead-journal.org/content/12141.pdf, last accessed on 21 March 2014.

Poffenberger, M. and B. Mcgean (eds) (1996) *Village Voices and Forest Choices: Joint Forest Management in India*, Delhi: Oxford University Press.

Rawat, A. (2003) 'History and Growth of Panchayati Forests in the Kumaon Himalaya', *Occasional Papers on Perspectives in Indian Development*, no. 13, New Delhi: Centre for Contemporary Studies, NMML Teen Murti House.

Sarin, M. (2001) 'Disempowerment in the Name of Participatory Forestry? Village Forest Joint Management in Uttarakhand', *Forest, Trees and People*, Newsletter 44, April.

7 Handling fishery conflicts in the context of legal pluralism

A case-study analysis of street-level bureaucracy in Tamil Nadu, India[1]

Maarten Bavinck

Introduction

Two legal systems emanating from different loci of authority determine the condition of fishing rights in Tamil Nadu, India. One stems from the state, the other from institutions in the fishing community. Both legal systems consist of rules rooted in a particular knowledge of marine ecology and the effects of human intervention. Fisher law generally has greater legitimacy among fishers; however, backed by the power of the state, official law dominates the formal landscape.

What we have here is a situation of legal pluralism, defined as 'different legal mechanisms applicable to identical situations' (Vanderlinden 1972: 20). This definition locates social dynamics within the reality that various legal systems, from which the parties concerned can draw according to their interests and beliefs, overlay a subject or situation. As each legal system may potentially be called upon, a complex process of interaction occurs (Benda-Beckmann and Benda-Beckmann 2006; Tamanaha et al. 2012). Academics in the field of legal pluralism have applied this schema to various domains, including fisheries (Bavinck 2005; Wiber and Recchia 2010; Wylie 1989).

Another category of academic literature examines the conditions under which property regimes demonstrate management effectiveness (Ostrom 1990, 2012). Management scientists have discovered non-state sea tenure systems co-existing with state-sponsored regimes, and demonstrated their vitality throughout the world (Berkes et al. 2001; Cordell 1989; Kurien 2002; McGoodwin 1991; Ruddle and Satria 2010; Schlager and Ostrom 1993). Very little thought in this perspective has, however, gone to analysing the consequences of the present state of legal pluralism for fishing practice (but see Bavinck et al. 2013; Jentoft et al. 2009).

Academics interested in legal pluralism have focused on the broad range of relationships between state law and non-state legal systems, often highlighting 'the penetration and dominance of state law and its subversion at the margins' (Merry 1988: 886). In this chapter, I focus on the position of what Lipsky (2010) has called the 'street-level bureaucrats', individuals in charge of and responsible for public services. In accordance with Lipsky's definition of street-level bureaucrats (2010: xvii), the officers of the Fisheries Department of Tamil Nadu charged with resolving the conflicts that emerge in the fisheries field, possess substantial discretion in exercising their authority.[2] Although improvisation is a core feature of their jobs, they also develop what he calls 'routines of practice' (2010: xi) to address situations that are essentially similar. In my experience (Bavinck 2001a), these 'routines' are communicated over time from one government officer to another, and become part of the larger administrative culture or toolbox.

The core difference between Lipsky's bureaucrats and my own is the incidence of legal pluralism. Lipsky's recipients of public services do not subscribe to alternative legal systems, and his bureaucrats therefore do not need to navigate the problems of linking various realms of law in a way that makes sense to those involved. In post-colonial societies such as India, this is, however, the living challenge (Baxi 1981; Merry 2012).

It is interesting to note that, despite its obvious utility in conceiving connections between the various parts of a plural order, the notion of street-level bureaucracy has rarely found its way into the scholarly literature on legal pluralism (but see F. von Benda-Beckmann 1989; K. von Benda-Beckmann 1989). With Malawi as the backdrop, Anders (2010) is one of the few who analyses the predicaments and dilemmas of street-level bureaucrats in a legal pluralist context.

In this chapter, I explore one particular case to understand how state officers – and, by implication, the state itself – adjust to fisher law. The setting for this exploration is the Coromandel Coast of Tamil Nadu, and the issue at hand is the regulation of the snail net, which many consider to be a detrimental form of fishing. By investigating a dispute over fisher law, I ask why the state has not established a consistent law practice either by imposing state fisheries law or by integrating fisher law into the formal system. What motivated the officers in charge of mediation to 'muddle through' (Lindblom 1973) in the way they did? I argue that the answer has roots both in the defects of state fisheries law and in governmental perceptions of the strength and value of fisher institutions.

Although the case study in question dates back to the mid-1990s, when I was first conducting ethnographical fieldwork in the area, I believe it continues to illustrate the complex relationship that persists between state and customary law in India.[3] In the postscript, I provide an update of the situation, realised through annual scholarly visits to the region.

The regulation of fisheries along the Coromandel Coast

Two hundred and seventeen fishing hamlets dot the Coromandel Coast of Tamil Nadu between Pulicat Lake in the north and Point Calimere to the south (calculated from CMFRI 2012). Most of these settlements date back many decades, if not centuries. Fishing is the traditional occupation, and most fishers belong to the Pattinavar caste. Each hamlet is administered by a council, or *uur panchayat*,[4] with a head who carries the title of *chettiyar* or *naaddaar*. Although their powers have been reduced and their structure modified, *uur panchayats* still regulate and control many local affairs (Bavinck 2001b).

At the time of the incident that makes up the centrepiece of this chapter, most fishers in this region used a small log craft called *kattumaram* to work the inshore waters close to their hamlets.[5] Contrary to first impression, their fishing technology is highly dynamic. A study of fishing gears indicates that new types of nets, as well as novel applications of old types, are adopted on a regular basis. Although income disparities exist even at the hamlet level, there are no significant economic differences between fishing households, a feature that is due in large part to the lack of variation in fishing technology.

The present-day system of fisher regulation on the Coromandel Coast is predicated on two principles. One of these stems from an awareness of the difficulty of defining property rights in the sea and concerns common access to inshore fishing waters. This principle is checked by another principle that states that the settlement adjacent to a fishing ground has the right to place limitations on its use. However, such conditions are not of a blanket variety, and instead pertain to specific locations, types of gear and periods of time.

One of the major instruments *uur panchayats* along the Coromandel Coast utilise to regulate fishing is the prohibition of a particular type of fishing gear or one of its applications. Such bans (*tadai*) may be pronounced for a limited or an indefinite period of time. Irrespective of duration, they apply to all users of a hamlet's 'territorial waters' and are vigorously enforced. Transgressors are tried by village leaders who impose fines or other sanctions in the event of a violation. Since each *uur panchayat* is autonomous, bans are sometimes very local indeed. In other cases, however, injunctions have a much broader geographical range and follow the distribution pattern of the new gear (for a history of gear bans in northern Tamil Nadu, see Bavinck and Karunaharan 2006).

In imposing gear bans, *uur panchayats* invariably refer to the potential harm that might be caused to the community. An analysis of a large number of bans reveals three recurring definitions of harm: damage to fish stocks on which fishers depend, threat to the majority's style of fishing, and injury to the community as a social entity. When fishers refer to harm imposed on the fish stock, they are concerned primarily with the species that are important to their livelihoods. That is, the variety of species they target because of market price and availability. The second kind of harm stems from competition within one and the same ecological niche (Tuomi-Nikula 1985). In this instance it refers to cases in which a minority employs a gear type that threatens the livelihoods of a larger group of fishers. Finally, harm can be social in nature; if a profitable gear type is too expensive for all but a few fishers, its use is thought to result in undesirable social differentiation.

A combination of all these motives played a role in the banning of the *kachaavalai*, or snail net, which took place along a large stretch of Tamil Nadu shore in 1995 and 1996 (see Bavinck 1996 for a regional analysis of this ban). It is to one incident that occurred in the margins of this larger exercise that we now turn. The reconstruction of events is based on repeated interviews with the Assistant Director of Fisheries, who was involved in the case, and whom I had come to know well through my other work, as well as on regular visits to the hamlets in question. The author was also able to attend the second, and final, peace meeting in full.

Case study: the *kachaavalai* conflict in Chennai

Crowds were congregating in the fishing hamlets of southern Chennai (then still called Madras) on 12 January 1996, in anticipation of one of the great festivals of Tamil Nadu, Pongal. The Minister of Fisheries had decided to hand out free clothing to all fishing families in the state, and Department officers had arrived to distribute the promised garb. In the midst of a throng of fishers awaiting the hand-outs, a fight suddenly erupted between fishers from three neighbouring hamlets: Nochchikuppam, Nadukuppam and Icehouse-Kuppam. As the fight quickly escalated, the police station was alerted. A short while later, the Assistant Commissioner (Law and Order) and five policemen arrived. The atmosphere was charged; many fishers carried weapons and three persons had already suffered injuries.

Managing to separate the warring parties, the police called a peace meeting with representatives of the three hamlet populations. Aware of the history of animosity and violence, and knowing that any incident, real or imagined, might trigger retaliations, one of the first tasks was to determine the source of conflict. The police soon learned that the skirmish had originated in a dispute over fishing rights. Fishers from two of the hamlets had been pushed by traders into trying a new kind of fishing gear, the *kachaavalai* or snail net,[6] but fishers from the third hamlet felt it was destroying the fish stocks on which most of them depended. The latter hamlet wanted this snail net prohibited and had told the users so a few days before the fight. The fishers using the net, however, had resisted, and a quarrel ensued. Hamlet leaders convened a joint meeting without notifying the state, and decided that the complainant *uur panchayat* would send a letter requesting that each of the other *uur panchayats* ban the use of the net. Before this decision could be implemented, however, some fishers had employed the net again, thus setting the scene for the fight that took place later that day.

Convinced that it was indeed the *kachaavalai* that triggered the skirmish, the Assistant Commissioner requested the three *uur panchayats* to ban the use of the net without further ado, and everyone present agreed. However, violations of the ban occurred almost immediately. In response, the Assistant Commissioner requested the Assistant Director of the Fisheries Department responsible for the Chennai region to initiate a second peace-making effort.

The Assistant Director took his assignment very seriously. He first arranged separate gatherings with the fishers of the three hamlets in order to hear them out, and learned that the fishers in favour of a ban actually formed a majority. These fishers explained that the *kachaavalai* had a number of disadvantages. Foremost, the snail net was baited with rotting ray fish or other meat, the smell of which scared off fish varieties on which most fishers depended. In addition, the *kachaavalai* removed snails from the sea floor, and in doing so robbed the inshore area of one segment of the marine food chain. This would naturally decrease the predatory fish population. Third, it was felt that the *kachaavalai* physically interfered with other kinds of fishing conducted in the inshore area. Finally, the fishers considered it unfair that a fishing technique used by a minority of fishers and which had substantial negative effects on the majority should be tolerated.

The Assistant Director had tested their resolve by arguing that the sea was so big, a small fishing appliance could not possibly have such serious results, but the fishers had stood by their assertions.

In the meantime, the same officer was being pressured from another quarter. A delegation of traders dealing in snail products and adversely affected by the fisher bans visited his office along with an important functionary of the ruling party to discuss the matter. Though the Assistant Director managed to rebuff their pleas, he was still unsure as to whether he could stay free from political interference. The Member of the Legislative Assembly (MLA) representing South Chennai might involve himself on behalf of one or the other party, or the Minister of Fisheries himself – native to Chennai – could request a particular standpoint; fisher organisations were also starting to come forward with their opinions.

The day of the second peace meeting arrived. Delegations from the three hamlets and the Fisheries Department had been invited to the Assistant Commissioner's office in South Chennai. The delegation from the hamlet where many fishers still opposed the imposition of a ban did not appear at the appointed time, however, and it was forcibly brought by police bus.

The Assistant Commissioner and the Assistant Director had prepared the meeting well. In advance, they had decided that they should avoid an open-ended debate, and should instead focus on discussing the proposal drafted by the Assistant Director. The latter thus opened the meeting by emphasising that he was interested in peace (*amaiti*) and wanted to have the problems (*pirachinai*) resolved. He also said that regardless of the decision, the three *uur panchayats* would be responsible for enforcement. At this point, playing the role of the devil's advocate, the Assistant Commissioner interrupted: 'Can these council members really control their fellow fishers? Are they at all capable of effectively enforcing rulings?' The fisher representatives maintained an appropriate silence.

The Assistant Director then delivered his proposal, which was largely a repetition of the arguments brought forward by the fishers themselves, yet coated in an aura of scientific veracity. Entreating them to prohibit the *kachaavalai*, he concluded: 'We must protect the main method of fishing of this region and the welfare of the majority of fishers, by prohibiting methods which affect it.'

A brief intermission to hear possible objections followed, but no one spoke up. A police inspector was quick to draft the text of the agreement. When it was read aloud, only the Assistant Commissioner demanded a change:

> Please add that if anybody uses the net in future, it will be considered treachery to the nation (*teesa turoogam*). The Police Department must be informed, and we will maintain law and order on the basis of legal articles prohibiting incitement to communal violence and breaches of the peace.

While the inspector typed out the final version, the Assistant Commissioner soothed the ruffled feelings of hamlet representatives with small-talk about vacancies in the Police Department and a request to propose suitable candidates. All present then signed the agreement, and the meeting concluded. The

Assistant Director later expressed great satisfaction about the calmness of proceedings and the achieved result. His confidence proved well-founded, for six months later the agreement was still in effect.

This case contains some unusual elements, in part because of the strong personalities involved. The policeman in charge happened to have experience with and interest in fishing communities. He thus took the case more seriously than others might have, and invited the Assistant Director to participate in its resolution. The latter was a diligent man, capable, at least to some extent, of keeping outside interests at bay and of judging the incident on its own merits. The relative lack of political meddling is another rare feature of the case. One can also surmise that this incident, which took place in the state capital a few months prior to elections, demanded and received more attention from the Police and Fisheries Departments than it might have done had it taken place at another time or location.

Particularly striking, however, is the Assistant Director's role in this incident. This officer can after all be assumed to be acting in accordance with bureaucratic convention. It is surprising, first of all, that his solution to the *kachaavalai* problem contained not one reference to state law or policy. Was this coincidence? Or are fishing rights issues tackled outside, or in the margin, of state law? One explanation is that state law has neither the range nor the flexibility to be used in cases such as this.

Marine fisheries regulation policy

The Tamil Nadu Marine Fishing Regulation Act of 1983 forms the main body of legislation on fishing within territorial waters. The troublesome circumstances that prevailed in the state's fisheries in the decade prior to its conception largely defined its content. Since the birth of the trawling sector in the 1960s, the conflict between trawler and small-scale fishers had developed to alarming proportions. Over the course of time, it claimed many lives, caused large-scale destruction of capital in the form of fishing gear, and triggered repeated law and order problems. The conflict became an important political issue after large-scale riots took place in Chennai in 1977 and 1978. The authors of the Act of 1983 aimed to defuse this intractable problem by separating the two groups of fishers geographically and in time. They paid less attention to other issues involving fishing rights, and opted for a formulation that left the possibility of further regulation open.

Accordingly, Section 5.1 (a–d) of the Act empowers the government to introduce supplementary regulations on fishing activity in certain areas, during defined hours, or with certain kinds of fishing craft and gear. Section 5.2 specifies the main grounds for such regulations as follows: the need to protect the interests of a particular group of fishers, the conservation of fish stocks, and the maintenance of law and order. The opportunities for supplementary regulation offered by Sections 5.1 and 5.2 have rarely been used, however. Except for the aforementioned restrictions on trawling, the Tamil Nadu government has very few time regulations, area closings or limitations on fishing craft or gear in the state. This means that the state regulation 'map' contains many white and uncharted patches.

It would be unfair, however, to blame this state of affairs on the Fisheries Department alone. In fact, the Department has submitted several suggestions for supplementary regulation to the state government, but these have been kept pending for no other plausible reason than bureaucratic inertia. Consequently, officers of the Fisheries Department are highly reluctant to propose use of the legislative opportunities offered by Sections 5.1 and 5.2 of the Act, and instead prefer other avenues.

Recently the Fisheries Department has sought to make more fundamental changes to the Act of 1983 by removing problematic sections and adding new clauses. One of the suggested changes relates to Section 5.1. As it stands, Section 5.1 provides the state government with the power to regulate, restrict or prohibit fishing activities. Henceforth, if the Department's advice is heeded, the power to issue notifications on fishing rights will be delegated to the district level. Department officers believe this would reduce bureaucratic red tape and hasten the process of state law-making. It would also make it easier to adapt regulations to the conditions of individual districts. If this amendment is passed, every administrative district may accordingly develop a different set of state fishing regulations.

These are all plans for the future. It is interesting, however, that the Fisheries Department's plan mirrors the current ground-level situation in Tamil Nadu. In fact, each district already has a different, albeit non-codified, set of fisheries regulations as a result of factors such as varying implementation of the Act of 1983, the existence of court orders applicable only to a particular district, and informal agreements between fisher groups (Bavinck 2003). The suggestion to amend the Act of 1983 and delegate powers to District Collectors would probably reinforce the current process of differentiation and give it a more stable legal basis.

As for the *kachaavalai* case, it is clear, first of all, that the state cannot utilise its legal system to regulate cases such as this for the simple reason that its marine fisheries law does not take account of them. Government officers find no legislative foothold with which to judge disputes over fishing practices in the artisanal sector.

Fisheries Department officers are free, however, to suggest supplementary regulation on the basis of Sections 5.1 and 5.2 of the Act of 1983. Such regulations could be drafted according to the insights of officers or fishers. In the *kachaavalai* case, the latter option is not necessarily ruled out. After all, fishers motivated the *kachaavalai* ban as a result of their concern about the future of the resource, and Section 5.2 of the Act of 1983 mentions conservation as a valid ground for supplementary regulation. Moreover, the *kachaavalai* ban was not a local affair, but instead one with a larger geographical reach. There is no reason why Department officers and scientists should not investigate the value of the ban according to their scientific norms and, depending on the result, submit it for codification. Important reasons they have not done so include the sluggishness of the bureaucracy and the overall reluctance of officers to draft new legislative proposals.

There are other factors to consider too, some of which are hinted at by a Fisheries Department officer's matter-of-fact answer to the question of why the Department did not codify the *kachaavalai* ban: 'It was simply not necessary.' This statement has two dimensions. It contains an implicit reference to the Fisheries Department's objectives with regard to regulation: 'It was simply not necessary [because we achieved our goals anyway].' A study of the Fisheries Department's regulatory practice reveals a concern less with resources than with conflict management (Martin 1979: 283–284). This sequence of priorities is also revealed in the history and content of the Tamil Nadu Marine Fishing Regulation Act of 1983. Although it mentions conservation, the legislation is mainly aimed at restoring harmony between warring factions of fishers.

The Fisheries Department officer's statement also intimates an approach other than legislative codification: 'It was simply not necessary [because the problem was solved differently].' At the heart of this other approach lie particular conceptions of fisher regulations and institutions that, from the viewpoint of many officers, are better left uncodified.

Before elaborating on this point, we still need to address the legal status of the agreement reached in the police station on the *kachaavalai* case. It is difficult to give an unequivocal answer to this question. It appears that agreements such as the one signed by the representatives of the three village councils on the *kachaavalai* can be and sometimes are taken to court. There they are challenged on the basis of the fundamental rights enshrined in the Constitution of India. Article 14 thus asserts that 'the State shall not deny to any person equality before the law' and Article 19 (g) provides that 'all citizens shall have the right to practise any profession, or to carry on any occupation, trade or business' (Republic of India 1995). Although these rights normally carry substantial weight in jurisprudence, informed officers of the Department feel that the judge would probably uphold the agreement in instances such as the *kachaavalai* case. For one, the agreement bears the signatures of two senior government officers. Furthermore, anyone who complains will inevitably be a member of the three hamlets concerned, and the judge will conclude that he is bound by the signatures of his representatives. This highlights a jurisprudential tradition of upholding local rulings. My informants emphasise, however, that they do not expect anyone to take this agreement to court, and thus the court scenario is only speculative.[7]

Attitudes towards fisher regulation

The peace meeting on the *kachaavalai* hinged on the presence of hamlet delegates, considered to be imperative. In fact, when one delegation failed to arrive, the Assistant Commissioner sent a police van to fetch it. From the onset of the meeting to its conclusion, the organisers were eager to avoid the impression that they were forcing a decision down the participants' throats. This meeting was not meant to announce a government order, but to bring the three *uur panchayats* together in a mutually acceptable agreement. Thus, when the Assistant Director launched his proposal to ban the *kachaavalai*, he chose his words carefully, avoiding terms that might suggest even the slightest directive. Although cloaked in government authority, the speech that followed contained no more than a summary of the arguments raised by the majority group of fishers opposing the ban. From beginning to end, the two officers stressed the responsibility of the *uur panchayats* for monitoring and controlling the agreement.

Such respect for *uur panchayats* is common in the Fisheries Department. It is rooted in an appreciation of both the continuing authority of these institutions within the fishing community and the limitations of the Department's influence. Fishers have a vibrant sense of self-determination and form a closed front against perceived intruders. People with business in the fishing community, such as officers of the Fisheries Department, are well advised to follow the community channels of authority.

However, officers' conceptions of the *uur panchayats* go further than a recognition of their mediating role. They include a sense that there is a separate field of jurisdiction that should not be infringed upon. The officer involved in the *kachaavalai* case thus proclaimed his indignation in another instance when a government department overruled an *uur panchayat* decision. He commented that '[o]fficers shouldn't get involved in council matters or in their fields of jurisdiction'. His dismay was based more on a body of collective experience than on a moral view. In fact, Fisheries Department officers have bad memories of times they have tried to steer events in fishing communities, only to find that their often well-intended efforts generated waves of resistance. Time and time again, Department officers stress with experience that fisheries regulations must emanate from the fishers themselves if they are to be successful. Otherwise, the officers explained, regulations would likely be dead on arrival. Introducing measures that lacked fishers' support was overplaying one's hand. From this point of view, the *kachaavalai* meeting was well executed. Rather than introducing 'foreign' measures, the officers made careful use of local knowledge and opinion in order to reach a locally acceptable solution.

Despite endorsement of the *uur panchayats*' right to manage local affairs, including the definition of fishing rights, Department officers do not always respect the councils' style of functioning. They blame the unevenness of council decisions and point out that the quality of *uur panchayats* depends on the availability of competent leadership. They also argue that hamlet leaders do not always act in the common interest and sometimes take money from interest groups in exchange for a favourable decision.

What then do Fisheries Department officers think of the regulations drafted by the *uur panchayats*? Do they feel that these regulations fit with the imperatives of scientific resource management? The speech given by the officer at the *kachaavalai* meeting suggests an endorsement of fisher regulation and the arguments on which it was based. The officer verbally accepted all the reasons fishers gave for banning the net and acted as if the reasons were part of a conventional scientific knowledge underwritten by the Department. This was not, however, the case. In truth, various officers and marine scientists who were consulted expressed strong opinions that the fishers' fears about the *kachaavalai* related more to superstition than to objective observation.

The scepticism with which Fisheries Department officers view fisher regulations and their underpinnings has a history that begins in the post-Independence era. Specific preconceptions of the nature of fishing communities and of fisher reactions to change underlay the modernisation drive that began in Indian fisheries in the 1950s. Written on the eve of the announcement of substantial government fisheries programmes, the *Handbook of Indian Fisheries* provides the following illustration of these early viewpoints: 'At present the fishing population is illiterate and occupy a very low position in the social scale. Consequently, they are highly conservative and reluctant to adopt new ways and methods in their profession' (Chopra 1951: 124).

The idea that fishers are inherently conservative shaped government thinking in subsequent decades. At regular intervals, Fisheries Department officers noted that the artisanal fishing population blocked well-intended changes. The introduction of nylon webbing in place of cotton, jute and coconut fibre in the fabrication of nets from the late 1950s on is a case in point. This resulted in extensive bans, for fishers down the coast feared that nylon caused excessive bleeding in fish and would force fish stocks to leave the inshore areas. In an interview, a senior staff member explained that he and other Department officers believed that this form of fisher regulation was rooted in illiteracy and 'crude notions':

> We knew the advantages of the technology, and wanted them to use it. We were confident that in the long run their attitude would change. We didn't counter it directly, no. But we let people who wanted to use the new filaments use them.

A full analysis of the history of interaction between the Fisheries Department and the fisher population of the northern Coromandel Coast must be left for another occasion (see Bavinck 2001a). The gist of contemporary bureaucratic opinion is clear, however. Officers feel that fisher regulation stems from unscientific, primitive thought and perhaps from jealousy, and that its content generally need not be taken seriously by modern fisheries managers. This attitude explains the lack of scientific follow-up to concrete instances of fisher regulation; for example, no effort is being made to discover whether the apprehensions fishers expressed about the use of the *kachaavalai* had a scientific foundation. It also helps to explain why Department officers neglected to submit the *kachaavalai* ban for codification in a standard legislative draft and to introduce it to other coastal areas, an action they might well have taken if the ban had been treated seriously.

So why did the Fisheries Department officer act as if he was taking the *kachaavalai* ban seriously, if he and his colleagues entertained fundamental doubts about its usefulness? I have already provided the contours of an answer to this question, but a final element that must be explored emerges in a review of the Tamil Nadu government's approach to incidents of social unrest in the fishing sector.

The law and order perspective

Let me repeat some crucial events in the *kachaavalai* incident. The *kachaavalai* ban captured the attention of the authorities only when it became so controversial among fishers of the area that it escalated into a major physical fight. At this point it attracted the attention of the Police Department, which was interested in restoring a semblance of normalcy. The Assistant Commissioner of Police invited the Fisheries Department to take part in deliberations only after the initial peace effort had failed. From the Assistant Commissioner's point of view, the Fisheries Department's involvement in the second attempt to make peace was intended to establish a solid foundation for a successful imposition of law and order. In this case the Assistant Director appears to have played no more than a supportive role. This is illustrated by the fact that the meeting took place in the police station and not in an office of the Fisheries Department.

Generally speaking, Fisheries Department officers seem to follow a reactive rather than a proactive policy towards fisher regulation. They become involved in matters of regulation only after problems arise and it is imperative that they take measures to prevent a potential disruption of law and order. Often, as in the *kachaavalai* case, this means that police take action first. The Fisheries Department is involved later, if at all, and its efforts are mainly aimed at mediating between police officers and the distrusting fishing community. From this point of view, agreements with and between *uur panchayats*, such as in the *kachaavalai* case, are more an instrument of law and order than of resource management.

However, it is not only in assisting the Police Department that Fisheries Department officers take on a law and order perspective. Numerous officers, the majority of whom do not come from the fishing community, confided their fear of fishers when they were incensed. Their anxiety stems from a popular perception in Tamil Nadu that fishers, more than other sections of the population, are both fearless and aggressive. In some cases, Department officers opted to risk incurring the wrath of their superiors rather than take measures that ran counter to the wishes of the fishing community.

Although they do not believe in fisher regulation as an instrument of resource management and do not give priority to resource management themselves, Department officers are required to play a part in quelling the disturbances sometimes caused by such regulation. Eager to achieve workable compromises, they don cloaks of opportunism and give agreements reached in peace meetings no more weight than necessary. When fishers forget them, the agreements fade into oblivion and retire to the Department's archives having outlived their purpose. This analysis holds true for the *kachaavalai* ban, as a later conversation with the Fisheries Department officer revealed. He emphasised that the settlement of the *kachaavalai* dispute had been no more, but also no less, than 'a matter of maintaining peace'.

Conclusions

The centrepiece of this chapter is a physical row that emerged in the streets of the city of Chennai over a regulation enacted by non-state fisher councils. This chapter highlights the reaction of the government officers involved in addressing this dispute, and concludes that they made no attempt whatsoever to interpret the dispute in terms of state fisheries law. Instead, they upheld the ban of the snail net according to an interpretation of fisher law. The efforts made by these street-level bureaucrats in doing so, however, remained half-hearted and the ban was neither formally promulgated nor extended to other parts of the coastline.

This raises questions as to the nature of the accommodation of the state to fisher law. In investigating the matter, three steps were undertaken. First, the chapter considered the state fisheries law map, discovering that this contains many voids and is not applicable to the issue at hand. Moreover, the procedures to convert fisher regulations into state law prove to be cumbersome. It then examined the bureaucrats' perceptions of fisher organisations and their rule-making, concluding that government officers respect fisher councils mainly because of their authority in the fishing community. The Fisheries Department conversely has a tradition of dismissing the substance of fisher regulations, considering them manifestations of superstition and unscientific thought. Finally, the chapter studies the approach of the Fisheries Department officers involved and concludes that it was dominated by a law and order perspective aimed at pacifying the conflict rather than addressing its origins. This is not only the role law enforcement agencies such as the Police Department expect them to play, but also the one implied by departmental policy, in which resource management has a low priority (but see the postscript).

It became clear from the analysis that, although state fisheries law theoretically applies to the same situations as fisher law does, the two legal systems largely lead a separate existence. State law ends where fisher law begins, and where fisher law is effective, the state sees little reason to become involved. It is only when fishers are unable or unwilling to resolve disputes themselves that the government intercedes. This conclusion was affirmed on the macro-level by the Marine Fishing Act of 1983, which addressed the conflict between artisanal and trawler fishers, but only after village councils demonstrated their powerlessness to contain it. The case study in this chapter is another example on a more local level.

The 'separateness' of the two legal systems manifests itself on a different plane as well. Economic concerns, which include notions of ecological harm, play an important role in fisher regulations. The state, however, approached the dispute that came to its notice mainly from the viewpoint of conflict management. This distinction is not always apparent. An innocent observer might thus conclude that the participants in the peace meeting on the snail net ban shared a concern about the ecological harmfulness of the net, whereas in truth their interests were quite different.

What does the snail net dispute teach us about the presumed dominance of the state in a situation of legal pluralism? The Fisheries Department officers I came to know in the course of my study proved quite sceptical. Their experience with fisheries disputes is one of limited manoeuvring space and even physical peril. For them it is clear that fisheries law cannot be imposed; one can only hope to convince or co-opt the hot-tempered group of individuals, or, more sensibly, to make use of their institutions to achieve one's own ends.

However, this ground-level perspective is not the only reality. After all, as was underlined by the ruthless crackdown of fisher riots in 1977 and 1978 in Chennai (Bavinck 2001a), the state does not lack an ability to impose its will if it commits its resources to this purpose. In practice, however, this is rarely mobilised. The actual influence of the state on a given sector differs from its potential power, exercised under special circumstances.

Three variations of the state's possible role in dealing with other legal systems emerge from the literature on the subject (see Bavinck et al. 2013; Benda-Beckmann and Benda-Beckmann 2006). At one end of the continuum stands the possibility of non-involvement or indifference; the state is not interested in activities that are governed by another legal system, possibly because of their economic unimportance. At the other end stands the possibility of a state that, for reasons of economics or ideology, is highly interested in the activities governed by another legal system and makes successful attempts to bring them under its own control.

A middle ground exists, however, between the two extremes of non-involvement and domination, in which the state wishes to gain (more) control but is ultimately unable to do so. Thus, in writing about irrigation policy in southern India, Wade (1988: 36) concludes that 'the state continues to have a limited ability to reach into villages and push aside or absorb systems of rule that stand in its way; that is, a limited ability to control or meddle'. The counterpart legal system in this situation is capable of partial resistance and generates what Moore (1973) calls a 'semi-autonomous social field'. This would appear to apply to the fisheries field in Tamil Nadu as well. The state might desire greater influence, but is countered by a strong sense of self-determination among the fisher population, which succeeds in committing collective resistance.

Enough has now been said about the systemic aspects of the case study. Just as fascinating, in my point of view, is the performance of the civil servants in charge of conflict management, which reached its zenith during the second peace meeting. The investigation of the way they handled the problem at hand throws light on the nature of public policy in the fisheries field. As Lipsky (2010: xii) points out, 'understanding public policies in street-level bureaucracies requires analysis of how the unsanctioned work of street-level bureaucrats combine with rules and agency pronouncements to add up to what the public ultimately experiences as agency performance'. In the case study at hand, the main performance delivered was the quelling of social disorder in the streets of the capital city, Chennai.

Postscript

Fifteen years have passed since the first version of this chapter was published – years in which some matters have inevitably changed and others have remained the same. The tsunami that struck the Coromandel Coast in 2004 was an important change agent, illuminating, among others, the important role of *uur panchayats* in coastal affairs (for a thoughtful reflection on this topic see Gomathy 2006). Generally speaking, however, the fisher councils of this shoreline seem to be doing what they were doing before, and my respect for their activities in the domain of fisheries management has not diminished. With the completion of the World Bank-/FAO-funded Fisheries Management for Sustainable Livelihoods (FIMSUL) project (https://sites.google.com/site/fimsul/), and other international exposure, the Tamil Nadu Fisheries Department does seem to be entering a new era, in which resource conservation and co-management are becoming keywords. In the course of time this might generate a more genuine official interest in the regulatory activities of village councils. For the moment, however, I am hesitant to believe that officers of the Fisheries Department have changed their policy with regard to problems such as those that emerged in the snail net case. 'Maintaining the peace' likely remains the prevalent motto.

What has happened to the fisher ban on the snail net? The only time I have come across a snail net being used since the ban was in 2009 during the closed fishing season for trawlers in Chennai. A small-scale fisher, who was in the company of a trader clearly interested in the marketing of produce, was cheerfully preparing the net for operation. Asked whether the use of the net was not prohibited, he said: 'yes, it is banned along other parts of the coast', suggesting that it was only in the city that he was able to do this kind of fishing with impunity. Indeed, urban-based *uur panchayats* in Tamil Nadu are generally much weaker than those in rural areas, and less capable of maintaining control (see Bavinck 2001a). I therefore take this incident as an – admittedly weak – indication of the fact that the ban is still in force, and that fisher management is less short-lived than sometimes imagined.

Notes

1 This is a revised version of an article that appeared earlier in the *Journal of Legal Pluralism*, vol. 40, pp. 151–171, under the title '"Maintaining the peace" – state accommodation to subordinate legal systems, the case of fisheries along the Coromandel Coast of India'. My initial intention was only to update the references and add a postscript. Going through the article again, however, I concluded that some more tweaking needed to be done, also in the conceptual realm. Rather than limiting myself to the structuralist argument about the adaptation of one legal system to another, I have now also chosen to highlight the agency of the 'street-level bureaucrats' (Lipsky 2010) involved. This emphasis has also resulted in a new title. It remains to be said that K. Subramanian, who is a magnificent fieldworker, helped to collect the original data, and that Phil van der Krogt has done a good language-editing job.

2 Lipsky (2010) was interested in the situation of lower-level bureaucrats located at the interface with the public they are supposed to serve. The civil servants I refer to in this case study are higher up on the administrative echelon, but have a similar public function.

3 The overall theme of the field research (1995–1996) was the conflict occurring in the inshore fisheries, most notably between artisanal and trawler fishers, and the role played by legal pluralism. For the methodology employed, see Bavinck (2001a).

4 The non-state *uur panchayat* is not to be confused with the lowest tier of the Indian administrative hierarchy, the *Gram Panchayat*. The authority of these caste councils has faded in many parts of Tamil Nadu, but is still particularly strong among fishers.

5 Another section of the population is engaged in trawl fishing. Following the tsunami of 2004, most of the small-scale fishers of Tamil Nadu exchanged their *kattumarams* for fibre-glass boats.

6 Rather than being a wholly new type of gear, the *kachaavalai* is more properly defined as a new fishing application. A net resembling the *kachaavalai* has long been used in various locations to catch crabs. Apparently, because of a growing demand for snails, the crab net was put to a new use.

7 One of the obvious reasons for public hesitancy in taking matters to court is the fact that 'courts cannot provide quick, decisive outcomes' (Mendelsohn 1981: 825) and cases are often kept pending for many years. Rather than looking to the courts for solutions to disputes, litigants are often more interested in furthering them (Cohn 1959: 90). The crisis of the Indian legal system (Baxi 1981) – which irrefutably influences the strategic actions of law-makers, enforcers and the public alike – is beyond the scope of this article.

References

Anders, G. (2010) *In the Shadow of Good Governance: An Ethnography of Civil Service Reform in Africa*, Leiden: Brill.

Bavinck, M. (1996) 'Fishermen regulations along the Coromandel Coast: a case of gear-banning', *Marine Policy*, vol. 20, pp. 475–482.

Bavinck, M. (2001a) *Marine Resource Management. Conflict and Regulation in the Fisheries of the Coromandel Coast*, New Delhi: Sage Publications.

Bavinck, M. (2001b) 'Caste panchayats and regulation of fisheries in Tamil Nadu', *Economic and Political Weekly*, vol. 36, no. 13, pp. 1088–1094.

Bavinck, M. (2003) 'The spatially splintered state – myths and realities in the regulation of marine fisheries in Tamil Nadu, India', *Development and Change*, vol. 34, no. 4, pp. 633–657.

Bavinck, M. (2005) 'Understanding fisheries conflicts in the South – a legal pluralist perspective', *Society and Natural Resources*, vol. 18, no. 9, pp. 805–820.

Bavinck, M. and K. Karunaharan (2006) 'A history of nets and bans: restrictions on technical innovation along the Coromandel Coast of India', *Maritime Studies*, vol. 5, no. 1, pp. 45–59.

Bavinck, M., D. Johnson, O. Amarasinghe, J. Rubinoff, S. Southwold and K.T. Thomson (2013) 'From indifference to mutual support: a comparative analysis of legal pluralism in the governing of South Asian fisheries', *European Journal of Development Research*, vol. 25, no. 4, pp. 621–640.

Baxi, U. (1981) *The Crisis of the Indian Legal System*, New Delhi: Vikas Publishing House Ltd.

Benda-Beckmann, F. von (1989) 'Scapegoats and magic charm: law in development theory and practice', *Journal of Legal Pluralism and Unofficial Law*, pp. 129–148.

Benda-Beckmann, F. von and K. von Benda-Beckmann (2006) 'The dynamics of change and continuity in plural legal orders', *Journal of Legal Pluralism*, vols 53–54, pp. 1–43.

Benda-Beckmann, K. von (1989) 'Comment on Simon and Lynch', *Law & Society Review*, vol. 23, no. 5, pp. 849–854.

Berkes, F., R. Mahon, P. McConney, R. Pollnac, and R. Pomeroy (eds) (2001) *Managing Small-scale Fisheries: Alternative Directions and Methods*, Ottawa: International Development Research Centre.

Chopra, B.N. (ed.) (1951) *Handbook of Indian Fisheries Prepared for the Third Meeting of the Indo-Pacific Council Madras, February, 1951*, Ministry of Agriculture, Government of India.

CMFRI (Central Marine Fisheries Research Institute) (2012) *Marine Fisheries Census 2010*, Cochin: CMFRI.

Cohn, B.C. (1959) 'Some notes on law and change in North India', *Economic Development and Cultural Change*, vol. 8, pp. 79–93.

Cordell, J.C. (1989) 'Defending customary inshore sea rights', in Ruddle, K. and T. Akimichi (eds), *Maritime Institutions in the Western Pacific*, Senri Ethnological Studies No. 17, Osaka: National Museum of Ethnology, pp. 301–326.

Gomathy, N.B. (2006) 'The role of traditional panchayats in coastal fishing communities in Tamil Nadu, with special reference to their role in mediating tsunami relief and rehabilitation', in *Proceedings Regional Workshop on Post-tsunami Rehabilitation of Fishing Communities and Fisheries-based Livelihoods, 18–19 January 2006, Chennai, India*, Chennai: ICSF, pp. 211–244.

Jentoft, S., M. Bavinck, D.S. Johnson and K.T. Thomson (2009) 'Fisheries co-management and legal pluralism: how an analytical problem becomes an institutional one', *Human Organization*, vol. 68, no. 1, pp. 27–38.

Kurien, J. (2002) 'People and the sea – a tropical majority perspective', *Maritime Studies*, vol. 1, no. 1, pp. 9–26.

Lindblom, C.E. (1973) 'The science of "muddling through"', in Faludi, A. (ed.), *A Reader in Planning Theory*, Oxford: Pergamon Press, pp. 151–169.

Lipsky, M. (2010) [1980] *Street-level Bureaucracy – Dilemmas of the Individual in Public Services, Updated Edition*, New York: Russell Sage Foundation.

McGoodwin, J.R. (1991) *Crisis in the World's Fisheries: People, Problems and Policies*. Stanford: Stanford University Press.

Martin, K.O. (1979) 'Play by the rules or don't play at all: space division and resource allocation in a rural Newfoundland fishing community', in Andersen, R. (ed.) *North Atlantic Maritime Cultures*, The Hague: Mouton, pp. 277–298.

Mendelsohn, O. (1981) 'The pathology of the Indian legal system', *Modern Asian Studies*, vol. 15, pp. 823–863.

Merry, S.E. (1988) 'Legal pluralism', *Law & Society Review*, vol. 22, no. 5, pp. 869–896.

Merry, S.E. (2012) 'Legal pluralism and legal culture mapping the terrain', in Tamanaha, B.Z., C. Sage and M. Woolcock (eds), *Legal Pluralism and Development: Scholars and Practitioners in Dialogue*, Cambridge: Cambridge University Press, pp. 66–82.

Moore, S.F. (1973) 'Law and social change: the semi-autonomous social field as an appropriate subject of study', *Law & Society Review*, vol. 7, pp. 719–746.

Ostrom, E. (1990) *Governing the Commons: The Evolution of Institutions for Collective Action*, Cambridge: Cambridge University Press.

Ostrom, E. (2012) *The Future of the Commons – Beyond Market Failure and Government Regulation*, London: The Institute of Economic Affairs.

Republic of India (1995) *Constitution of India (11th ed.)*, Lucknow: Eastern Book Company.

Ruddle, K. and A. Satria (2010) *Managing Coastal and Inland Waters – Pre-existing Aquatic Management Systems in Southeast Asia*, Dordrecht: Springer.

Schlager, E. and E. Ostrom (1993) 'Property-rights regimes and coastal fisheries: an empirical analysis', in Anderson, T.L. and R.T. Simmons (eds), *The Political Economy of Customs and Culture: Informal Solutions to the Commons Problem*, Lanham, MD: Rowman & Littlefield, pp. 13–41.

Tamanaha, B., C. Sage and M. Woolcock (eds) (2012) *Legal Pluralism and Development – Scholars and Practitioners in Dialogue*, Cambridge: Cambridge University Press.

Tuomi-Nikula, O. (1985) 'The cultural-ecological aspect of culture change', *Studia Fennica*, vol. 30, pp. 147–163.

Vanderlinden, J. (1972) 'Le pluralisme juridique: essai de synthèse', in Gilissen, J. (ed.), *Le pluralisme juridique*, Brussels: Editions de l'Université de Bruxelles, pp. 19–36.

Wade, R. (1988) *Village Republics: Economic Conditions for Collective Action in South India*, Cambridge: Cambridge University Press.

Wiber, M.G. and M. Recchia (2010) 'Legal pluralism and integrated management in Saint John Harbour, Canada', *Maritime Studies*, vol. 9, pp. 81–101.

Wylie, J. (1989) 'The law of the streets, the law of the courts, and the law of the sea in a Dominican fishing village', in Cordell, J. (ed.), *A Sea of Small Boats*, Cambridge, MA: Cultural Survival Inc., pp. 152–176.

8 A political ecology of legal plural disconnection in the marine fishery of Junagadh District, Gujarat, India

Derek Johnson

Introduction

In the past 30 years, there has been a fruitful collaboration between social scientists and ecologists on community-based management in fisheries. Scholars working in the areas of maritime anthropology, commons theory, institutional economics, local ecological knowledge and social-ecological resilience have contributed to this area. At the same time, there has been strong interest among scholars in how community-based informal systems can productively relate to formal government systems of fisheries regulation. Scholarly work in this area has been predominantly in the areas of co-management and governance, but the similar interests of legal pluralism offer further opportunities for synergy here. Some of the possibilities for connection have already been explored elsewhere (Bavinck 2001; Jentoft et al. 2009). In this chapter I am interested to bring another combination to the mix. I look at how legal pluralism is enriched when looking at attempts to build formal–informal relations of governing in fisheries by connection to political ecology.

The linking of legal pluralism to political ecology foregrounds three major concerns (Biersack and Greenberg 2006; McCarthy 2007; Meinzen-Dick and Pradhan 2001): the drivers of change; the construction of knowledge and meaning; and power in social relations. Together, emphasis on these areas reinforces arguments for plural legal arrangements that are dynamic, co-constituting of multiple interpretational possibilities and reflective of competing as much as collaborating interests. In a single chapter, it is not possible to explore all of the intersections of legal pluralism and political ecology. I will explore the major ones of relevance to the analysis of my focus case.

My analysis considers the fishery of Junagadh District[1] in Gujarat State, India, a subject that has occupied me for nearly 20 years. The case offers not only a rich basis for exploring the intersection of the various focus perspectives of this chapter, but their particular combinations also shed new light on the Gujarat fishery itself. The Gujarat fishery is striking for its size and economic importance, but also for its marginality to mainstream Gujarati society. That distinctive broad backdrop has been shaped by a specific social and developmental history that has had important implications for the expression of legal pluralism in the fishery.

Legal pluralism is very present in the fishery but I argue that it is largely defective, in the terms that have been used elsewhere (Bavinck et al. 2013), because state officials and fisher leaders have failed to build connections among their institutions for managing the fishery. The why of that failure holds lessons not only for understanding the ecologically unsustainable development path of the fishery, but also reinforces the importance of considering legal pluralism not as a fixed system property, but as something that is contingent and unstable over time.

Legal pluralism, political ecology and the assessment of management institutions in small-scale fisheries

Interactive governance and institutions in fisheries

Since the 1980s, as the ecological and political-economic precariousness of fisheries has increasingly become a concern for social scientists, an important focus of research has been non-state fisheries management institutions. These have been seen as not only critically important to the resilience of small-scale fisheries but also as a potentially valuable complement to state efforts at fisheries management. Non-state fisheries institutions are also held as a fundamental corrective to reductionist approaches to fisheries governance – the latter often drawing on Hardin's logic (Hardin 1968) – that see either the state or the market as the key to fisheries management but overlook the rich social, cultural and geographical particularities of different small-scale fisheries. In recent years various efforts have been made to synthesise that work theoretically (e.g. Charles 2001; McGoodwin 1990). Here I will use the perspective of interactive governance theory to do that service.

A central concern of interactive governance theory is institutions. Institutional theory is diverse and the meaning of institutions is debated (Jentoft 2004). In broad terms, however, institutions consist of not only intangible rules or norms but also tangible organisational bodies that monitor and enforce regulations (Bavinck et al. 2013). Institutions are also nested or embedded features of human life: they intersect and interrelate with other institutions and they are influenced by, and draw strength from, broader social relations and cultural ideas. In interactive governance terms, they are a meso order of governance that links meta-order understandings of the world to the practical first-order efforts to address particular needs or problems on a day-to-day basis (Kooiman et al. 2005).

An important advantage of the interactive governance approach to institutions is how it deliberately positions them within larger social and cultural relations, and other features of the landscape of particular fisheries. Unlike some applications of commons theory or co-management approaches that look at institutions narrowly as defined and relatively static sets of rules or relationships, interactive governance predisposes analysis in systemic or holistic terms and with emphasis on dynamics. The attention of interactive governance to institutional embeddedness highlights the complexities, or 'wickedness', of governance (Jentoft and Chuenpagdee 2009). That attention is also an important link to complementary insights in legal pluralism and political ecology.

The interactive governance perspective on institutions provides a useful framework for analysing the institutions that fishers devise to manage their fisheries. Those management institutions are composed of rules both tacit and more formalised that are anchored in fishers' organisations. So, for example, in Bavinck's (2001) work on small-scale fisheries management institutions in Tamil Nadu, caste councils are the organisations responsible for coordinating and enforcing a collectively understood set of rules regulating access to and use of village territorial waters. The leaders of these organisations are responsible for dispute resolution and for acting as intermediaries with the caste councils of other villages or the urban boat owners' associations that in some ways represent a similar institutional mechanism in urban areas. Since his earlier research in Tamil Nadu, however, conditions have changed considerably with decreasing fish catches, major technological changes following the 2004 tsunami and, most recently, a dramatic surge in outmigration of fishers from his villages of study. These changes are putting pressure on the capacity of caste councils to adapt, and serve as an example of how management institutions in fisheries must be seen in dynamic terms (Bavinck 2008).

Legal pluralism and fisheries

It should be evident from Bavinck's work on institutions for fisheries governance in Tamil Nadu that there is a clear potential for interweaving such holistic governance perspectives with legal pluralism. Bavinck himself has recognised that potential and uses legal pluralism as a primary point of reference in his work on fisheries. Bavinck contrasts three legal spheres of law in the Tamil Nadu fishery: those of the small-scale beach-based fishing villages; the urban trawler boat associations; and the state fisheries regulatory bodies. The juxtaposition of these different coexisting regulatory bodies entails an uneasy and ongoing regulation of fishing activities and space. In some instances, such as the effective alternation of access to fishing grounds between trawlers and small-boat fishers in Ramnathapuram District, interacting legal systems of regulation can be quite effective (Bavinck and Karunaharan 2006).

Fisheries globally are highly diverse. In India this diversity is evident in the range of activities that fishing includes, from beach-based gleaning for shells to month-long trips by mechanised vessels. In general, however, like the institutions of which they are composed, fisheries are embedded within particular contexts: ecological, geographic, economic, historical, social, political and cultural. The historical prevalence of *kattamuram* vessels on the southern and eastern coasts of India, for example, was a technological innovation appropriate to heavy surf and locally available, low-cost, construction materials. Reflecting the particular conditions that shape the fisheries of different places, there is a global diversity of local-level legal institutions for managing small-scale fisheries. These vary even at the micro-scale of contrast between different fishing villages in the same region (cf. Benda-Beckmann 2001 for agriculture).

Aside from recognition of the common presence of institutions adapted to local conditions, a legal pluralist perspective on fisheries by definition also points to the necessity of fishers' legal institutions coexisting with other legal systems. Acknowledgement of the state of legal pluralism in fisheries has become all the more pressing as all scales of fisheries have increasingly come under the scrutiny of state agencies for purposes of sectoral development and social welfare, as conflicts amongst fishing sectors have intensified and as the resources on which fishers depend have become increasingly attractive to other users such as property developers, industrialists and tourists. The literature on legal pluralism is well aware of these sorts of dynamics with regard to resource access and use, and the challenges that the interactions of users and different legal systems pose (Benda-Beckmann and Benda-Beckmann 2006; Meinzen-Dick and Pradhan 2001). The legal pluralist perspective suggests that greater awareness of the existence of alternative legal forums by resource users may help to build common understanding and even create a useful flexibility in establishing legal institutional arrangements. It also, however, recognises that different social positions may create less desirable forms of legal pluralism, where privileged groups are able to influence or use legal institutions to the disadvantage of more poorly endowed groups (McCarthy 2007). Such considerations of power and social structural difference lead to the value of political ecology in rounding out an analytical package for understanding legal pluralism in the Gujarat fishery.

Political ecology and fisheries

Biersack and Greenberg (2006) argue that political ecology in its present form has emerged out of two contrasting theoretical traditions within the social sciences: political economy and post-structuralism. While these approaches recognise the legacy of more deeply ecological approaches to human–environment relations, they are social relational rather than ecological in emphasis. The political economy stream of political ecology broadens Marxist and neo-Marxist insights into the dynamics of capitalism to include attention to the ecological consequences of capitalist change. It attends to how the relative power of different individuals and groups shapes access to and use and perceptions of resources and the environment and how those interests are facilitated or constrained by changing opportunities for production and exchange. The post-structuralist position is linked to Marxist political ecology in its central interest in change and how relations of power shape environmental perception but it decentres the Marxist perspective, seeing it as a valuable critical discourse on human–environment relations under capitalism but also a perspective with its own blind spots (Escobar 1999). Post-structuralist political ecology especially emphasises how understandings of the environment and relations with the environment are socially and culturally constructed. In some formulations it links with practice theory, looking at how the imperfections and contradictions of ways of knowing create opportunities for agency (Idrobo and Davidson-Hunt 2012). In practice, much contemporary political ecology cannot easily be associated exclusively with either stream of political ecology but rather draws inspiration from both, while also drawing inspiration from feminist theory and other sources.

Political ecology is motivated by what it sees as an unfolding global crisis in human–environment relations; a crisis that has significant social justice implications (Foster et al. 2010). Political ecology is thus centrally concerned with change and the corresponding intensification resources use. That intensification is resulting in resource degradation at multiple scales and erosion of resource access by resource users and communities globally. Political ecology questions pathways of development or governance that undermine the capacity of populations to engage in meaningful practices of engagement with the environments on which they depend.

The literature overtly on the political ecology of change in small-scale fisheries is small (e.g. Greenberg 2006; Pálsson 2006), but there is a much larger body of writings that deal with related themes while not necessarily adhering to the formal label. An old and rich stream of this literature looks at the distinctive social organisational, cultural and knowledge features of small-scale fisheries. It challenges assumptions about the inevitability of industrial transition in fisheries (Apostle and Barrett 1992; Menzies 1997; Sinclair 1985) and valorises the distinctive and particularistic contributions of these fisheries (Ram 1992). This work provides an antidote to other more gloomy, if nevertheless also accurate, accounts of dispossession and marginalisation (Carothers 2010; Greenberg 2006; Pálsson 2006). Yet another important sociological and historical literature looks at change and socio-economic differentiation in fisheries (Butcher 2004; Idrobo and Davidson-Hunt 2012; Neis 1999; Ommer 1989; Sider 1986; Sinclair 1985) and how these processes may be shaped profoundly by particular cultural logics (Coulthard 2011; Sider 1986). Another major thread in the fisheries political ecology literature is critical attention to developmentalism (Bailey 1988; Greenberg 2006; Kurien and Achari 1994; Kurien and Mathew 1982; Platteau 1989) and neo-liberalism in fisheries governance as drivers of change for small-scale fisheries (Butler 2006; Johnsen 2013; Pálsson 2006). This work links to recent critical reflections on discourse and relations of power in fisheries governance (Bavington 2010; Béné et al. 2009; Johnsen 2013; Johnsen et al. 2008).

The purpose of this first theoretical section of my chapter has been to explore conceptual relationships linking legal pluralism to interactive governance and political ecology. In broad terms, the three perspectives are interested in the conditions that shape small-scale fisheries institutions. Their differences with regard to that focus can be characterised by orientation. In interactive governance theory, the balance with regard to institutions is optimistic: the theory leans towards arguments to strengthen cooperation. In political ecology, the balance is the reverse: political ecology draws attention to the ways in which institutions are marshalled to favour some interests over others. Legal pluralism is analytically more neutral: it can be employed to illustrate constructive legal plural interactions or it can demonstrate how dominant legal regimes systematically disrupt subordinate ones (McCarthy 2007; Moore 2011).

Data sources and methods of data collection

The empirical portion of this chapter is a synthesis of data from two long-term periods of research and a series of short visits and correspondence with contacts in the Gujarat fishery. The two major periods of research were from September 1997 to January 1999 and for a total of six months in 2004 and 2005.[2] During these longer periods of research and during the shorter visits, the core research methodology was participant observation. This was supplemented during the longer periods by surveys designed to understand variables at the population level. During the first period, I conducted a household census of the village where I was based for a year. During the second period, in collaboration with Dr Jyothis Sathyapalan, I coordinated a survey of the entire district. The majority of the individuals with whom I have interacted and interviewed over the years in Junagadh District were fishers from all caste groups. I have also met formally and informally with numerous other participants in the fishery including government officials, traders, processors, and suppliers of ancillary services to the fishery.

The bulk of my research has been conducted in the fishing harbour of Veraval and in the smaller village landing centre where I lived during my first major research period. I have spent time in all of the landing centres of the district and Diu, however. I have also made research visits to Porbandar District and to the Fisheries Department headquarters in Gandhinagar. I sought to balance my more ethnographically rich work in the village landing centre and Veraval with the large-scale district survey.

Legal plural disconnection in Junagadh District

In the remainder of the chapter I use the Junagadh fishery case to support the argument that the analytical perspective of legal pluralism may be enhanced by coupling it with interactive governance theory and political ecology. Specifically, while legal pluralism provides a way to highlight and examine crucial social relational and normative aspects of the fishery, it is only through a political ecology lens that a full sense of the historical factors driving the current governance contradictions in the fishery becomes evident. My approach proceeds in layers. I start with some basic orienting considerations on the Junagadh fishery. From there I use some of the fisheries system descriptive tools of interactive governance, with some attention to prevailing relations of power, to describe the heterogeneous social and economic groups in the fishery and their inter-relations. I then proceed to describe the non-state and state regulations that structure fishers' lives and reflect on the degree to which they also shape relations among groups in the fishery. In the discussion section that follows, I elaborate an historical argument for understanding the virtually intractable division between the state and the non-state legal systems. Only by drawing together the three theoretical perspectives of the chapter to analyse the Junagadh case is it possible to get a holistic sense of the obstacles to establishing a legal plural governance approach for the Junagadh fishery.

Orientation to the Junagadh fishery

Junagadh District is the southernmost district on the central Saurashtra peninsula of Gujarat State (see Figure 8.1). The district's coastline is 156 kilometres in length and is a mix of sandy beaches frequently interrupted by large limestone outcroppings. The high productivity of the fishery is in large part due to the broad gently sloping continental shelf of Gujarat, which extends at least 100 kilometres to the south of Junagadh's main trawler port of Veraval. According to our estimates in 2005, the total fishing population of the district was almost 100,000 (Johnson and Sathyapalan 2006). Veraval is the main fishing centre of the district. It has the largest fishing population, lands most of the district's catch, and is the main fish processing and trading hub for the entire state. Junagadh has 22 other significant fish landing centres and a couple of additional tiny fishing hamlets. In addition to Veraval, there are five other landing centres with dedicated port infrastructure for fisheries. The remaining fishing settlements are beach-based, most of which are protected by headlands or other geographical features from the direct force of the sea.

As is typical of tropical fisheries, the fishery of Gujarat targets dozens of species. Fishers reported catching 120 different species, most of which have market value (Johnson and Sathyapalan 2006). The most important species by total value are croakers, cuttlefish and squid, catfish, ribbonfish, shrimp, white pomfret, Bombay duck, shark and Jew fish (Gujarat 2008). Most of these species owe their

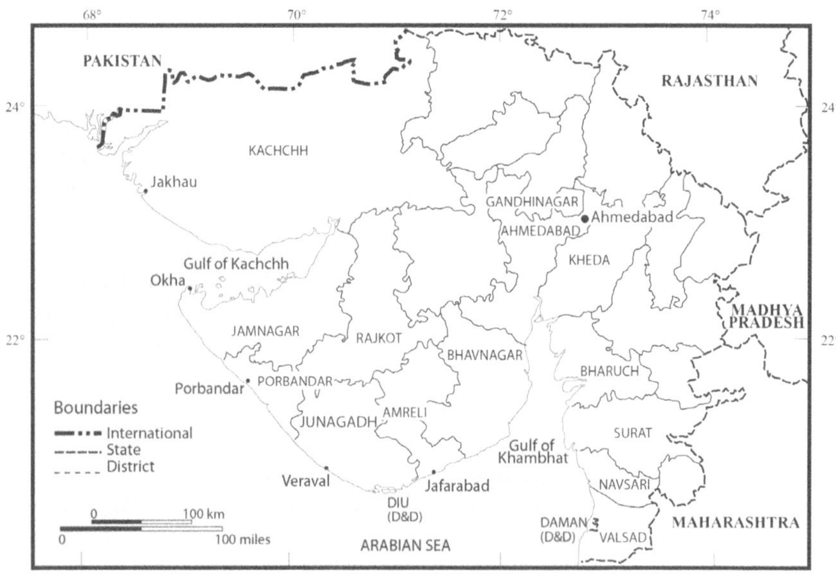

Figure 8.1 Map of Gujarat coastal districts.

Source: Author.

importance to their status as targets of the trawler fleet, which produces by far the highest volumes of catch in the district. Nonetheless, gill net fishers catch many of the same species targeted by trawlers and are the primary producers of high-value white pomfret. The bag net fleet is the primary supplier of Bombay duck and also catches significant quantities of shrimp.

The fishery is driven by an annual cycle that revolves around the monsoon, which usually begins around mid-June and begins to taper off by mid-August. Good-quality monsoon rains are critical for the productivity of the fishery. In addition to its ecological function, the rough seas of the monsoon also impose a break on fishing activity; one reinforced by the national ban on monsoon fishing that has been in effect since 2003. The monsoon period gives fishers a chance to rest and the opportunity to repair boats and gear. Fishing is at its peak in the months after and immediately before the monsoon. In the winter months from December to March, there is normally a significant dip in productivity in inshore waters, even in a good year.

Socio-economic diversity in the Junagadh fishery

The Junagadh fishery is heterogeneous in multiple ways, including with regard to the legal systems that shape the actions of different groups of participants in the fishery. That heterogeneity is one factor among others that contributes to the difficulty of governing the fishery. At the same time, the diversity of social groups provides a potential, although untapped, resource for the fishery's governance.

The very marine ecological diversity of the area has facilitated the development of different strategies for catching fish and thus socio-economic differentiation. The principle ecological division of relevance for differentiation in the practice of fishing is between the eastern quarter of the district, from Navabandar to Rajpara, and the remaining western stretch of coast. Strong currents, likely in conjunction with tidal flows in the Gulf of Khambhat, appear to be associated with a particularly rich production of small shrimps and other species, including Bombay duck in particular, in eastern Junagadh District. The intensity of currents makes fixed bag nets (or *dol* nets) particularly effective and they have become the dominant fishing method in the area. In the remainder of the district fishers are divided into the trawl-based sector and a sector that uses gill nets and hook and line technology. The former is a highly effective active gear but one that is also very ecologically damaging. The latter gears are passive in that they entrap fish rather than pursue them. They are also more selective in their operation. Each sector can be further divided into finer technological sub-sectors based on vessel size, gear complement and engine power but I will not delve further into those details here (but see Johnson and Sathyapalan 2006). In addition to these primarily commercially oriented fisheries, it is also important to acknowledge the beach-based subsistence fishery using cast nets, hooks and lines and stake nets, which is important for household food security.

In India, trawling is distinguished from the other fishing methods with the label mechanised. Other technological sectors of the fishery are motorised, non-motorised or artisanal. Here I will identify the trawl sector as industrial and the remaining sectors as small-scale. This helps to the make the connection to the broader economic dimensions of each sector. While virtually all boat-based fishing is commercially oriented, there are important qualitative differences between the trawler sector and the other sectors. Most trawlers are now operated as business ventures in the sense that they are an investment producing fish for trade and are run using wage labour. They feed directly into the export-oriented processing plants of Veraval and Mangrol and many are owned by processing plant owners, indicating some degree of vertical integration. The fishers running the inboard and outboard motor boats of the gill net sector and those operating *dol* net boats also direct their catches primarily to commercial purposes, and much of that also goes to the major processors, but the logic of production is different. The small-scale sector is organised at a household level and crew are employed using a share system. This social relational difference in the economic organisation of the small-scale and the trawler sector is reinforced by a strong sense of antipathy by small-scale fishers to trawlers. This is primarily due to their perception of the ecological destructiveness of trawling and the frequent destruction of small-scale gear by trawlers. While I have not studied this systematically, I think that the difference also reflects the perception by small-scale fishers that trawling represents a different logic of fishing.

The small-scale/trawler division to an important degree corresponds to class differences in the fishery. The economic elite of the Junagadh fishery controls the fishery's most productive capital: the family enterprises in this group own multiple trawler vessels, reportedly as many as 40 per enterprise, and are also involved in fish trading, processing and export. There are also small-scale fishing-based families that own multiple craft and are involved in fish trading, but the most successful families in this group cannot approach the economic clout of the urban-based trawler-owning families and they are ultimately dependent on the latter for processing and the upper links in the fish market chain. Below both groups in terms of economic status are boat owners not involved in the fish trade and crew without fixed capital in the fishery.

Diversity in the fishery is heightened further by caste and religion. As a whole, fishers in Gujarat, as elsewhere in India are considered to be low caste by virtue of their profession. Amongst the fisher population, the major caste groups are the Hindu Kharvas and Kolis, each of which is further subdivided into two sub-caste groups. Both of these major caste groups are Hindu. Kharvas dominate the trawler sector, while Kolis dominate the *dol* net sector. Hindus comprise about 90 per cent of the fishing population of Junagadh, with Muslims making up the rest of the population. Muslim fishers are mostly of the Machhiyara caste, which also has sub-caste divisions. In addition to the Machhiyaras, there is also a significant group of Bhadela Muslim fishers who are primarily involved in *dol* net fishing at Navabandar. Muslim Machhiyaras largely practice gill net and long line fishing. There is a sprinkling of other Muslim and Hindu caste groups involved in the fishery but the vast majority of participants in the fishery are from the Kharva and Machhiyara fishing castes and from the low status Koli caste. The most lucrative processing and international trading areas of the fishing economy are dominated by Kharvas and some other Hindus, with one or two Muslim exceptions. The domestic fish trade is dominated by Muslim Memons, Patnis and Sheikhs. Members of Hindu and Muslim groups involved in the fishery dominate the local fish trade. This is the only sector of the economy where women play a significant and often lead role. The only other major area of Hindu and Muslim female employment is as wage labourers in the processing sector.

The Junagadh fishery's legal plural matrix

This complex social landscape provides a significant portion of the canvas on which legal pluralism plays out. The other portion, of course, is supplied by the state. I turn to the state legal system after describing fisher legal institutions. Fishers and fish processors have a number of institutions that aim to regulate action and relationships (Johnson and Sathyapalan 2006). Of these, only three, caste councils, boat owners' associations and a Gujarat-level fisher organisation, have direct relevance for the actual conduct of fishing. Their activities with regard to fishing are primarily in the areas of conflict resolution and distribution of state-subsidised fuel. They enforce only a few regulations that can be linked to resource management.

Caste councils, or *samaj* or *nath*, are present for all caste groups involved in fishing and are instituted at the fishing settlement level. In some instances, multiple *samaj* for a single caste exist in particular settlements, reflecting past unresolved conflicts within the caste leadership. *Samaj* are led by a leader (*patel* or *nath pramukh*) who is supported by a number of respected senior men (*agewano*) and, for big *samaj*, office staff. Leadership positions in the *samaj* are supposed to be rotating but in my experience particularly influential or effective *patels* and *agewano* may retain their posts for years at a time. The *samaj* function as a local level of administration for members of a given caste. While not formally recognised by the state, for members of the caste the *samaj* is often more important to the conduct of their day-to-day lives than the state. *Samaj* power varies by caste group and by place: the Kharva *samaj* organisations, for example, are particularly powerful, while those of the Machhiyaras are relatively weak. Nonetheless, for the resolution of disputes and other local matters, the *samaj* is the first recourse for all caste groups.

The main legislative body for the *samaj* is the caste court for which the *patel* is the ultimate arbiter of decisions, after consultation with his *agewano*. Depending on the wealth and size of the caste group, the *samaj* may have its own building to house the court. The Veraval Kharva *samaj* is large enough to have a small complex of additional buildings, including a temple and a jail. The Veraval Kharva *samaj* meets twice daily; *samaj* in smaller centres meet less frequently, sometimes on an ad hoc basis only. The main task of the caste court is to uphold caste regulations. These are primarily moral and social relational in nature. The court upholds caste rules regarding endogamy, monogamy and public sobriety, passes judgement on crimes such as theft and battery, and arbitrates conflicts amongst caste members. The *samaj* also act as an intermediary in relations with other *samaj*, whether of the same caste or others. The *samaj* of each fishing caste group are linked together in a larger caste-wide organisation that meets periodically to discuss caste affairs.

In relation to fishing, the primary role of the *samaj* is to mediate conflicts that cannot be resolved by the boat owners' association, when the latter are present. Disputes may occur at different levels of the production chain. They may be between crew and owners about compensation or working conditions; they may be between boat owners and fish suppliers or moneylenders, or they may be between owners of vessels if there is an accident or incident of gear destruction at sea. In the small-scale sector, an example of the kinds of norms of fishing practice that that *samaj* may enforce concerns distance between nets, and the orientation of nets, set by separate boats. The spirit of the rule here is that a fisher who comes to a fishing spot after another fisher has set his nets should not block the passage of fish to the net of the first. He also must ensure that his nets are set at a sufficient distance so that they will not become entangled with others' gear. If these rules are violated, the offended party may seek compensation from the *samaj*.

The only directly ecological regulation that may be enforced by *samaj* relates to the religious calendar. Hindu small-scale fishers are expected to not fish (or consume fish) on the eleventh day of every fifteen-day cycle (*aigyaras* in Gujarati) of the Hindu lunar calendar and on the thirtieth day of the lunar month (*amas*) as these are considered particularly sacred days. A similar but less well-observed proscription applies to fishing during the holiest month of the Hindu calendar year, *Sravan*, towards the end of the monsoon period. These restrictions apparently used to apply to the trawler sector as well, but have since lapsed. Muslim fishers generally are not subject to similar restrictions with the exception of the Machhiyara fishers of Hirakot who the *samaj* prevents from fishing on Fridays.

The boat owners' associations are less common than the *samaj* and are for the most part associated with large fishing harbours where an administrative division of labour makes sense. The boat owners' associations represent the trawler sector, with the exception of the boat owners' association of Ghoghala, which represents the small-scale sector. The primary function of the boat owners' associations is to act as an intermediary with the state for the purpose particularly of accessing subsidised fuel. The boat owners' associations do also advocate on behalf of fishers and are a first level for dispute resolution and redress among fishers. The associations are linked closely to the *samaj*, with the association head generally sitting in the *samaj* court as an *agewan*.

I have not systematically conducted research on the state-level fisher organisation that is known as the *Gujarat Machhimara Sangharthan*. The *sangharthan* is composed of fisher leaders at various levels, regional and fishing-harbour wise. It meets periodically to discuss matters of common concern to fishers in Gujarat. It has had inputs into the regulations imposed by the state Fisheries Department with regard to mesh size and the monsoon ban. In 2014 it imposed an extended monsoon fishing ban in Gujarat, with a starting date more than a month earlier than usual on 7 May. Normally, the ban starts on 10 June.

In addition to the formal, if not state recognised, sphere of the *samaj* and boat owners' associations, I did come across some evidence of informal norms on fishing practice. My data on the topic come largely from the fishing village where I have had long-standing ties. In that village, Hindus and Muslims alike state a deep respect for certain forms of marine life that they consciously try to avoid harming. Dolphins, sea turtles and whales are considered to be sacred animals that should not be targeted.

The most important state agency responsible for implementing fisheries law is the Gujarat Department of Fisheries. The department is complemented by a number of other organisations at the federal and state level that provide financial, technological, informational and regulatory support either to the department directly or to various sectors of the fishery. These other organisations have been instrumental in the development of the Gujarat fishery, and the Customs and Coast Guard authorities have some enforcement and regulatory roles, but the coordination and implementation of fisheries regulation, particularly in the area of resource management, has fallen almost entirely upon the Fisheries Department. In the period following the terrorist attacks on Mumbai in late 2008, port security tightened considerably and inspections at sea by the Coast Guard significantly increased. These have not materially affected fishers' livelihoods but they have meant that fishers have had to even more strictly adhere to licensing and identity card regulations when at sea.

The capacity and function of the Fisheries Department changed considerably in 2003 with the passing of the Gujarat State Fisheries Act. To that point, the department's main role had been to increase production in the fishery through a variety of technical and subsidy interventions. It also played and continues to play an important role in data gathering, although the quality of the data it collects as compared to that collected by the Central Marine Fisheries Research Institute is increasingly doubtful. The Fisheries Act on paper gives the department considerable power to control how the fishery is practised. The department's most significant and enforced rules with regard to the fishery concern licensing, area-wise boat registration, seasonality of fishing and targeting of select charismatic species. Nonetheless, there are limitations to the effectiveness by which the Fisheries Department is able to enforce each of these regulations. The department has set a ceiling on the number of licences for trawler vessels in Gujarat that it appears to have maintained. This restriction on increase in trawler capacity has been to some degree compromised by the replacement of lower capacity vessels with higher capacity ones. Area-wise boat registration is effective for small boats of relatively limited range and compels trawlers to return their catch to their home port. The great range of trawler and inboard motor gill net vessels due to the lengthy periods they spend at sea – up to a month – however, limits the effectiveness of this regulation in terms of restricting them to a certain fishing area. By seasonality of fishing I mean the monsoon ban, which is fully effective for trawler vessels, although enforcement is poor for small-scale vessels, which take advantage of protected harbours or days when the sea is less rough to engage in highly productive local fishing. The ban on the fishing of turtles, dolphins and whales has been effective as fishers historically did not target these species for the cultural reasons noted above. The one exception to this was the fishery for whale sharks, which surged in the mid-1990s. Whale sharks are not considered sacred by fishers and thus were targeted when the market for their flesh and oil developed. At the end of the 1990s, led by the Forest Department, which is responsible for enforcing the protection of endangered species under the Indian Wildlife Protection Act (1972), the Fisheries Department assisted in stopping the whale shark fishery. The 2003 Fisheries Act includes an article on enforcement of the Wildlife Protection Act.

The Fisheries Act is also striking for several important resource management articles that are unenforced. The Act imposes a minimum mesh size of 40 millimetres on the cod end of *dol* nets and trawl nets, which fishers ignore with impunity. Fishers say that an important part of their income comes from the small fish and shrimp that they catch in the tiny mesh size cod ends of their nets. For the *dol* zone, where small shrimp are a major contributor to the catch, fisher arguments for a small cod end mesh size have merit. Trawler fishers have a much less convincing argument. Other articles that are obviously not enforced are a ban on the trade of undersized or juvenile fish, a ban on the catching of brooding or egg-bearing fish, the reservation of waters up to nine kilometres from shore for the small-scale sector, and a ban on the release into the sea of polluted waters that might damage fish. The Act also gives the department the right to set quotas and to restrict fishing in certain areas. It has exercised neither right. Finally, fisheries officers have the 'duty to protect the interest of traditional fishermen such as country craft or canoes'. There is little evidence that the Fisheries Department has been proactive in its interventions on behalf of this group.

As I will describe in the next section, the potential for coordination between fisher and state legal systems is poorly met. Nonetheless, there are areas in which state and non-state regulations are complementary. The problem is that these complementarities coexist with major production maximisation pressures that significantly compromise possibilities for achieving a sustainable fishery.

Legal plural complementarity exists with regard to the monsoon ban and with regard to charismatic species, although not out of a deliberate effort at coordination. For fishers, particularly trawler fishers, the monsoon ban takes place at a time when fishing is difficult and dangerous anyway. The ban not only facilitates safety at sea but it also provides a valuable opportunity for rest and refitting of vessels. The ban on fishing charismatic species directly fits with local norms about target species. At the same time, however, fishing, and trawler fishing in particular, do incidentally impact charismatic species. On numerous occasions I saw dead dolphins and sea turtles washed up on the beach from injuries due to encounters with or entanglement in fisher gear. These examples of legal plural complementarity are the minority, however, with most fisher and government regulations poorly coordinated or absent altogether.

The historical basis for defective legal pluralism in the Junagadh fishery

From two sides, there is potential for a robust legal pluralism in the Junagadh fishery: fishers have deeply rooted *samaj* institutions that have some role in regulating fishing and there is a dedicated state Fisheries Department that historically played a powerful role in developing the fishery. The potential for linking these two institutions into a legal plural governance structure that builds on their relative strengths has to date largely been missed, however, with major threats to the long-term viability of the fishery. Why this opportunity has been missed requires a consideration of the historical trajectory of development of the fishery and attention to the specific social and cultural context in which that development took place. Political ecology provides useful reference points in mapping that background with its attention to history, relations of power and cultural constructions of resources.

The fishery of Gujarat has been in growing ecological crisis since the late 1990s (Armitage and Johnson 2006; Bavinck et al. 2013; Johnson 2001). Should that crisis deepen abruptly, it will necessarily entail an economic and social crisis as well. The origins of the crisis lie in the production orientation of state-led fisheries development since the 1950s. That orientation has taken a distinctive path in the Gujarat fishery, reflecting its particular social and cultural conditions, and has left a deep legacy, of which the failure to pursue the possibility of some kind of co-governance drawing on fisher as well as state legal systems is a major result.

The origins of the contemporary Junagadh fishery lie in the post-Independence modernisation phase of development in India (Johnson and Bavinck 2010). Fisheries development, led by the Gujarat Fisheries Department, began in the 1950s but only began to have a significant impact on the fishery in the 1960s. While some attempts were made to foster fisher cooperatives, effort in the main was focused on increasing the production and productivity of the fishery through the provision of technological inputs. Synthetic twine for nets, motorisation, and the introduction of trawlers were some of the major interventions that were undertaken with foreign development assistance. By the 1990s, the small-scale subsistence and dry-fish trade oriented fishery of Junagadh had been fully transformed. The fishery was motorised and mechanised, catch levels had increased by a factor of ten and it was driven by large and lucrative domestic and export markets (Johnson 2001, 2002).

By the mid-1990s it appeared that the Gujarat Fisheries Department had accomplished its mandate: the fishery was vastly more productive and income generating. From the late 1990s to the present, however, the steady upward trajectory of the fishery has reached a bumpy plateau, with good and bad years interspersed. Fishers point to various indicators of resource decline, including significantly greater effort to secure consistent levels of income and declining sizes of target species. Economic insecurity has been cushioned by high prices for fish, but those high prices are helping to drive unsustainable levels of fishing.

The production-oriented development emphasis of state agencies itself acted against developing a legal plural basis for management of the fishery. The Fisheries Department paid little if any attention to resource management, and even less did it consider the possibility of involving fishers in such management. It was not until the sudden realisation of the ecological limitations of the fishery in the late 1990s that attention shifted to include resource management in Fisheries

Department policy. Thirty years of focus on the top-down delivery of technological intensification, however, has meant that Fisheries Department culture places very little value on outreach with fishers.

Underlying the separation of fisheries officers from their fisher clients is the deeper and more widespread cultural perception of fishing in Gujarat. The middle and upper castes of Gujarat are largely vegetarian, and vegetarianism is a powerful reference value and status indicator in the state. Fishing and the eating of fish thus go against the grain of mainstream values and fishers and fishing are consequently stigmatised. Historically this meant that fishers were treated similarly to *dalits*, or untouchables. Older fishers told me, for example, that they were compelled to use separate drinking vessels than others in public places. Such overt discrimination has disappeared but fishing continues to be perceived, if it is thought of at all, as a dirty and marginal activity. Fisheries management is thus not a priority area for the Gujarat government, the status of the Fisheries Department is relatively low among other agencies, and fisheries work does not confer prestige on fisheries officers. Policy attention and funding to the Fisheries Department has consistently and significantly declined since the 1980s, leaving the Fisheries Department little more than a shadow of its former self. The department used to have considerable research capacity, for example, which has now been completely lost. Current officers do little more than administer licensing and subsidy programmes. Institutionally, therefore, there has been little interest in or capacity to support initiatives to build links with fisher organisations. I suspect that the low status of fishing also explains why fishers' rights have figured so little in the intensification of coastal zone industrialisation in recent years. That industrialisation is a continuation of the production-orientation of the Fisheries Department up to the 2000s through a different coastal-based sector. Now that fisheries are no longer a growth sector, the attention of the state has shifted elsewhere.

On the fishers' side, the resource management potential of fisher legal institutions was left untapped throughout the period of rapid growth from the 1960s to 1990s as fishers seized on the opportunity to increase their incomes. That history has left significant barriers to strengthening the fisher legal system. The first of these is simply one of scale. The rapid growth of the fishery has meant that it is now the basis of livelihood for a large fishing population. This population has multiple internal divisions by caste, religion, craft and gear, and geography, all of which pose a major coordination problem. More seriously, from a social relational point of view, is the emergence of a capitalist class for which the fishery is just a business. The profits of this group come principally from trawler fishing and processing, so it has an incentive to maintain and, indeed, expand production from that ecologically destructive sector. The fishery's elite also has investments in other areas, including supporting the advanced education of its children, which reduces its dependence on, and commitment to, fishing. This business orientation pits the fishery's economic elite directly against the interests of the numerically preponderant small-scale sector. As the trawler elite dominates the Kharva *samaj*, the most powerful fisher institution in Junagadh, it seems unlikely that any significant proposals for restrictions on trawling can emerge from the fisher side. It is also doubtful whether, after years of neglect, the potential fisheries governance functions of the *samaj* can be reenergised. The production-orientation of the fishery has had an impact on more than just the trawler elite. Technological intensification, increased capacity, increasing exchange-value-oriented production, and declining catch per unit of effort has created a race for fish for all fishers. This is manifested in a sense of futility amongst fishers about the possibility of institutional innovations to secure the future of the fishery. It is also represented symbolically in fisher usage where fish is identified as 'material'[13]: an exchange value rather than a use value.

The history of fisheries development, in combination with the particular social and cultural context of Junagadh District, has created path dependency in the fishery. This path dependency is constituted by a production orientation, a conception of the environment in largely instrumental terms, a separation of fishing and its negative characterisation by mainstream Gujarati society, and a highly deficient institutional framework for governing the fishery. The potential fisher and state legal instruments that have been and are present in the fishery have hardly been effective and certainly have not been creatively drawn together into some kind of governance framework based on legal pluralism.

Conclusion

The combination of legal pluralism with political ecology and governance provides valuable analytical depth to understanding the origins and manifestations of particular human–ecological challenges. That understanding, in turn, contributes to the basis for attempting to address such challenges. In the Junagadh case, a legal pluralist perspective draws attention to the coexistence of multiple different sets of rules by which fishers and fishing are constrained and enabled. These sets of rules exist at different levels of formality and explicitness, they change over time, and they are to a greater or lesser extent respected. While legal pluralism is analytically sensitive to contextual factors, power, perception and history, coupling it with political ecology provides an explicit yet complementary framework for addressing these factors. In the Junagadh case, political ecology thus points to the great significance of the development orientation of the state in the formative period of the Gujarat fishery's modernisation from the 1950s to the 1990s. In the context of a Hindu vegetarian majority state, the possibility for building a robust legal plural system for managing the fishery has largely been bypassed and, indeed, potentially compromised. Fortunately for the fishers of Junagadh, the productivity of the area they fish is among the highest and apparently most ecologically resilient of South Asia. This has given the fishery a continued viability and space, if the will can be mustered, to build more effective management institutions.

The focus of the main part of this chapter has been on the intersection of legal pluralism and political ecology. Nonetheless, the question of effective governance has underlain the entire chapter. As I note early on, my primary reference point for governance is the interactive governance perspective on fisheries. From the interactive governance perspective, there are clear analytical complementarities with legal pluralism and political ecology. Interactive governance is grounded in the study of institutions; it is interested in their capacities and their ability to effectively collaborate. Law, in the broad legal plural sense, is a central feature of institutions, and legal complementarity or incommensurability is a central area of overlap between the two perspectives. As with its value for legal pluralism, political ecology heightens the understanding of the strengths and weaknesses of legal systems, and legal plural interactions. In Junagadh, some tools for fisheries management exist, such as useful regulations at the Gujarat state level and the existence, at least on paper, of a cadre of officers who could be tasked with management responsibilities. More broadly, elements of a possible fisheries governance platform exist as well, with the various fisher and state institutions and their legal frameworks, including the state Fisheries Act. To date, however, as I have tried to show above, there has been a strikingly lack of vision and capacity to transform these various elements into an enduring and adaptive governing system for the fishery.

The Junagadh fishery continues to generate considerable economic and livelihood benefits for fishers and industry along the coast, but significant institutional change will be required to avoid ecological crisis. Fishers are acutely aware that the fishery is in a highly vulnerable state but feel trapped in a cycle of intensifying competition for fish. To break that cycle, fisher and state institutional change is urgently needed. From the point of view of effectiveness, resource efficiency, and legitimacy, a legal pluralist perspective argues that that institutional change will require much greater communication and collaboration between state and fisher institutions. In order to force that institutional shift, however, some kind of substantial and sustained intervention will be needed. I think the most probable source for such an intervention would be from the fisher side, with the *Gujarat Machhimara Sangharthan* the most promising driving force for change. Given the dominance of that group by the industrial sector, however, I have reservations about how well it would represent small-scale interests and how effectively it would push for restrictions on ecologically destructive trawling.

To date the history of the fishery has been one of surprise, with the biggest being its very endurance in the face of the massive increase in effort of the past 40 years, so any prediction about the future of the fishery can only be extremely contingent. I can only hope that somehow the fishery's currently grim outlook will yield to some new coalition of interests which can develop a robust governance framework for the fishery that learns from history and builds on its legal pluralist institutional wealth.

Notes

1 In 2013, Junagadh District was divided into two parts. Most of the coastal belt became Gir-Somnath District, with Mangrol remaining with the now largely inland remainder of Junagadh. Given that the research on which this chapter is based took place before the change, I use the old district name and boundaries.

2 I would like to acknowledge the financial support of the Social Sciences and Humanities Research Council of Canada, the International Development Research Centre and the Indo-Dutch Program on Alternatives in Development for making this research possible. I owe thanks also to my research collaborators and research assistants over the years and, of course, to the fishers of Gujarat.

3 A direct translation of the Gujarati word *mal*.

References

Apostle, R. and G. Barrett (1992) *Emptying Their Nets: Small Capital and Rural Industrialization in the Nova Scotia Fishing Industry*, Toronto: University of Toronto Press.

Armitage, D. and D. Johnson (2006) 'Can resilience be reconciled with globalization and the increasingly complex conditions of resource degradation in Asian coastal regions?', *Ecology and Society*, vol. 11, no. 1.

Bailey, C. (1988) 'The political economy of fishery development', *Agriculture and Human Values*, Winter–Spring, pp. 35–48.

Bavinck, M. (2001) *Marine Resource Management: Conflict and Regulation in the Fisheries of the Coromandel Coast, Volume 5*, New Delhi: Sage Publications.

Bavinck, M. (2008) 'Collective strategies and windfall catches: fisher responses to tsunami relief efforts in South India', *Transforming Cultures*, vol. 3, no. 2, p. 17.

Bavinck, M. and K. Karunaharan (2006) 'A history of nets and bans: restrictions on technical innovation along the Coromandel Coast of India', *Maritime Studies*, vol. 5, no. 1, pp. 45–60.

Bavinck, M., D. Johnson, O. Amarasingh, J. Rubinoff, S. Southwold-Llewellyn and K.T. Thomson (2013) 'From indifference to mutual support – a comparative analysis of legal pluralism in the governing of South Asian fisheries', *European Journal of Development Research*, vol. 25, pp. 621–640.

Bavington, D. (2010) 'From hunting fish to managing populations: fisheries science and the destruction of Newfoundland cod fisheries', *Science as Culture*, vol. 19, no. 4, pp. 509–528.

Benda-Beckmann, F. von (2001) 'Legal pluralism and social justice in economic and political development', *IDS Bulletin*, vol. 32, no. 1, pp. 46–56.

Benda-Beckmann, F. von and K. von Benda-Beckmann (2006) 'The dynamics of change and continuity in plural legal orders', *Journal of Legal Pluralism*, vols 53–54, pp. 1–43.

Béné, C., E. Belal, M.O. Baba, S. Ovie, A. Raji, I. Malasha, F. Njaya, M.N. Andi, A. Russell and A. Neiland (2009) 'Power struggle, dispute and alliance over local resources: analyzing 'democratic' decentralization of natural resources through the lenses of Africa inland fisheries', *World Development*, vol. 37, no. 12, pp. 1935–1950.

Biersack, A. and J.B. Greenberg (eds) (2006) *Reimagining Political Ecology*, Durham, NC and London: Duke University Press.

Butcher, J.G. (2004) *The Closing of the Frontier. A History of the Marine Fisheries of Southeast Asia c.1850–2000*, Singapore: ISEAS Press.

Butler, C. (2006) 'Understanding the coho crisis: political knowledge in a fractured salmon fishery', *Maritime Studies*, vol. 4, no. 2, pp. 73–92.

Carothers, C. (2010) 'Tragedy of commodification: displacements in Alutiiq fishing communities in the Gulf of Alaska', *Maritime Studie* s, vol. 9, no. 2, pp. 95–120.

Charles, A. (2001) *Sustainable Fishery Systems, Volume 5*, Oxford: Blackwell Science.

Coulthard, S. (2011) 'More than just access to fish: the pros and cons of fisher participation in a customary marine tenure (Padu) system under pressure', *Marine Policy*, vol. 35, no. 3, pp. 405–412.

Escobar, A. (1999) 'After nature: steps to an antiessentialist political ecology', *Current Anthropology*, vol. 40, no. 1, pp. 1–30.

Foster, J.B., B. Clark and R. York (2010) *The Ecological Rift: Capitalism's War on the Earth*, New York: Monthly Review Press.

Greenberg, J.B. (2006) 'The political ecology of fisheries in the upper Gulf of California', in Biersack, A. and J.B. Greenberg (eds), *Reimagining Political Ecology*, Durham, NC: Duke University Press, pp. 121–148.

Gujarat (2008) *Gujarat Fisheries Statistics 2006–07*, Gandhinagar: Commissioner of Fisheries, Government of Gujarat.

Hardin, G. (1968) 'The tragedy of the commons', *Science*, vol. 162, no. 3859, pp. 1243–1248.

Idrobo, C.J. and I. Davidson-Hunt (2012) 'Cercos flutuantes in Ponta Negra, SE coastal Brazil: the paradox of social-economic differentiation through livelihood diversification', *Maritime Studies*, vol. 11, no. 3, p. 22.

Jentoft, S. (2004) 'Institutions in fisheries: what they are, what they do, and how they change', *Marine Policy*, vol. 28, pp. 137–149.

Jentoft, S. and R. Chuenpagdee (2009) 'Fisheries and coastal governance as a wicked problem', *Marine Policy*, vol. 33, pp. 553–560.

Jentoft, S., M. Bavinck and D. Johnson (2009) 'Co-management and legal pluralism: how a methodological problem becomes and institutional one', *Human Organization*, vol. 68, no. 1, pp. 27–38.

Johnsen, J.P. (2013) 'Is fisheries governance possible?', *Fish and Fisheries*, vol. 15, no. 3, pp. 428–444.

Johnsen, J.P., P.R. Sinclair, D. Bavington and P. Holm (2008) 'The cyborgization of the fisheries: on attempts to make fisheries management possible', *Maritime Studies*, vol. 7, no. 2, pp. 9–34.

Johnson, D. (2001) 'Wealth and waste: contrasting legacies of fisheries development in Gujarat since 1950s', *Economic and Political Weekly*, vol. 36, no. 13, pp. 1095–1102.

Johnson, D. (2002) 'Emptying the sea of wealth: globalisation and the Gujarat fishery, 1950 to 1999', PhD, University of Guelph.

Johnson, D. and J. Sathyapalan (2006) 'Legal pluralism in the marine fisheries of Junagadh District and the Union Territory of Diu', in *Working Papers Series 2006*, Delhi and The Hague: Indo-Dutch Program for Alternatives in Development, p. 80.

Johnson, D. and M. Bavinck (2010) 'Social justice and fisheries governance: the view from India', in Metzner, R., D. Isokawa, Y. Liu, and F. Wells (eds), *Proceedings of the Sharing the Fish Conference, Freemantle, Australia 2006*, Rome: FAO.

Kooiman, J., M. Bavinck, S. Jentoft and R. Pullin (eds) (2005) *Fish for Life: Interactive Governance for Fisheries*, Amsterdam: Amsterdam University Press.

Kurien, J. and S. Mathew (1982) *Technological Changes in Fishing: Its Impact on Fishermen*, Trivandrum: Centre for Development Studies.

Kurien, J. and T.R. Thankappan Achari (1994) 'Overfishing the coastal commons: causes and consequences', in Guha, R. (ed.), *Social Ecology*, Oxford in India Readings in Sociology and Social Anthropology, Delhi: Oxford University Press, pp. 218–244.

McCarthy, J. (2007) 'Shifting resource entitlements and governance reform during the agrarian transition in Sumatra, Indonesia', *Journal of Legal Pluralism*, vol. 55, pp. 95–122.

McGoodwin, J.R. (1990) *Crisis in the World's Fisheries: People, Problems, and Policies*, Stanford, CA: Stanford University Press.

Meinzen-Dick, R.S. and R. Pradhan (2001) 'Implications of Legal pluralism for natural resource management', *IDS Bulletin*, vol. 32, no. 4, pp. 10–17.

Menzies, C.R. (1997) 'Class and identity on the margins of industrial society: a Breton illustration', *Anthropologica*, vol. 34, pp. 27–38.

Moore, S. (2011) 'Parchedness, politics, and power: the state hydraulic in Yemen', *Journal of Political Ecology*, vol. 18, pp. 38–50.

Neis, B. (1999) 'Familial and social patriarchy in the Newfoundland fishing industry', in Newell, D. and R. Ommer (ed.), *Fishing Places, Fishing People: Traditions and Issues in Canadian Small-Scale Fisheries*, Toronto: University of Toronto Press, pp. 32–54.

Ommer, R.E. (1989) 'Merchant credit and the informal economy: Newfoundland, 1919–1929', *Historical Papers/Communications historiques*, vol. 24, no. 1, pp. 167–189.

Pálsson, G. (2006) 'Nature and society in the age of postmodernity', in Biersack, A. and J.B. Greenberg (eds), *Reimagining Political Ecology*, Durham, NC: Duke University Press, pp. 70–93.

Platteau, J.-P. (1989) 'Penetration of capitalism and persistence of small-scale organisational forms in Third World fisheries', *Development and Change*, vol. 20, pp. 621–651.

Ram, K. (1992) *Mukkuvar Women: Gender Hegemony and Capitalist Transformation in a South Indian Fishing Community*, New Delhi: Kali for Women.

Sider, G. (1986) *Culture and Class in Anthropology and History: A Newfoundland Illustration*, New York: Cambridge University Press.

Sinclair, P.R. (1985) *From Traps to Draggers: Domestic Commodity Production in Northwest Newfoundland, 1850–1982, Volume 31*, St John's, Newfoundland: Institute for Social and Economic Research.

9 Institutional pluralism, multi-level arrangements and polycentricism

The case of Chilika Lagoon, India

Prateep Kumar Nayak

Introduction

This chapter is about institutional challenges to the governance of small-scale coastal fisheries. Using Chilika Lagoon, India as a case study it deals with the institutional arrangements and processes to understand their linkages across levels of social and political organisations. I particularly examine inter-institution dynamics to explore alternate ways to bring a new institutional balance and achieve a more functional but equitable multi-level institutional network based on polycentric governance arrangement. I discuss how even in situations of institutional plenty there could still be critical gaps or a lack of linkages and, at the same time, trends of scale dominance (the influence of higher scale organisations over lower level institutions) and cooptation of ground-up institutional processes by top-down authority. The chapter analyses various institutional issues in Chilika from the point of both historical developments and current trends, and attempts to identify what type of institutional arrangement could possibly lead to successes in the governance of commons.

Chilika Lagoon is located in Odisha state, eastern India near the Bay of Bengal and covers an area of approximately 1,200 sq. km of wetland. A unique mix of estuarine, marine and freshwater ecosystems characterises Chilika, which is a Ramsar wetland of global conservation importance. The lagoon ecosystem nurtures a wide diversity of species including some that are recorded in the International Union for Conservation of Nature Red List of Threatened Animals. About 400,000 fisher people, belonging to specific caste groups, who have customarily engaged in capture fishery for their livelihoods (Nayak and Berkes 2010), live in and around the lagoon. The lagoon had historically provided a multi-species and small-scale capture fishery. However, in the 1980s, the sudden boost in the international shrimp markets and increase in export prices made shrimp aquaculture a major driver of change in the lagoon. The socially powerful local elites began to encroach customary capture fishery areas belonging to caste-based fishers and converted them into aquaculture farms. This has led to severe resource conflicts as the caste-based fishers protested the activities of non-fisher elites. In 2001 a second important event took place. The state government created an artificial sea mouth with the Bay of Bengal through a hydrological intervention to deal with persisting siltation problem in the lagoon. The results of the sea mouth created direct impacts on the lagoon ecosystem by altering the frequency and intensity of interaction of the lagoon with the Bay of Bengal.

The synergistic impact of the shrimp aquaculture and sea mouth on the social-ecological system of the lagoon was enormous. Ecologically, these included disturbance in daily water inflow and outflow altering the saltwater–freshwater balance, reported damage of the habitats of key species of fish, crab and shrimps, along with associated species such as Irrawaddy dolphins (*Orcaella brevirostris*) and migratory birds, change in species composition and altered food webs in the lagoon indicating an ecological crisis. There were related impacts on the social subsystem as well. Fish production decreased dramatically and the small-scale fish economy including its management and institutional structures began to collapse. Policy and institutional responses to this crisis further aggravated the situation instead of bringing long-term resolution.

This chapter uses data from a longitudinal study that is ongoing in Chilika since 2007. The study used qualitative and participatory research approaches and implemented three sets of data collection methods: (1) a variety of surveys involving fisher villages and households; (2) consultations and interviews across multiple stakeholders; and (3) accessing secondary data sources including both village records and policy documents. Surveys were undertaken at three different levels: (1) household (N = 160) surveys in two selected fisher villages (Berhampur and Badakul); (2) monthly household-level (N = 30) monitoring; and (3) general surveys in fisher villages (N = 150). Several consultations and interviews with multiple stakeholders (e.g. members of village-level institutions, representatives of Chilika Fisher Federation, tourist boat associations, owners of ice factories, fish traders, representative of relevant ministries and bureaucracy, a number of non-fisher caste villages) were conducted. Village elders, some of whom are actively involved in fish cooperatives, were important sources of information. Interviews with the members of the traditional village institutions were conducted, and focus group discussions were held to elicit views of women and other vulnerable groups. Views of non-governmental organisations (NGOs), relevant government departments, political representatives, fish traders, officials of the tourist boat associations, and representatives of fishers' federations were collected to understand perceptions of a cross-section of stakeholders. A number of policy workshops were organised with selected representatives from various fisher villages of Chilika to discuss and come up with recommendations on specific issues linked to the lagoon management. A wide variety of secondary data sources including the written records of traditional village institutions/cooperatives, account books of fish traders, records of tourist boat associations, proceedings of a fishers' federation, lease records from the Fishery Department, government orders, legislative assembly proceedings, development plans and policies on lagoon management has been analysed.

Following a brief discussion on alternative institutional arrangements that draws on existing scholarly literature, I briefly outline the structural and functional layout of various institutions in Chilika Lagoon at three different levels: local, Chilika/district and state. Based on this, I then focus on some emerging trends and the overall status of institutional processes in Chilika. In the concluding section, I try to deal with the questions of 'how to bring new institutional balance' and 'how to achieve a more functional but equitable multi-level institutional network' in Chilika by suggesting that a polycentric governance arrangement is the way to go.

Institutional arrangements in theory

Commons scholars tend to differ in their focus on the importance of community institutions. While some believe that communities in themselves are able to create the conditions for successful commons regimes, others argue in favour of building stronger institutions as a precursor (Berkes 2004; Ostrom 2005a). Communities are generally seen as multidimensional, cross-scale, socio-politically complex entities changing through time (Carlsson 2000). Consequently, Berkes (2004) suggests that it is more logical and effective to focus, not on communities per se, but on their pertinent institutions. The strength of institutions and their arrangements lies in their ability for renewal and reorganisation, learning and adaptation, and for dealing with change (Berkes et al. 2003; Holling 2001). Thus, community-based institutions, not communities themselves, can create conditions for sustainability of the commons (Berkes et al. 2003). However, because cross-level linkages are so pervasive, attention to community-level institution-building alone may not be sufficient to provide for effective management (Berkes 2006). Management at all levels is required but the local level is important as the starting point (Berkes 2007a); therefore, we need to move in a bottom-up direction in our effort to build successful institutions for management of the commons. Higher levels may be necessary but not at the cost of the local level. Failure to recognise both the local-level institutions along with bottom-up arrangements, and giving them the political space to continue may lead to the marginalisation of institutions and people.

There is a need to recognise that a large variety of institutional arrangements in itself may not lead to sustainable management. Appropriate linkages among these institutions across multiple scales and levels are essential. Recent work has identified 'missing institutions' and 'missing linkages' as factors for looming multi-scale failures as well as obstacles to empowerment (Walker et al. 2009; Almudi and Berkes 2010). Therefore, institutions in themselves would not lead to sustainable resource management but attention to the extent to which these institutions are able to connect to each other transcending multiple geographical, administrative, political and social-ethnic boundaries (Ostrom et al. 1999; Young 2002; Adger 2001, 2003; MEA 2003; Cash et al. 2006). However, only some of the commons literature, in the area of co-management in particular, explicitly deals with multi-level management necessitating additional empirical knowledge on the impact of the higher scale on the lower scale, and forms of commons institutions with potential for cross-scale governance (Berkes 2006).

In theory, multi-level linkages in a globalised world are important (Lebel et al. 2005; Adger et al. 2006; Berkes 2008) but they require significant attention to the risk of cooptation (Lele 2000; Glecich et al. 2006; Nayak and Berkes 2008). In practice, for example, better linkages to the global shrimp market may bring short-term economic gains but may lead to large-scale changes in the lagoon ecosystem and jeopardise the livelihoods of fishers. Therefore, institutional linkages that help avoid cooptation and promote the strengthening of institutions across all levels are required. The lack of linkages across scales and levels, and problems associated with the cooptation of institutional processes including scale dominance (the impact of higher scales on lower scales) may be addressed through creating institutional arrangements that provide an arena for trust-building, sense-making, learning, knowledge co-production, vertical and horizontal collaboration, and conflict resolution (Hahn et al. 2006; Berkes 2009). These arrangements are referred to as bridging organisations (Brown 1991; Cash 2001; Folke et al. 2005) or boundary organisations (Guston 1999; Cash and Moser 2000; Berkes 2009)[1] and the functions they carry out are known as bridging functions (Olsson et al. 2007).

Bridging organisations can create the space for institutional innovations and the capacity to deal with abrupt change and surprise in social-ecological systems (Olsson et al. 2007). They explicitly focus on the differences across levels about what is perceived as salient, credible and legitimate, and what is perceived as the important scale or level of the problem and play an intermediary role between different arenas, levels or scales (Cash et al. 2006). The role of bridging organisations includes creating effective local organisations, horizontal linkages across sectors, and vertical linkages that enable grassroots influence on national policy-making (Brown 1991). Thus, bridging organisations are not only effective in dealing with the problem of scale and levels but also the outcomes of bridging functions could potentially create effective checks and balances against scale dominance and cooptation. Moreover, these intermediary organisations seem to play a central role in stimulating, facilitating and sustaining adaptive co-management and adaptive governance (Folke et al. 2005), which are key instruments for bringing together multiple institutional and individual stakeholders onto a common platform.

In a complex and multi-level world, the task of dealing with institutional plurality where there can be different institutions that overlap in jurisdiction and capabilities is a real challenge. While there is a lot of meaning in having strong community-based and smaller-scale institutions at the helm of resource management, attention to the community level alone is never likely to be sufficient to provide for effective management (Berkes 2006), and such an overemphasis runs the risk of defining issues at one level instead of many (Cash et al. 2006). Andersson and Ostrom (2008: 71) observed that

> while we certainly do not deny the importance of local institutions, we argue that institutional arrangements operating at other governance scales – such as national government agencies, international organisations, NGOs at multiple scales, and private associations – also often have critical roles to play in natural resources governance regimes, including self-organised regimes.

In this context, smaller-scale, community-governed resource institutions may be more effective than centralised government in achieving many aspects of sustainable development but, at the same time, the absence of supportive, large-scale institutional arrangements may be just as much a threat to long-term sustenance as the presence of pre-emptive large-scale governmental agencies (Ostrom 2005a). The critical challenge is 'how to build relationships among these multiple authorities with overlapping jurisdictions', which is an area dealt with by scholars working on *polycentricity* (McGinnis 1999, 2000; Oakerson 1999; Ostrom 2005a; Andersson and Ostrom 2008).

Vincent Ostrom (1999: 57) defined a polycentric order as 'one where many elements are capable of making mutual adjustments for ordering their relationships with one another within a general system of rules where each element acts with independence of other elements'. A recent paper noted that polycentric inter-unit relationships may be independent or interdependent, informal interactions can be as important as formal ones, and cooperative and competitive feedback loops intersect (Brewer 2010). Such a diverse notion of polycentricism hints at high levels of uncertainty and unpredictability in resource management situations, and helps to analyse the role of institutions in the management of complex systems. Ostrom (2005a) explains polycentric as a system where citizens are able to organise not just one, but multiple governing authorities at different levels. While large-scale units are part of effective governance, small and medium-scale units are also necessary components; simply recommending a single government unit to solve global collective action problems needs to be seriously rethought and the important role of smaller-scale effects recognised (Ostrom 2009, 2010). Rather than a neatly nested and discrete array of organisational units, however, polycentricism envisions less orderly networks of governing bodies with partly overlapping jurisdictions (Brewer 2010).

In summary, increasing complexities in resource management systems require particular attention to appropriate institutional design and arrangements. In particular, effective institutional arrangements are necessary in order to deal with a situation of 'institutional mess', i.e. too many institutions with conflicting jurisdictions and adversely overlapping responsibilities that become a mismatch with the resource governance system. Governance theory has particularly focused on concepts such as coordination and collaboration (Olsson et al. 2006), interactions (Kooiman and Bavinck 2005; Armitage and Plummer 2010), linkages and networks (Pretty and Ward 2001; Folke et al. 2005; Armitage 2008), recognition of diversity, flexibility and monitoring (Walker and Salt 2006), processes of negotiation, integration and learning (Plummer and FitzGibbon 2007; Armitage et al. 2012) as key elements that are useful to deal with this mess. There are, in fact, several other possibilities, the success of which would depend on specific resource management contexts. As discussed above, analysis of existing literature on the subject emphasises four interrelated areas: (1) focus on institutions and institutional complexity with attention to the local level first and then moving in a bottom-up direction; (2) institutional linkages across scales and levels in view of 'missing institutions' and the role of bridging functions; (3) possibilities for co-management but with attention to scale dominance and cooptation; and (4) institutional plurality in the context of overlapping jurisdictions and the need for polycentric institutional arrangements.

Layout of the institutional arrangements in Chilika

Institutional arrangement with regard to Chilika can be divided into five broad levels, e.g. local, Chilika regional/district, state, national and international. In this section, I discuss some of the key institutions with a specific focus on the local, Chilika/district and state levels, which are important to understand the current state of the fisher organisations that had sustained the lagoon fishery management for a long time.

Local and Chilika regional/district level institutions

In Chilika the organisation of fishing hamlets and villages has both a customary and a revenue orientation. Customarily, most of these villages are distinguishable based on the caste system, where a village would be inhabited by a particular caste group or several caste groups with one or two castes forming the majority of households. These villages all along Chilika combine a variety of demographic arrangements such as villages with only fisher castes (one particular fisher caste or several fisher castes); villages with only non-fisher castes (mostly higher castes engaged in farming and other non-fishing activities); villages with a combination of both fisher and non-fisher castes where the fisher castes are located in a specific hamlet within the larger revenue village. From a revenue point of view, a village is the smallest area of habitation with a definite surveyed boundary, officially recognised as a separate administrative unit and may have one or more hamlets, which are customarily oriented. Known as a revenue village, this is considered as the lowest administrative unit for all purposes regarding civil and judicial administration.

As it precedes the establishment of revenue villages, the customary orientation of fisher hamlets and villages in Chilika has not only influenced the reorganisation of village boundaries in the post-independence period but has also remained a dominant feature of how they are arranged even today. This offers an important background to any discussion on local level fishers' institutions in Chilika. Table 9.1 lists some of the key local and Chilika regional/district level institutions with their brief profile.

Traditional village institutions

Traditional village institutions, or *Panchayat* (one or a combination of revenue villages), form the core of the institutional rubric in Chilika (Bavinck 2001a). Typically, each fisher village has one traditional institution with strong normative and functional characteristics. These institutions are often as old as the village itself. Deeply rooted in the local culture and history the traditional

Table 9.1 Local-level institutional arrangement in Chilika

Name of institution	*Level of formation*	*Who are members?*	*Key functions*	*Current status*
Traditional village institution and *Panchayats*	Hamlet, village or more than one village	All households represented by adult members	Overall village management including fishing	Exist in all villages but growing powerless to deal with issues of fisheries management
PFCS	Single or combination of villages	All fisher households	All fishing related matters including fishing area lease	Exist on paper, used for annual lease but otherwise either dormant or dysfunctional
CFCMS	All fishing villages in Chilika having a PFCS	All PFCSs and their members	Take bulk lease from revenue department and sub-lease to PFCS	Dissolved and powers were given to the FISHFED in 1988
Jati Panchayats or caste assemblies	Regional, i.e. all fishers belonging to a particular fishing caste irrespective of villages they live in	Fishing villages or fishers belonging to a particular fishing caste	All matters relating to the particular fishing caste including fishing-related conflicts	Exist but with weak structure and functions
Fisher Federation	At the level of the lagoon	All fisher villages in Chilika	Front organisation of the fishers: think tank and political voice, conflict resolution	Divided into five groups based on caste and location of villages
Village *Panchayat*	One or more revenue villages	All households of the member villages	*Panchayat*-level decision-making on all matters	Functional with election every five years

Source: Author.

institutions were organised primarily around fishing activities but most of them evolved into including other aspects of village life. Box 9.1 outlines the profile of the traditional village institution in Berhampur (one of the study villages) as an example.

Box 9.1 Profile of traditional village institution in Berhampur village

In Berhampur, a single traditional village institution was in charge of the overall village management. However, because of its large fisher population and two different fishing areas, the entire village was divided into two groups under two sets of leaders. Created specifically for fishing-related activities, these two groups were known as the big group (*Bada dala*) and the small group (*Sana dala*) based on their membership size. However, all fishing-related norms and rules of operation were made by the council of elders under the traditional village institution and were uniformly applied to both groups. These rules were operationalised to ensure that the groups engaged in fishing activities without serious contestations or conflicts.

With the passage of time, however, these two groups separated out and have emerged as two different institutions that are now largely based on political party lines and they manage their own fishing areas with rules that each of them make for their respective groups. The interesting aspect of this multi-institutional arrangement in Berhampur is the latent presence of the concept of a single traditional village institution whereby the two largely conflicting groups come together at least once a year to rotate the fishing areas between them. Other occasions when they come together include village functions (both religious and cultural) including matters linked to the village temple, dealings with government departments including annual lease of fishing areas, and conflicts involving both the groups or between Berhampur village and outside villages.

Source: Author.

The structure of traditional village institutions included all households represented by adult members; either the village headman or a council of elders provided leadership. Though there were broad similarities, the institutions differed with regard to the finer details of membership composition and structural layout. On a normative plane, all traditional village institutions were involved in making rules not only for overall village governance but also for the management of fishery resources. In these predominantly fisher caste villages, rules regarding general village life were very much linked to the relationship of people to the lagoon. Table 9.2 shows various types of fishing related norms and rules that were made and implemented by the traditional village institutions, some of which were in operation until about 2005. Only glimpses of these rules are seen today in a few fisher villages around Chilika. These norms and rules addressed areas related to both fishing behaviour and fishing actions thereby offering an orientation to the fishers to engage in responsible fishing. The functional responsibilities of traditional village institutions pertained to the implementation of rules for day-to-day village governance; functions with regard to fishing broadly included implementation of fishing-related rules and dealing with deviations from these.

Table 9.2 Fishing-related norms and rules followed by traditional village institutions: Primary Fishermen's Cooperative Society (PFCS)

Areas of rule making	*Nature of village norms and rules*
No fishing on specific days of the year	• *Ekadashi* – Eleventh lunar day of a fortnight in the lunar month. There are more than 24 *Ekadashis* in a year • *Sankranti* – Transmigration of the Sun from one '*Rāshi*' (zodiac in Indian astrology) to the other. There are 12 *Sankrantis* in a year • Major festival days during the year • Day on which someone dies and on the tenth, eleventh and twelfth day of the death • Days on which someone in the village is getting married
Restrictions on fishing gear	• Certain gears are not allowed for certain types of fishing
Strict seasonality of fishing	• Shrimp in summer, fish in winter and crabs in rainy season • Fishing areas and fish species were declared as restricted to ensure seasonality
Distribution of fishing locations and fish species	• Assigning areas to village groups to fish in different locations and prescribing the species (shrimp or fish) they could catch on that particular day (similar to *padu* system in South India and Sri Lanka)
Management related	• Fixed days for meetings of village traditional fishery institutions • Resolution of conflicts in the village or at the caste assembly

Source: Author.

Chilika Lagoon was handed over to the government of Odisha by the then king of Parikuda in 1953 following which the government started the system of fishing area leases to villages. During 1956–1959 the government appointed a fisher leader (known as *bahania*) who received the fishing area lease from the *anchaladhikari* (Regional Officer) on behalf of the village and remained responsible for effective management of the specific fishing areas.[2] By 1959 a total of 22 PFCSs were organised involving 41 fisher villages of Chilika and the government started giving fishing area leases to these village cooperatives. The PFCSs were organised under the Odisha Cooperative Societies Act of 1951, which thereby formed the basis of first legal institutional arrangement in Chilika fisher villages.[3] The structure, rules and functions of the PFCSs were prescribed under the cooperative act thereby a uniform village institutional arrangement was put in place across fisher villages in Chilika, which continues until today through the enactment of the Odisha Self-help Cooperative Act 2001. However, leaning towards the rich practice of traditional village institutions the fisher villages continued to retain most of their rules and functions even under the cooperative structure.

Two major shifts were observed with the change from traditional village institutions to the PFCSs: (1) the sphere of the institution moved outside the village boundary as two or more fisher villages were combined to form a PFCS; and (2) the individual fisher villages continued to retain the influence of their traditional village institutions over fishery-related activities, which led to the establishment of sorts of parallel fisheries institutions at the local level. Thus, in effect, while villages under a single PFCS worked together as a cooperative institution that received the lease of a fishing area from the government (i.e. acting outside the sphere of village boundary), they reverted back to their respective traditional village institutions for management and use of the leased area (i.e. acting within the sphere of traditional village boundary) after acquiring their share of the fishing area.

Central Fishermen's Cooperative Marketing Society (CFCMS)

Soon after the transfer of Chilika from the king, the state government realised that dealing with the complex access and rights system with regard to the village specific customary fishing areas was not an easy task. The distribution of leases became all the more difficult as Chilika was never surveyed therefore there was no systematic written record of rights regarding which area belonged to which village, and whatever records existed were misplaced during the transition from the king to the state government. Partly for this reason and also because of the influence of the larger cooperative movement that supported a multi-layer cooperative structure, a CFCMS was created in 1959 with all the PFCSs as its primary members. Table 9.3 on the structure of the CFCMS shows that the central cooperative had 10 out of 13 boards of governors from the PFCSs and thereby helped the fishers to retain a lot of influence on how fishery resources in the lagoon should be managed. The main function of the CFCMS was to manage the lease of Chilika fishing sources, i.e. receive the bulk lease from the revenue department, distribute fishing areas to PFCSs through written lease agreements, collect lease fees from PFCSs and deposit the total lease fees with the revenue department. However, as already mentioned in Table 9.1, the CFCMS was dissolved in 1988 to give way to a state-level organisation known as FISHFED.

Caste assembly

Jati Panchayats or caste assemblies were another prominent institutional arrangement created by specific caste groups for their overall development, which built

Table 9.3 Structure and functions of the CFCMS

Levels of representation	*Number of members from each level (Total 13 on Board of Directors)*
Village	Ten members from the PFCSs
District	Three District Collectors (with whose jurisdiction comes Chilika)
Others	Director, Fishery Department as the Ex-Officio President of CFCMS

Source: Author.

on the strengths of the traditional village institutions. All the five fisher castes in Chilika have specific *Jati Panchayats*. Since these are caste-based institutions they are not limited by any geographical boundary. Rather, anyone belonging to a particular caste automatically becomes a member of that *Jati Panchayat*.Structurally, the *Jati Panchayats* included one member from each of the villages where people of that particular caste reside, and also a number of selected/elected office bearers such as a *Mukhia* (President), *Sachiba* (Secretary), *Malika* (Assistant Secretary), *Tahala* (Public relations), Cashier, *Dakua* (Messenger), *Behera* (in charge of guests and visitors) who performed different roles and responsibilities (Table 9.4). Over the years the *Jati Panchayats* have been able to develop an elaborate rule system through which they manage various issues linked to their caste members and it also includes major fishery related issues.

Chilika Matsyajibi Mahasangh *(Chilika Fisher Federation)*

The Chilika *Matsyajibi Mahasangh* (CMM – translates as Chilika Fisher Federation) is an umbrella organisation of fishers in Chilika. All fisher villages are primary members of CMM that are represented by their village leaders. The origin of the CMM dates back to the late 1950s when fisher villages had a chance to interact on a regular basis through the CFCMS at Balugaon. There were also issues around fishing area leases that the fisher villages occasionally took up as an informal group. During that time the need to have a formal structure of the CMM was not felt by the fisher leaders because the CFCMS fulfilled this requirement as the apex cooperative institution. At times of need it also acted as the front organisation of the fishers to represent their issues at different levels of government. However, there were two developments that made it necessary for the CMM to emerge as a more formal apex organisation of the fishers. First, the dissolution of the CFCMS in 1988 and the transfer of its responsibilities to the FISHFED (discussed subsequently) brought an end to the existing structure

Table 9.4 Roles and responsibilities of various office bearers in caste assemblies

Office bearers	*Key roles*
Mukhia	President of the assembly and its main leader
Sachiba	Secretary of the assembly and maintains the proceedings
Malika	Assistant Secretary who takes charge in the absence of the Secretary
Tahala	In charge of public relations
Cashier	In charge of finance and maintains books of records
Dakua	Messenger – main responsibility is to inform the members
Behera	In charge of guests and visitors to the caste assembly and cooks food at meetings

Source: Author.

of the fishers' apex organisation. Second, starting in the late 1980s Chilika came under heavy pressure for potential tiger shrimp production through aquaculture, which gave rise to serious problems of encroachment of fishers' rights and fishing areas by powerful higher castes and outsiders. To deal with such issues on a regular basis the CMM began to consolidate its position and finally emerged as a formal apex organisation of the fishers in 1991 and led many successful protest movements against the state and other outside forces including the Tata Integrated Shrimp Project.

The CMM's structure included a general body consisting of all caste-based fisher villages and an Executive Committee elected by the members whose numbers changed from time to time. With growing instances of shrimp aquaculture in Chilika, CMM became a lead organisation of the fishers and took on several issues on behalf of the fisher villages. However, politicisation became intense in Chilika starting in the mid-1990s and that put a dent on the unity of the fishers and also their institutions including the CMM. Differences based on caste and geo-political locations became strongly visible. Moreover, the political affiliations of different fisher villages became an important factor contributing to discomfort and disagreements within the CMM.[4] While there was unanimous agreement among its members on the question of opposing shrimp aquaculture in Chilika, CMM members could not come to an agreement on the issue lagoon management including the 2001 artificially opened sea mouth. Such factors gradually destabilised the CMM giving rise to internal conflicts. Slowly, smaller groups within the CMM started to break away and formed their own smaller federations. Figure 9.1 shows a timeline of emerging factions within the CMM that had a total of six break-away groups as of 2014.

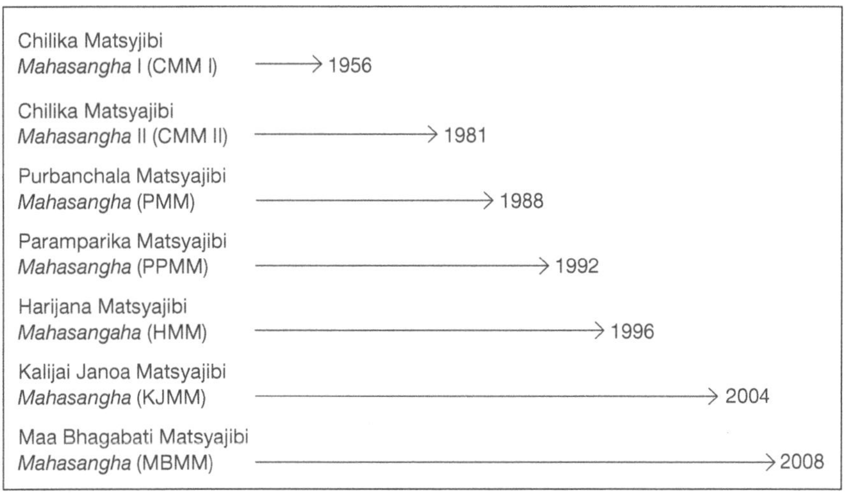

Figure 9.1 Institutional processes regarding CMM and emerging factions.

Source: Author.

State-level institutions

A number of government departments

Regarding lagoon management there is a large concentration of institutions at the state level. Most of these institutions are government organisations that have either direct or indirect responsibilities regarding Chilika. From the point of view of their involvement, government organisations can be divided into four groups (details in Table 9.5): (1) departments that have a direct responsibility in Chilika-related matters (e.g. revenue department responsible for annual lease of fishing areas); (2) departments that are indirectly involved in the matters of Chilika Lagoon (e.g. Department of Agriculture and Department of Water Resources dealing with their respective issues in the Chilika area); (3) departments that

Table 9.5 Government departments, nature of jurisdiction in Chilika and the legal acts they follow

Ministries and departments	*Nature of jurisdiction*	*Acts, laws, rules and policies*
Cooperation Department Directorate of Registrar of Cooperative Societies Director of Cooperation in Fisheries	Registration of new cooperatives, monitoring of existing cooperatives, dealing with offences and disputes, undertaking annual audit of books of records of all cooperative societies	Odisha Self-help Cooperative Act 2001
Coastal Aquaculture Authority	Regulation of activities connected with coastal aquaculture in coastal areas	Coastal Aquaculture Authority Act 2005
	Take measures necessary for regulation of coastal aquaculture by prescribing guidelines, to ensure that coastal aquaculture does not cause any detriment to the coastal environment and implement the concept of responsible coastal aquaculture to protect the livelihood of various sections of people living in the coastal areas	Coastal Aquaculture Authority Rules, 2005 Coastal Aquaculture Authority Guidelines
Wildlife Forest and Environment	Protecting, propagating and developing wildlife including birds, fish, dolphins and its environment, managing Nalabana Bird Sanctuary	Indian Wildlife Protection Act, 1972
Departments authorised by central government	Prevention, control and abatement of environmental pollution	Environmental Protection Act, 1986
Forest and Environment	Conservation of forest areas adjacent to the Lagoon through implementation of laws	Forest (Conservation) Act, 1980

Central and State Pollution Control Boards	Prevention and control of water pollution in India	Water Act, 1974
Water Resources		National Water Policy, 2002
Environment and Forests National Coastal Zone Management Authority	Impose restrictions on prohibited activities within the coastal regulation zone	Coastal Regulation Zone Notification, 1991 replaced by CRZ Notification, 2011
Forest and Environment National Biodiversity Authority	Ensuring conservation of biological diversity and their sustainable use	The Biological Diversity Act, 2003
CDA Revenue Administration Fisheries and Animal Resources (FISHFED)	Regulation of fishing and other activities including fishing area lease in Chilika Lagoon	Fishing in Chilika (Regulation) Bill 2002
Fisheries and Animal Resources	Regulation and registration of boats playing inside Chilika Lagoon for fishing purposes	Odisha Marine Fishing Regulation Act 1982
Inland Water Transportation	Regulation and registration of boats playing inside Chilika Lagoon for tourism	Odisha Boat Rules 2004
Revenue Administration (through District Collectors)	Eviction of encroachment, leasing of water bodies for fishing activities	Odisha Prevention of Land Encroachment Act 1972
Revenue Administration	Extraction of minor minerals such as lime shells, silt, etc.	Odisha Minor Mineral Concession Rules 2004

Source: Author.

have a specialised responsibility in Chilika-related matters (e.g. Chilika Development Authority (CDA), an autonomous government organisation with overall Lagoon responsibility, Department of Forest and Environment responsible for Lagoon conservation, Department of Wildlife for Sanctuary Management, Tourism Development Corporation with a focus on lagoon tourism); (4) departments that are more focused on the sea or marine system but have jurisdiction over parts of the lagoon because of its physical linkages with the Bay of Bengal (e.g. Department of Marine Resources, which administers the lagoon side of the sea mouth area).

While it is convenient to understand the nature of involvement of these government institutions by separating them into groups, there are distinct overlaps among these categories. Based on their activities in Chilika (Table 9.5), many of these government institutions will easily fit into more than one of the four groups. However, the point of focus is both on the total number government departments with varying degrees of responsibility in the lagoon and, to a great extent, their overlapping jurisdictions. In the absence of proper inter-departmental coordination, this has resulted in operational and management-related confusion. The fact that these departments draw their administrative powers from different pieces of legislation (Table 9.5) often makes coordination rather impossible and brings the interdepartmental power dynamics to the forefront.

Two key state government institutions

Two developments with regard to government institution-building in the early 1990s were considered important landmarks in the erosion of the institutional base for commons management in Chilika. First, in 1991, FISHFED was created as the apex organisation of all the fishers' cooperatives in the state, including Chilika. This institution replaced the CFCMS (the apex cooperative of Chilika fishers), which, being a local institution, was able to function in close collaboration with village level fishers' cooperatives. In contrast, the creation of FISHFED at the state level took away the locus of decision-making control from the local fishers and gave it to a centralised administrative. This severed any direct linkages between the Chilika fishery institutions and the state revenue department.

Second, the creation of the CDA in 1992 as the nodal institution to manage Chilika added to the confusion by creating additional power structures, which, on the one hand, conflicted with the existing government departments and their jurisdiction in Chilika, and resulted in the complete neglect of village and regional level fisheries institutions by denying them any share in the decision-making process concerning Chilika, on the other. However, the role of the CDA in the management of Chilika has continuously been questioned not only by the local fishers and civil society organisations, but also recently by India's Auditor General's report, which identified irregularities such as fund mismanagement, improper planning, and inaction against encroachment and illegal shrimp aquaculture farms by the CDA (CAGI 2008). Paradoxically, it also recommended for larger financial and administrative powers for the CDA as a way to improve its operations. I am not aware of any specific new actions initiated by the CDA or the state government to address the long list of comments and observations made by the Auditor General's report. As a noted fisher leader in the state put it: 'it is business as usual despite such scathing comments from the top Auditor in the country'. Table 9.6 gives key details of the Auditor General's report.

Other institutions at the state level

The other institutions at the state level include NGOs, academic and research institutions and a host of others at the level of the judiciary, politics and the media. NGOs working in Chilika are not generally as influential as is the case for other resource sectors in Odisha, especially forests (Interviews with NGOs and funding agencies in Bhubaneswar). For example, there is a strong NGO and civil society movement around forests and mining issues in the state. In the case of Chilika, there have been strong civil society movements such as the *Chilika*

Table 9.6 Key observations in the Auditor General's report on the CDA's role in Chilika

Areas of review	*Specific observations*
Funds allocation and expenditure	• Non-utilisation of funds • Irregular diversion of funds towards establishment expenditure • Non-utilisation of money collected out of ferry services
Programme implementation	• Absence of perspective plans and actions plans for the activities undertaken • Funds for multidisciplinary and multidimensional activities for preservation and restoration of the lagoon were used for stand-alone activities • No action plan for economical disposal of dredged minor mineral materials • No action plan to address the adverse impacts of the dredged sea mouth on biodiversity. No disaster management plan exist to tackle possible adverse effects of artificial opening of the mouth
Treatment of catchment areas	• Wasteful expenditure of 21 million rupees due to failure of plantation • Improper maintenance of plantation journal/muster rolls – complete details of plantation labour charges not maintained • Forest department norms were not followed in undertaking the plantation
Conservation of biodiversity and genetic resources	• Total indifference of district administration to evict shrimp aquaculture gherries in the lagoon • Ecological restoration work was limited to the bird sanctuary area only and not to other ecologically critical areas of the lagoon • Illegal fishing and boating activities in dolphin habitation areas
Underutilisation of assets	• Underutilisation of existing ferry crafts • Non utilisation of survey and patrolling boats after construction
Regulatory issues	• Illegal fishing activities going on unabated • Unauthorised playing of tourist boats • Absence of a proper legal framework for CDA and to manage the lagoon • Monitoring mechanisms though in place largely remained non-functional

Source: Compiled from the report of the Comptroller and Auditor General of India (CAGI) 2008.

Banchao Andolan (Save Chilika Movement), which took leadership at the time when the state government handed over parts of Chilika to the Tata Company for intensive industrial shrimp aquaculture. However, such movements have often died out once the issue became dormant, which implies that there are informal institutional arrangements that appeared and disappeared with specific issues around the lagoon. There are, however, permanent NGOs that work with local fishers on different issues around the lagoon. The judiciary is yet another institution that has played a key role in providing direction to the management of Chilika Lagoon through court orders. The 1993 Odisha State High Court order banning shrimp aquaculture in the lagoon was considered a major institutional intervention that upheld the customary rights of the fishers. The support of political parties at the state level, more prominently the support of the Communist Party of India – Marxist for the fishers on the sea mouth issue, was considered by the fishers to be critical institutional support.

Thus, three trends in institution-building were observed at the state level and its comparison with the local-level institutions: (1) creation of institutions that had specific focus on Chilika only, such as the CDA; (2) creation of another set of institutions that dealt with matters of Chilika as part of their overall responsibilities, such as the FISHFED; and (3) the gap between traditional and state-created organisations can be characterised in terms of their historical roots, support base, mutual distrust and legal structure.

Understanding the institutional mess in Chilika

Incapacitation and elimination of local-level institutions

The Chilika case shows an overall increase in the number of institutions involved in governance over the last two decades. These institutions fall into several categories such as government, quasi-government, non-government, private, and community-owned, and span multiple horizontal and vertical scales. However, while their numbers have increased not all the institutions have gained the required autonomy and authority to function as independent entities. There is an uneven growth in institutional arrangements whereby some of the institutions have gained excess authority and power at the cost of others. Specifically, higher-level government institutions have become powerful either by taking over existing power structures or creating new levels of authority for themselves. In the process there has been large-scale incapacitation and, in certain cases, even elimination of lower-level institutions.

An institutional analysis of Chilika suggests that the incapacitation of local institutions happened in several ways. My study found that the village-level fishery institutions in Chilika have evolved over a long period of time and are specifically tied to the resource and its ecological status, and the nature of fishing activities that the resource can sustain (Sekhar 2004; Nayak and Berkes 2010). Such a close link between the resource and the institutions suggests that the very survival of fishery institutions would be dependent on the status of the lagoon itself. In 1970, an area of 1553 hectares of the lagoon fishing grounds was withdrawn from four *Tiara* caste villages in Banapur region and the same area was declared by government as a sanctuary (restricted area). This break in the link between customary fishing area and the village resulted in the loss of functional capacity of the village fishery institution. Moreover, the continuous degradation of the lagoon ecosystem through the impacts of shrimp aquaculture and the new sea mouth radically changed the condition of the resource with serious impacts on fishers' livelihoods. The condition of the resource and loss of fishery-based livelihoods have led to the weakening of these institutional arrangements.

Owing to the livelihoods crisis, increased out-migration has led to a physical disconnect between fishers and the lagoon, which has accelerated the process of institutional redundancy. In Berhampur and Badakul villages, the PFCSs are dysfunctional and traditional village fishery institutions struggle because of stagnant and ineffectual leadership. The pool of potential leaders has dwindled due to population loss and because many returned migrants are no longer interested in participating in village affairs (Robson and Nayak 2010).

The elimination of institutions has resulted in either complete eradication of certain institutions or putting them on a pathway towards closing down. In 1988, the CFCMS, which was the apex body of all PFCSs, was dissolved by the government and replaced with a state-level bureaucratic institution called the FISHFED. This shifted the locus of decision-making from the villages and Chilika as a region to the state capital in Bhubaneswar. With the elimination of the CFCMS, many of the PFCSs now exist on paper alone, used only to secure the fishing area lease but are no longer performing any of their traditional duties. Several other institutions had a similar fate. Once regarded the hub of inter-community decision-making, the *Jati Panchayats* (or caste assemblies) have been severely weakened. Moreover, once a symbol of unity amongst Chilika fishers, the Fisher Federation is currently in crisis due to internal conflicts and division into six splinter groups. Part of the reason for why these two institutions did not survive well goes to a lack of adequate policy support and negative political party dynamics that increasingly became a part of these groups since the early 1990s.

Top-down institutions overwhelming bottom-up institutions

Institutional history in Chilika offers evidence of a rich tradition of diverse institutional arrangements spanning from single fisher villages to the lagoon as a social-ecological unit (Nayak 2014). Of course, there were higher-level institutions beyond the lagoon that had existed from the king's time to the *Zamindars* to the democratic government in post-independence years. However, it is important to note that for a considerable period of time the local and regional institutions, made and run by the fishers, were able to manage the lagoon resources in a considerably effective manner, with limited external influence (Nayak and Berkes 2011). Of course, there were conflicts and issues around resource sharing but there were also mechanisms at multiple levels to deal with them, often with a fair amount of success. There were also significant issues between these community institutions and other institutions at a higher level (mainly state-run institutions such as the Revenue Department for lease and rent collection).

Much of the problem relating to institutional crisis appeared when there was an accumulation of institutions at higher levels; institutions whose numbers and authority became a formidable force in suppressing the legitimacy of existing community-level institutional arrangements. While the creation of the CDA and FISHFED are examples of new institutions at higher levels, new lease policies in 1991 and the implementation of wildlife and other conservation acts added extra ammunition to the armoury of both Revenue and Forest Departments. There were not only missing linkages between these institutional levels clearly distinguishable on the basis of the power and authority they hold, but there was also a total lack of downward accountability (Béné and Neiland 2006) on the part of the higher-level institutions. Some of the examples of missing linkages between these layers of institutions in Chilika context include: (1) lack of collaboration on lagoon management policy such as the controversial Chilika Bill of 2001 and increasing the annual fee for fishing area lease; (2) absence of any community consultations on major decisions such as restricting rights in customary fishing areas through the declaration of Nalabana Bird Sanctuary and opening of the controversial new sea mouth; (3) deficiencies in inter-departmental coordination on matters pertaining to Chilika, and specific departments focus exclusively on their jurisdictional matters with an approach of specialised management (e.g. Revenue Department dealing only with fishing area lease and law and order, Marine Affairs focusing on the portion of Chilika in the proximity of the sea mouth, and Ministry of Tourism exclusively dealing with eco-tourism activities).

The emerging patterns indicate the taking over of power and authority by senior-level governing institutions, at the expense of local power and control. The increasing dominance of higher-level institutions in the context of Chilika Lagoon is an example of how top-down institutions are overwhelming bottom-up institutions thereby gradually replacing a bottom-up process of institution-building with a top-down structure. Consequently, the bottom-up link, which had emerged out of years of traditions and practice, is becoming fragile and the top-down link is consolidating its position, even with an absence of a downward accountability. In such a situation the scope of lower-level institutions to influence policies and functions of the higher-level institutions is reduced. This situation in Chilika is not different from what scholars have found elsewhere. Berkes' (2006) Kerala example regarding cross-scale governance in Lagoon shrimp management is a classic example of how clusters of institutions may take up a position at one particular level of the geo-political scale without having any cross-scale linkages, both vertical and horizontal (Bavinck 2001b; Jentoft et al. 2009). Olsson et al. (2007) figure representing co-management in Kristianstads Vattenrike Biosphere Reserve, Sweden prior to 1989 shows clusters of institutions at multiple levels but with a narrow focus and without any linkages beyond the scale at which the cluster exists. However, the Chilika case stands out prominently because of the large number of institutions that exist in relation to the lagoon as well as the absence of linkages between the institutions in each cluster and across clusters at multiple scales and levels.

Management 'at all levels' (Cash et al. 2006) is a fundamental problem, especially in the context of scale mismatches (Cumming et al. 2006; Anderies et al. 2006). Thus, it may be useful to keep a community-based focus in the context of an increasingly globalised (i.e. multi-level) world (Berkes 2005, 2007a; Brosius et al. 2005). However, overemphasis on community-based management runs the risk of defining issues at one level instead of many (Cash et al. 2006; Berkes 2006). We need to move in a bottom-up direction (Berkes 2006, 2007a) in our effort to build stronger institutions and create institutional sustainability that may be based on partnerships and networks. There is no panacea (Ostrom 2007; Ostrom et al. 2007) in dealing with problems of institution-building. Even though there is a general preference for building resource management institutions as a bottom-up process it may not always work well. Depending upon the context and policy environment both bottom-up and top-down processes could be useful. The key is to start building from where the foundation lies. Where there is a rich tradition of successful local-level management, as in the case of Chilika, it could offer a good starting point for both building new institutions and establishing appropriate linkages between them. In this context, a bottom-up approach is the de facto rule. Inversely, successful government programmes and institutions running them, wherever in existence, can be used to develop the process of institution-building with a top-down approach, however, with adequate attention to downward accountability and cooptation.

Institutional vacuum in bridging functions

In the case of Chilika, the entire institutional arrangement not only looks lopsided (e.g. increasing role of new or existing government institutions in the management of Chilika compared to removal of responsibilities from local-level institutions and decreasing their numbers through closure, i.e. CFCMS) but also there are gaps or missing links between institutions (e.g. absence of interaction between state-level institutions such as the CDA and Chilika-related bureaucracy and the fishers' institutions including the traditional institutions and CMM) across multiple levels. There is also a large concentration of different institutions across administrative and geographical levels. However, even in the midst of such numerous institutions there seems to be an institutional vacuum in Chilika. As discussed above, the vacuum is due to the disappearance of several institutions representing different levels and also due to the absence of institutions at appropriate levels, referred to as 'missing institutions' by Walker et al. (2009). Incapacitation of certain institutions along with missing linkages between them has also contributed to this vacuum. All of these have resulted in a problem of 'institutional fit' (Folke et al. 1998; Young 2002) whereby there is a mismatch between ecological and social dynamics, and the institutional boundaries deviate from the resource or ecosystem boundaries. Moreover, this has also led to problems in 'institutional interplay', which allows institutions to interact both horizontally and vertically across all levels of organisation (Young 2002, 2006).

The critical question is how to deal with this growing institutional vacuum and the gaps before they become pervasive? The Chilika case has already shown that networks (Carlsson 2000) and partnerships, even though they had a prominent history in the LAGOON'S management, have not been fully effective in dealing with the complexities and dynamics associated with resource management. Rather, these institutional arrangements have been rendered dysfunctional to varying degrees owing to intense political and bureaucratic pressures, and several local/regional caste, class and resource dynamics. However, it may be wrong to visualise the network and partnerships as no longer relevant to the Chilika situation as they may revert back to prominence with support from alternate forms of institutional arrangements regarding lagoon management. There is a need to create arrangements that bridge these gaps by connecting local actors and communities with other organisational levels (Olsson et al. 2004).

Bridging organisations can provide strategies for managing social and policy networks and partnerships in order to deal with uncertainties in the social-ecological context (in the sense of Koppenjan and Klijn 2004). They can thereby become agents for reviving the lost institutional linkages and filling in the institutional gaps as seen in the case of Chilika. These intermediate institutions are important because they provide a package of services and facilitate other linkages (Berkes 2009), in the absence of which, existing resource management systems may end up separately engaging several 'proxy' organisations, agencies and partners to satisfy a diversity of needs (Berkes 2007b).

Even though bridging organisations can play key roles in building local institutions, creating horizontal and vertical linkages, increasing grassroots influence on policy, disseminating new visions and institutional innovations, and create conditions for sustainable development (Brown 1991), there may not be any long-term guarantee that they will continue to do so, or that the corresponding social-political circumstances will allow them to function unhindered. The case of Chilika is a good example to explain this process. In Chilika, there is, of course, a clear absence of bridging organisations (e.g. between the local and state-level institutions) at the present time but that was not the case historically. Institutions that were meant to play bridging roles have either taken clear hierarchical positions (CDA and FISHFED) or been rendered dysfunctional (Fisher Federation) or been coopted or disappeared (CFCMS). Institutions that are currently in a position to take up bridging roles, such as many regional, district and state-level agencies including the CDA and FISHFED, do not seem to be responsive to the users and they are not downwardly accountable, both in terms of structure and function.

The situation of the current institutional crisis in Chilika Lagoon would require several bridging organisations across multiple levels. However, it may not be possible, or even logical, to create a large number of bridging organisations. Due to past experience in Chilika, there would always be an apprehension that such organisations, even if they are successfully created, would eventually take positions of power and may become instruments of further cooptation (Nayak and Berkes 2008). Considering the ephemeral nature of the bridging organisations it may be more appropriate to talk about bridging functions instead of bridging organisations. This would facilitate existing institutions in key positions to take up bridging functions as part of their regular activities without having to create totally new organisations for this purpose. For example, CDA will potentially be able to undertake bridging functions that connect and create effective interaction between Chilika community-level institutions and the state government. An outcome of this function will be more collaborative and interactive processes of policy-making and efficient implementation in managing the social-ecological system of the Chilika Lagoon. Moreover, given the complexity and uncertainty in the resource management context it may be appropriate to spread bridging functions across the institutional spectrum, i.e. from local Chilika level to the state. While I argue in favour of a shift of focus to bridging functions instead of bridging organisations, in practice, a number of bridging organisations can coexist with a good number of existing institutions taking up bridging functions simultaneously. Such an arrangement could potentially accord continuity to the importance of 'bridging' as a key factor in institutional sustainability.

Linkages across scales and levels, scale dominance and politics of cooptation

There is a general agreement that forces or drivers at various levels of organisations often impact resource management systems (MEA 2003; Berkes 2004) including their institutions. There is also a recognised need to consider multiple levels of management (Ostrom et al. 1999; Young 2002; Adger 2003) with attention to cross-scale linkages (Cash et al. 2006). The Chilika case shows that there are several clusters of institutional arrangements that are located at different scales and levels. However, what is important to note is the lack of linkages between institutions in different clusters as well as between institutions within a cluster. The study also observed that any such linkages, which were mostly found at the level of the lagoon and some at the district or state levels, have been eroded to a considerable extent in recent years. Such erosions have occurred through resource conflicts and caste dynamics at the local level, and through the centralisation of resource administration and changes in government policies at higher levels. This has also significantly affected linkages between the higher- and the lower-level management institutions, especially between the non-government or community institutions and the government departments and ministries. Instead, most institutional linkages are observed at the higher levels of management whereas lower-level departmental units (such as *Tahasildar* (Officer in charge of Land Revenue Collection), Forest Range Officer, etc.) report to their line departments (Sub-collector, Divisional Forest Officer, etc.) and receive formal instructions for day-to-day functions. Similarly, non-government or community institutions are linked to the government institutional structure only to the point where they are legally obligated to follow the provisions of the law in managing lagoon resources. However, such relationships are often seen as one way (community to government) and characterised by a lack of downward accountability.

Since scales are a joint product of social and biophysical processes (Lebel et al. 2005) it is important to understand the many politics they entail. In diverse resource management contexts, different social actors constrain, create and shift scales and levels (Cash et al. 2006) to serve their own interests (Swyngedouw 1997a, 1997b). Actors can change power and authority by working at different spatial levels, and they can alter the access to resources, and the decision-making processes with respect to those resources. Therefore, scale choices can be a means of exclusion and inclusion (Lebel et al. 2005). Scale is shaped by the understanding of actors, and is likely to be an ongoing, dynamic, economic and political process (Delaney and Leithner 1997). Therefore, in our efforts at building stronger institutions and maintaining appropriate linkages between them we need to be careful of the dynamics associated with what Lebel et al. (2005) have termed the 'politics of scale' by paying attention to 'politics of position' and the 'politics of place'.

Experience in Chilika with regard to the 'politics of scale' and its implications for multi-level institutional linkages indicate a higher degree of 'scale dominance' – impact of higher scale on lower scale. Berkes (2002) observes that commons literature is full of examples of the impact of the higher scale on the lower scale, some of which include centralisation of decision-making, shifts in systems of knowledge, nationalisation of resources, influence of national and international markets, and development policies and projects.

In the case of Chilika, the problem of scale (linked to the 'politics of scale') and multi-level linkages along with scale dominance have clearly resulted in the cooptation of institutional processes. Theoretically, there are many types of institutional cooptation seen in Chilika, some of which include incapacitation and elimination of institutions, breaks in the bottom-up institutional processes, and the creation of institutional vacuums. The first level of cooptation occurred when traditional fisheries institutions were ignored with the establishment of PFCSs in 1959; the second level of cooptation occurred with the replacement of CFCMS by FISHFED in 1991; and the third level of cooptation occurred with the creation of the CDA, which virtually brought functional death to many existing institutions, both at the government as well as community levels. Table 9.7 outlines some of the key actions of the state government that have contributed to institutional cooptation in Chilika Lagoon, which suggest that cooptation took place in a number of ways, prominent among them being the creation of Nalabana Bird (Wildlife) Sanctuary, formalising shrimp aquaculture, entry of non-fishers (by caste) as formidable competitors of customary fishers, and enacting Fishing in the Chilika Lake Bill.

Table 9.7 Government actions contributing to increased cooptation of fishery institutions

Actions leading to cooptation	*Instruments of cooptation*
Creating higher-level institutions	FISHFED, CDA
Making new acts, policies, rules and their application	Chilika Bill, Odisha Marine Fisheries Regulation Act, Wildlife Act, Environmental Acts (see Table 9.5)
Extensive use of scientific research and knowledge	Sea mouth creation without consultation with village institutions
Changing practices	Capture to culture fishery Three year to one year lease system Increase in lease fees

Source: Author.

In a complex resource management scenario such as in Chilika, we require institutional arrangements not only with attention to the 'politics of scale', 'scale dominance' and the 'politics of cooptation', but also to designing forms of institutions with potential for cross-scale and cross-level linkages. With plenty of institutions already in place, of course with varying degrees of functionality, a true governance foundation might emerge only if political space is created for institutions across every level (Agrawal 2002; Ostrom 2005a).

Summing up: towards a polycentric institutional arrangement

In addition to the presence of a large number of institutions at the level of the government, discussions on institutional arrangements in Chilika reveal a number of issues: (1) a constant weakening of smaller-scale institutions with a number of them already dysfunctional; (2) bottom-up institutional processes overwhelmed by top-down control; (3) missing institutions and absence of linkages between existing institutions; (4) the creation of institutional vacuums and a lack of bridging functions; and, (5) breaks in cross-linkages, scale dominance and the cooptation of institutions. How do we bring a new balance rather than a top-heavy institutional network? How to achieve a more functional but equitable multi-level institutional network? In this section I will deal with some of these questions by focusing on available alternatives in the institutional arrangements that could offer a way forward. In this context, I consider the alternative of polycentric institutional arrangement in the context of Chilika.

A polycentric arrangement is thought to be possible because the range of institutions required is already present in the case of Chilika. Polycentric systems are characterised by multiple governing authorities at differing scales rather than a monocentric unit (V. Ostrom 1999). Each unit within a polycentric system exercises considerable independence to make norms and rules within a specific domain with partly overlapping jurisdictions (Ostrom 2010; Brewer 2010). Irrespective of the diversity of institutions and their hierarchical position across scales and levels, it is necessary to give due recognition to the role of every institution, be it at the community, regional or higher government levels. However, scholars caution against possible cooptation of institutional processes (Lele 2000; Nayak and Berkes 2008), especially in situations such as Chilika where a large number of higher-scale formal organisations exist. In view of this, they stipulate careful attention to power dynamics and institutional politics with an objective to strengthen the lower-level institutions (Berkes 2006), which are often left to deal with powerlessness. Yet, other scholars see possibilities of enhanced mutuality and trust (Ostrom 2005b; Armitage et al. 2009) between institutional levels that could become a fundamental basis for polycentric institutional arrangements.

There are certainly advantages and limits associated with a fully decentralised system where all responsibilities for making decisions related to small-scale common-pool resources are localised (Ostrom 2005a). In a polycentric system, the common-pool resource user institutions will have some authority to make at least a portion of the rules related to how that particular resource will be utilised. This helps these institutions to achieve most of the advantages of utilising local knowledge as well as the potential to learn from others who are also engaged in a similar trial-and-error learning process in parallel systems (Folke et al. 1998). However, problems associated with local tyrannies and inappropriate discrimination can be addressed by larger, general-purpose governmental units that are responsible for protecting the rights of all citizens and for the oversight of appropriate exercises of authority within smaller units of government (Ostrom 2005a).

Because polycentric systems have overlapping units, information about what has worked well in one setting can be transmitted to others who may try it out in their settings. When smaller units fail, there are larger systems to call upon – and vice versa (Brewer 2010). When there is only a single governing authority, policy-makers have to experiment simultaneously with all of the common-pool resources within their jurisdiction with each policy change (Ostrom 2005a). Moreover, higher-level institutions primarily focus on single problems, ignoring system-wide interactions (Walker et al. 2009). The effective presence of institutions can complement these inadequacies, and promote polycentric institutional arrangements in a bottom-up manner.

Polycentricism, in the context of Chilika, could be thought of in terms of institutions' roles in rule and decision-making, rule implementation and adjudication. Thus, it calls for an appropriate distribution of power and authority amongst all available institutions for their participation in operational, collective-choice and constitutional rule-making, and their involvement in monitoring and sanctioning process (E. Ostrom 2007; V. Ostrom 1999). In doing so, attention to 'scale mismatches' and 'scale dominance' is crucial within an institutional context, as, in its absence, institutions may exceed their functional and formal jurisdictions, and end up encroaching on each other's playing fields. In such situations, polycentricism's role in facilitating greater institutional interplay in which institutions may interact horizontally, i.e. across the same level (e.g. interactions and collaborations among village institutions and within the Fisher Federation–CMM), and vertically across all levels of organisation (e.g. interactions between village institutions, CMM with the state-level government institutions) is of critical importance (Young 2002, 2006; Berkes 2006).

From the viewpoint of formal government institutions such as the CDA, polycentric governance is unlikely to maintain complete independence from hierarchical arrangements, because they draw on essential legal, monetary and physical resources from the state. Polycentricism's particular relevance to the present discussion is that it permits more flexible and opportunistic institutional design, more mutable boundaries and less fixed and exclusive loyalties among members (Brewer 2010: 289). This potentially makes an institutional arrangement better equipped to deal with complex system problems that are characterised by uncertainty and unpredictability. Polycentric governance institutions are less permanent; they may arise, reform or dissolve in response to functional needs and do not offer the same breadth of goods or services provided by conventionally hierarchical organisations (Brewer 2010). Thus, in Chilika, polycentricism can potentially offer a versatile institutional design that promotes institutional capacity and resilience, maintain a rhythm between bottom-up and top-down institutional processes, mend institutional vacuum and bridge gaps, and guard against possible cooptation and scale dominance.

In the past, a diversity of local-level institutional arrangements symbolised the collective strength of Chilika fishers. There is evidence that the fishers have a long history of organising against external forces, including the Odisha state, Tata Company and higher caste aquaculture owners, to protect their interests in the lagoon. However, in the current circumstances the small-scale fishers are less powerful than elite aquaculture owners. For development to take place in the social, economic and ecological aspects of Chilika fishers' lives, appropriate institutions need to be put in place across different levels and linkages amongst them established. Fishers' marginalisation can be addressed by a process of empowerment of appropriate institutions that can help revive fishers' collective strength to negotiate their rights with multiple contesting stakeholders.

Notes

1 Bridging organisations are similar to boundary organisations, as originally described for the two-way translation between science and policy spheres (Cash and Moser 2000), but are considered to have a broader scope than boundary organisations (Hahn et al. 2006).

2 The lease was given to the leader (*bahania*) because in the judgement of the government there were no institutions at the village level that could take the lease until cooperatives were organised. Such a step proved that there was no recognition of the traditional village institutions by the government.

3 The first cooperative society was organised in 1873 under the leadership of Utkal Gaurav Madhusudan Das at Cuttack. Till the formation of a separate state of Odisha in 1936 the cooperative societies were regulated by Bihar-Odisha Cooperative Act. After Independence, The Odisha Cooperative Societies (OCS) Act, 1951 was enacted and this was substituted by the OCS Act 1962 with major amendments in 1991 and 1996. The Odisha Self-help Cooperative Act, 2001 has been enacted in 2002 to foster cooperative societies as self-help and democratically managed business enterprises. This new enactment shall be a milestone in the cooperative movement in Odisha since it will give wide scope to the cooperatives to be self-reliant to meet the emerging challenges of eliminating the interference of the government.

4 Out of the six breakaway groups within the CMM at least four have major affiliations with different political parties and the other three are based on geographical location of the fisher villages. Moreover, at least four groups are also distinguishable by their specific caste identities based on which they are organised.

References

Adger, W.N. (2001) 'Scales of governance and environmental justice for adaptation and mitigation of climate change', *Journal of International Development*, vol. 13, pp. 921–931.

Adger, W.N. (2003) 'Building resilience to promote sustainability', *International Human Dimensions Programme IHDP Update* vol. 2, 1–3, Bonn, Germany.

Adger, W.N., K. Brown and E.L. Tompkins (2006) 'The political economy of cross-scale networks in resource co-management', *Ecology and Society*, vol. 10, no. 2, p. 9. Online at: www.ecologyandsociety.org/vol10/iss2/art9.

Agrawal, A. (2002) 'Common resources and institutional sustainability', in Ostrom E., T. Dietz, N. Dolsak, P.C. Stern, S. Stonich and E.U. Weber (eds), *The Drama of the Commons*, Washington, DC: National Academy Press, pp. 41–86.

Almudi, T. and F. Berkes (2010) 'Barriers to empowerment: fighting eviction for conservation in a southern Brazilian protected area', *Local Environment*, vol. 15, no. 3, pp. 217–232.

Anderies, J.M., B.H. Walker and A.P. Kinzig (2006) 'Fifteen weddings and a funeral: case studies and resilience-based management', *Ecology and Society*, vol. 11, no.1, p. 21. Online at: www.ecologyandsociety.org/vol11/iss1/art21/.

Andersson, K.P and E. Ostrom (2008) 'Analyzing decentralised resource regimes from a polycentric perspective', *Policy Science*, vol. 41, pp. 71–93.

Armitage, D. (2008) 'Governance and the commons in a multi-level world', *International Journal of the Commons*, vol. 2, no. 1, pp. 7–32.

Armitage, D. and R. Plummer (eds) (2010) *Adaptive Capacity and Environmental Governance*, Berlin Heidelberg: Springer-Verlag.

Armitage, D., R. de Loe and R. Plummer (2012) 'Environmental governance and its implications for conservation practice', *Conservation Letters*, vol. 5, no. 4, pp. 245–255.

Armitage, D.R., R. Plummer, F. Berkes, R.I. Arthur, A.T. Charles, I.J. Davidson-Hunt, A.P. Diduck, N.C. Doubleday, D.S. Johnson, M. Marschke, P. McConney, E.W. Pinkerton and E.K. Wollenberg (2009) 'Adaptive co-management for social–ecological complexity', *Frontiers in Ecology and the Environment*, vol. 7, pp. 95–102.

Bavinck, M. (2001a) 'Caste panchayats and regulation of fisheries in Tamil Nadu', *Economic and Political Weekly*, vol. 36, no. 13, pp. 1088–1094.

Bavinck, M. (2001b) *Marine Resource Management. Conflict and Regulation in the Fisheries of the Coromandel Coast*, New Delhi: Sage Publications.

Béné, C. and A.E. Neiland (2006) *From Participation to Governance*, Penang, Malaysia: WorldFish Center and Colombo, Sri Lanka: CGIAR Challenge Programme on Water and Food.

Berkes, F. (2002) 'Cross-scale institutional linkages: perspectives from the bottom up', in Ostrom, E., T. Dietz, N. Dolsak, P.C. Stern, S. Stonich and E.U. Weber (eds), *The Drama of the Commons*, Washington, DC: National Academy Press, pp. 293–322.

Berkes, F. (2004) 'Rethinking community-based conservation', *Conservation Biology*, vol. 18, no. 3, pp. 621–630.

Berkes, F. (2005) 'Why keep community-based focus in times of global interactions?', *Topics in Arctic Social Sciences*, vol. 5, pp. 33–44.

Berkes, F. (2006) 'From community-based resource management to complex systems: the scale issue and marine common', *Ecology and Society*, vol. 11, no. 1, p. 45. Online at: www.ecologyandsociety.org/vol11/iss1/art45/.

Berkes, F. (2007a) 'Community-based conservation in a globalised world', *Proceedings of the National Academy of Sciences*, vol. 104, pp. 15188–15193.

Berkes, F. (2007b) 'Adaptive co-management and complexity: exploring the many faces of co-management', in Armitage, D., F. Ferkes, N. Doublday (eds), *Adaptive Co-management*, Vancouver: University of British Columbia, pp. 19–37.

Berkes, F. (2008) 'Commons in a multi-level world', *International Journal of the Commons*, vol. 2, no. 1, pp. 1–6.

Berkes, F. (2009) 'Evolution of co-management: role of knowledge generation, bridging organizations and social learning', *Journal of Environmental Management*, vol. 90, pp. 1692–1702.

Berkes, F., J. Colding, and C. Folke (eds) (2003) *Navigating Social-Ecological Systems: Building Resilience for Complexity and Change*, Cambridge: Cambridge University Press.

Brewer, J.E. (2010) 'Polycentrism and flux in spatialised management: evidence from Maine's lobster (*Homarus Americanus*) fishery', *Bulletin of Marine Science*, vol. 86, no. 2, pp. 287–302.

Brosius, J.P., A.L. Tsing and C. Zerner (2005) *Communities and Conservation: Histories and Politics of Community-based Natural Resource Management*, Walnut Creek, CA: Altamira Press.

Brown, D.L. (1991) 'Bridging organisations and sustainable development', *Human Relations*, vol. 44, no. 8, pp. 807–831.

CAGI (Comptroller and Auditor General of India) (2008) 'Functioning of Chilika Development Authority, Bhubaneswar. Audit Report (Civil), Orissa for the Year 2007–08', New Delhi: Government of India, pp. 94–104.

Carlsson, L. (2000) 'Policy networks as collective action', *Policy Studies Journal*, vol. 28, pp. 502–520.

Cash, D.W. (2001) 'In order to aid in diffusing useful and practical information: agricultural extension and boundary organisations', *Science, Technology, and Human Values*, vol. 26, pp. 431–453.

Cash, D.W. and S.C. Moser (2000) 'Linking global and local scales: designing dynamic assessment and management processes', *Global Environmental Change*, vol. 10, pp. 109–120.

Cash, D.W., W.N. Adger, F. Berkes, P. Garden, L. Lebel, P. Olsson, L. Pritchard and O. Young (2006) 'Scale and cross-scale dynamics: governance and information in a multilevel world', *Ecology and Society*, vol. 11, no. 2, p. 8. Online at: www.ecologyandsociety.org/vol11/iss2/art8/.

Cumming, G.S., D.H.M. Cumming and C.L. Redman (2006) 'Scale mismatches in social-ecological systems: causes, consequences, and solutions', *Ecology and Society*, vol. 11, no. 1, p. 14. Online at: www.ecologyandsociety.org/vol11/iss1/art14/.

Delaney, D. and H. Leitner (1997) 'The political construction of scale', *Political Geography*, vol. 16, pp. 93–97.

Folke, C., L. Pritchard, F. Berkes, J. Colding and U. Svedin (1998) *The Problem of Fit Between Ecosystems and Institutions*. IHDP Working Paper No. 2. International Human Dimensions Programme, Bonn, Germany.

Folke, C., T. Hahn, P. Olsson and J. Norberg (2005) 'Adaptive governance of social-ecological systems', *Annual Review of Environment and Resources*, vol. 30, pp. 441–473.

Glecich, S., G. Edward-Jones, M.J. Kaiser and J.C. Castilla (2006) 'Co-management policy can reduce resilience in traditionally managed marine ecosystems', *Ecosystems*, vol. 9, pp. 951–966.

Guston, D.H. (1999) 'Stabilizing the boundary between politics and science: the role of the Office of Technology Transfer as a boundary organization', *Social Studies of Science*, vol. 29, pp. 87–112.

Hahn, T., P. Olsson, C. Folke and K. Johansson (2006) 'Trust-building, knowledge generation and organizational innovations: the role of a bridging organization for adaptive co-management of a wetland landscape around Kristianstad, Sweden', *Human Ecology*, vol. 34, pp. 573–592.

Holling, C.S. (2001) 'Understanding the complexity of economic, ecological, and social systems', *Ecosystems*, vol. 4, pp. 390–405.

Jentoft, S., M. Bavinck, D.S. Johnson and K.T. Thomson (2009) 'Fisheries co-management and legal pluralism: how an analytical problem becomes an institutional one', *Human Organization*, vol. 68, no. 1, pp. 27–38.

Kooiman, J. and M. Bavinck (2005) 'The governance perspective', in Kooiman, J., M. Bavinck, S. Jentoft and R. Pullin (eds), *Fish for Life: Interactive Governance for Fisheries*, Amsterdam: Amsterdam University Press, pp. 11–24.

Koppenjan, J.F.M. and E.H. Klijn (2004) *Managing Uncertainties in Networks: A Network Approach to Problem Solving and Decision Making*, London: Routledge.

Lebel, L., P. Garden and M. Imamura (2005) 'The politics of scale, position, and place in the governance of water resources in the Mekong region', *Ecology and Society*, vol. 10, no. 2, p. 18. Online at: www.ecologyandsociety.org/vol10/iss2/art18/.

Lele, S. (2000) 'Godsend, sleight of hand, or just muddling through: joint water and forest management in India', *ODI Natural Resource Perspectives*, vol. 53, pp. 1–6, London: Overseas Development Institute.

McGinnis, M.D. (ed.) (1999) *Polycentric Governance and Development: Readings from the Workshop in Political Theory and Policy Analysis*, Ann Arbor: University of Michigan Press.

McGinnis, M.D. (ed.) (2000) *Polycentric Games and Institutions: Readings from the Workshop in Political Theory and Policy Analysis*, Ann Arbor: University of Michigan Press.

MEA (Millennium Ecosystem Assessment) (2003) 'Ecosystems and human well-being: a framework for assessment. Chapter 5: Dealing with scale', in *Millennium Ecosystem Assessment*, Washington, DC: Island Press, pp. 107–126.

Nayak, P.K. (2014) 'The Chilika Lagoon social-ecological system: an historical analysis', *Ecology and Society*, vol. 19, no. 1, p. 1. Online at: http://dx.doi.org/ 10.5751/ ES-05978-190101.

Nayak, P.K. and F. Berkes (2008) 'Politics of cooptation: self-organised community forest management and joint forest management in Orissa, India', *Environmental Management*, vol. 41, pp. 707–718.

Nayak, P.K. and F. Berkes (2010) 'Whose marginalisation? Politics around environmental injustices in India's Chilika Lagoon', *Local Environment*, vol. 15, no. 6, pp. 553–567.

Nayak, P.K. and F. Berkes (2011) 'Commonisation and decommonisation: understanding the processes of change in Chilika Lagoon, India', *Conservation and Society*, vol. 9, pp. 132–145. Online at: http://dx.doi.org/10.4103/0972-4923.83723.

Oakerson, R. (1999) *Governing Local Public Economies: Creating the Civic Metropolis*, Oakland, CA: ICS Press.

Olsson, P., T. Hahn and C. Folke (2004) 'Social-ecological transformation for ecosystem management: the development of adaptive co-management of a wetland landscape in southern Sweden', *Ecology and Society*, vol. 9, no. 4, p. 2. Online at: www.ecologyand-society.org/vol9/iss4/art2.

Olsson, P., L.H. Gunderson, S.R. Carpenter, P. Ryan, L. Lebel, C. Folke and C.S. Holling (2006) 'Shooting the rapids: navigating transitions to adaptive governance of socio-ecological systems', *Ecology and Society*, vol. 11, no. 1, pp. 1–18. Online at: www.ias.unu.edu/sub_page.aspx?catID=155&ddlID=299.

Olsson, P., C. Folke, V. Galaz, T. Hahn, and L. Schultz (2007) 'Enhancing the fit through adaptive comanagement: creating and maintaining bridging functions for matching scales in the Kristianstads Vattenrike Biosphere Reserve Sweden', *Ecology and Society*, vol. 12, no. 1, p. 28. Online at: www.ecologyandsociety.org/vol12/iss1/art28/.

Ostrom, E. (2005a) *Understanding Institutional Diversities*, Princeton, NJ: Princeton University Press.

Ostrom, E. (2005b) 'Towards a behavioural theory linking trust, reciprocity, and reputation', in Ostrom, E. and J. Walker (eds), *Trust and Reciprocity: Interdisciplinary Lessons for Experimental Research*, New York: Russell Sage Foundation, pp. 19–79.

Ostrom, E. (2007) 'A diagnostic approach for going beyond panaceas', *Proceedings of the National Academy of Science*, vol. 104, no. 39, pp. 15181–15187.

Ostrom, E. (2009) 'Polycentric approach for coping with climate change', *Policy Research Working Paper 5095*, Washington, DC: World Bank.

Ostrom, E. (2010) 'Polycentric systems for coping with collective action and global environmental change', *Global Environmental Change*, vol. 20, pp. 550–557.

Ostrom, E., J. Burger, C.B. Field, R.B. Norgaard and D. Policansky (1999) 'Revisiting the commons: local lessons, global challenges,' *Science*, vol. 284, pp. 278–282.

Ostrom, E., M.A. Janssen and J.M. Anderies (2007) 'Going beyond panaceas', *Proceedings of the National Academy of Science*, vol. 104, no. 39, pp. 15176–15178.

Ostrom, V. (1999) 'Polycentricity (Part I)', in McGinnis, M.D. (ed.), *Polycentricity and Local Public Economies*, Ann Arbor: University of Michigan Press, pp. 52–74.

Plummer, R. and J.E. FitzGibbon (2007) 'Connecting adaptive co-management, social learning and social capital through theory and practice', in Armitage, D., F. Berkes and N. Doubleday (eds), *Adaptive Co-management: Collaboration, Learning and Multi-level Governance*, Vancouver: University of British Columbia Press, pp. 38–61.

Pretty, J. and H. Ward. (2001) 'Social capital and the environment', *World Development*, vol. 29, no. 2, pp. 209–227.

Robson, J.P. and P.K. Nayak (2010) 'Rural out-migration and resource dependent communities: lessons from Mexico and India', *Population and Environment*, vol. 32, pp. 263–284.

Sekhar, N.U. (2004) 'Fisheries in Chilika lake: how community access and control impacts their management', *Journal of Environmental Management*, no. 73, pp. 257–266.

Swyngedouw, E. (1997a) 'Excluding the other: the production of scale and scaled politics', in Lee, R. and J. Wills (eds), *Geographies of Economies*, London: E. Arnold, pp. 167–176.

Swyngedouw, E. (1997b) 'Neither global nor local: "globalization" and the politics of scale', in Cox, K. (ed.), *Spaces of Globalization: Reasserting the Power by the Local*, New York: Guildford Press, pp. 137–166.

Walker, B. and D. Salt (2006) *Resilience Thinking: Sustaining Ecosystems and People in a Changing World*, Washington, DC: Island Press.

Walker, B., S. Barrett, S. Polasky, V. Galaz, C. Folke, G. Engström, F. Ackerman, K. Arrow, S. Carpenter, K. Chopra, G. Daily, P. Ehrlich, T. Hughes, N. Kautsky, S. Levin, K. Mäler, J. Shogren, J. Vincent, T. Xepapadeas and A. Zeeuw (2009) 'Looming global-scale failures and missing institutions', *Science*, vol. 325, no. 5946, pp. 1345–1346.

Young, O. (2002) *The Institutional Dimensions of Environmental Change: Fit, Interplay and Scale*, Cambridge, MA: MIT Press.

Young, O. (2006) 'Vertical interplay among scale-dependent environmental and resource regimes', *Ecology and Society*, vol. 11, no. 1, p. 27. Online at: www.ecologyandsociety.org/vol11/iss1/art27/.

10 Legal pluralism and the governability of fisheries and coastal systems in the world

A conceptual enquiry[1]

Svein Jentoft

Introduction

This chapter discusses how interactive governance and legal pluralism may mutually benefit from each other, particularly in highlighting the factors that help to inhibit and enhance the governability of fisheries and coastal systems. Governability, on the one hand, is here understood as 'the overall capacity for governance of any societal entity or system' (Kooiman 2008: 173). Governance, on the other hand, is basically seen as an interactive and collaborative process involving government and civil society, the latter also in a proactive role.

Zips and Weilenmann (2011: 7) observe, 'governance and legal pluralism belong to separate academic idioms'. A reason for this is perhaps that, whereas governance theory has evolved from a government centric perspective and the idea of government failure, the legal pluralism perspective has largely arrived 'from below', i.e. from the level of the local community. Still, at closer inspection there is obviously considerable common ground between the two analytical perspectives, most prominently in their similar insistence on the need to look beyond state law for governance mechanisms and actions. The move from government to governance is reflected in a more 'heterogeneous state' and a more complex and 'hybrid' legal system (Sousa Santos 2006). The fallacy of regarding the government as the only governor is juxtaposed by the argument that 'the longstanding vision of uniform and monopolistic law that governs a community [or a fishery, for example] is obsolete' (Tamanaha 2008: 409). This is an opinion that most scholars working in the field of interactive governance would support.

Interactive governance theory stresses the complexity, diversity, dynamics and scale of social and ecological systems. Legal pluralism is obviously one of several causes and outcomes of these traits. Studying multiple normative orders, legal pluralism asks questions about what norms and rules exist in particular situations, how they connect and add up, what social values underpin them and what mechanisms are working to reconcile legal differences that may exist at temporal and spatial scales (see Griffiths 1986; Pimentel 2010). A particular concern is the mutual influence of state and local law and the degree to which one has hegemony over the other (Guillet 1998; Tamanaha 2008). Interactive governance theory is concerned with ways to recognise and reconcile inconsistencies and conflicts between different governance norms and principles, and to identify potential for enhancing governability where this is essential for solving important ecological and societal problems, such as overfishing and marine ecosystem degradation (Kooiman and Jentoft 2009). This is a political ambition that interactive governance shares with legal pluralism. Legal pluralism would here be seen to involve a potential hindrance but also an opportunity, which may provide governors with a toolbox to govern better. For this reason, interactive governance would be particularly interested in governing institutions that are hybrid, flexible and adaptive (Kickert 2001).

In what follows, I start out by comparing the two perspectives: how do they relate to each other, what overlaps exist, how can they be of mutual benefit? The next section presents the essential features of interactive governance, stressing the need to distinguish between interactive governance as an empirical phenomenon, a normative theory and an analytical perspective. Interactive governance as an analytical perspective is then the topic of the next section, which gives an introduction into its particular conceptual framework, and explores how it may be applied in the context of legal pluralism.

Comparing perspectives

Analytical perspectives such as interactive governance and legal pluralism are ways of searching and seeing. They are places to start from and maps to navigate by. They make things stand out, they sharpen our vision, and they help us see the trees in the forest. Franz von Benda-Beckmann (2001: 54) makes this case when he states: 'thinking in terms of legal pluralism can help in providing better insight into the complexities around law and rights'. The same thing can be said about interactive governance. It is meant to help the analysis with a sharp focus on the things that matter from a governability perspective (Bavinck et al. 2013). Still, analytical perspectives are also 'prejudgments', as Gadamer coined it; while they highlight some issues, they leave others out of focus. Needless to say, this is also the case for legal pluralism and interactive governance. Therefore, it is important to be aware of the bias that comes with a particular perspective (see Gadamer 2003: 269).

Notably, not only do analytical perspectives make us look at things in a certain way; they also compel us to see one thing at a time. This can be illustrated with the famous image of the young and the old woman in one and the same sketch (www.exploratorium.edu/exhibits/postcard_illusions); we are not capable of seeing both women simultaneously. Even so, what makes this image particularly interesting is the fact that we know that it is possible to identify both of them if we switch between perspectives. Without that knowledge, once we have identified one of the women, we will be inclined to stop looking for the other, and we will have missed something very essential. This is what academic disciplines tend to do and why cross-disciplinarity is such a rare occurrence. The specificity that comes with disciplines induces us to stay put within one perspective. They make us believe that we have seen it all. Clearly, in fisheries and coastal governance, a limitation of governability is hidden here. It is an area of research that requires the perspectives of several disciplines; yet the extent of cross-fertilisation between disciplines is remarkably low (Buanes and Jentoft 2009). This seems to be true for the crossing between governance theory and legal pluralism as well.

Together, I argue that interactive governance and legal pluralism present a richer picture and a more nuanced set of policy options for fisheries governance. As far as interactive governance is concerned, it is essential to recognise the fact that multiple normative orders, be they formal or informal, exist in the real world. Consequently, governors must learn to deal with norms and principles that differ and are sometimes in conflict. For legal pluralism, however, a governance perspective may help to bridge theory and research with policy recommendations and implications. Interactive governance may help to answer the question of what it would take to bring the insights of legal pluralism into the governance process in a way that has real consequences for decision-making and outcomes.

Both perspectives share the observation that the state is not, and in this day and age cannot possibly be, the only governor; that one should not underestimate the fact that markets and civil society are also governing systems in their own right with a collective capacity for societal governance (Donahue and Zeckhauser 2011; Kooiman 2003; Offe 2009). They are not passive recipients of rules and regulations but are often involved in shaping them. Just think of a business corporation, an interest organisation or a religious institution (Berman 2007; Blacket 2001). Not only are they active in influencing the rules that the state in the next instance is imposing on them but also people who work within such systems are themselves subjugated to rules that have been internally generated – they are indeed plural legal systems in themselves. Thus, legal pluralism aligns well with interactive governance thinking. Legislation is, after all, an act of governance that results from a course of action that involves state as well as non-state actors.

Involving stakeholders in governance has obvious functional (governability) merits. Governments cannot expect citizen support if the law contradicts perceptions of fairness prevalent within society as a whole and stakeholder participation may be a way to avoid this. How popular perceptions of justice originate and become the law of the community or the land is therefore an interesting research issue within both legal pluralism and interactive governance. One should not expect such a process to be smooth. Why are they in some instances different from community to community and from community to state? And how do they score relative to each other with regard to good governance indicators such as effectiveness, legitimacy and hence governability? These are all relevant research questions whether one commences in interactive governance theory or in legal pluralism.

Interactive governance is the younger perspective of the two. However, it is a broader perspective, at least when we think of legal pluralism as a governance perspective, which it is also. This does not imply that I believe that interactive governance has nothing to gain from legal pluralism or that the need for learning only goes in one direction, quite the contrary. Thanks to those who work within legal pluralism and whose publications I have learned from, I have long been convinced that interactive governance theory has to assume a sharper focus on legal orders, that they are essential to understanding the complexity of governance challenges, and that they may help augment governability; for instance as far as poverty alleviation is concerned (Jentoft and Eide 2011; Meinzen-Dick 2009). But I also believe that it is important not to be oblivious to the possibility that legal pluralism may complicate governability in some instances, as when rival stakeholders claim competing rights by referring to different legal norms (Meinzen-Dick and Pradham 2002). The need to recognise legal pluralism in particular social and ecological contexts as conditions for governability is consistent with the general argument that both perspectives are advancing. This overlap stems from the fact that the two analytical perspectives often apply to similar research settings. As far as fisheries and coasts are concerned, one cannot think about governance without assessing the role of law. Omitting normative orders and legal institutions from empirical investigation of fisheries governance would clearly be a mistake.

Another common denominator between legal pluralism and interactive governance is that the two perspectives draw from the same classical thinkers. Bavinck (2001), for instance, refers to Max Weber when he argues that as far as legal systems are concerned, we cannot just focus on norms and rules but also on the institutions that are upholding them, such as courts and those agencies that enforce them. This is also an idea expressed by Francis Fukuyama (2011: 259–260) in his recent book on the origins of political order:

> The rule of law rests on the law itself and on the visible institutions that administer it ... It also rests on the formal procedures by which those institutions operate. But the proper functioning of a rule of law is as much a normative as an institutional or a procedural matter.

Explaining interactive governance

As does legal pluralism (see Rouland 1994; Woodman 1999), governance comes with different definitions. Fundamental is the perception of governance as a conscious, collaborative, deliberative and goal-oriented steering process involving both public and private actors, often organised in a formal partnership arrangement (for definitions see, for example, Ansell and Gash 2007; Offe 2009; Stoker 1998). Kooiman and Bavinck's idea of 'interactive governance' is: 'The whole of public as well as private interaction taken to solve societal problems and create societal opportunities. It includes the formulation and application of principles guiding those interactions and care for institutions that enable them' (Kooiman and Banvick 2005: 17).

The prominence of interaction in this particular definition highlights communication, negotiation and exchange. It also implies a focus on process as well as institutional design beyond the realm of the state. This is how legal pluralism, as expressed by Zips and Weilenmann (2011: 7–8), sees it:

> While it may be overstating the case to claim that governance and legal pluralism are two sides of the coin, the very fact of a particular constellation of legal pluralism brings about pressure to employ a set or network of institutions, actors and practices different from (state) government.

From both perspectives, it is essential to discern what the rules are, and where, when and how they apply in real settings and institutions, and who gains or loses because of them. It is also equally as important to assess how institutions, within which rules play a part, come about, and how they shape (restrict or enable) social interaction and collective action (Ostrom 1993). The dynamic aspects of rules are as relevant as their static dimensions, and there is no implicit assumption either within interactive governance or legal pluralism that arrangements, rules, procedures and outcomes are necessarily socially just (Benda-Beckmann, F. von 2001; Kooiman et al. 2005; Pimentel 2010). Rather, the justice implications of both are essential research issues.

Empirical and normative aspects of interactive governance

As a partnership, governance typically involves sharing power, but not necessarily in an equal or equitable manner (Jentoft 2007a). How power is actually shared may determine whether a social and ecological system is governable or not. Some management functions may be delegated to stakeholder organisations through a co-management arrangement, such as with fisher associations or multi-stakeholder organisations (Wilson et al. 2003). In other instances, stakeholder organisations play a more reactive and advisory role, as with the Regional Management Councils in the case of European Union fisheries (Linke et al. 2011; Long 2010). The balance between 'state-centred' and 'society-centred' governance may vary and, as Pierre and Peters (2000) argue, it therefore makes more sense to think of the two as forming a continuum rather than a dichotomy.

Moving from government to more capable governance (Kooiman 2003; Rhodes 1996) by including stakeholders in societal steering is essentially thought of as a means of enhancing governability; it is expected to provide more legitimate and effective governing by forming a more committed and responsible stakeholder community and a broader knowledge base. In fisheries and coastal management, for instance, it is assumed to induce more compliance to harvest regulations (see Jagers et al. 2012).

Interactive governance theory does not think of governance as a necessarily formal mechanism – which is consistent with what legal pluralism argues when emphasising the importance of both state and non-state law ('living law') and non-state law as not necessarily informal. As with legal pluralism, governance can be unofficial and tacit. Neither must governance be 'good' (as defined by the World Bank http://en.wikipedia.org/wiki/Worldwide_Governance_Indicators;

see also Kjær 2004). Despite the common assumption, there is no guarantee that a move from government to governance will enhance governability. In fact, the outcome might be the opposite. As governance blurs the distinction between the subject (governor) and object (those that governing is targeting), governance risks being captured by powerful stakeholders who take the opportunity 'to usurp genuinely public tasks' or to engage in 'outright corrupt practices' (Offe 2009: 553). Therefore, we must investigate the conditions under which governability increases or falters. Many of those conditions are likely to be highly contextual, suggesting that there is no single governance formula for all situations. This is also the idea behind the concept of 'adaptive governance' (Folke et al. 2005), i.e. a less uniform and standardised form of governance, one that is more tailored to particular circumstances and more sensitive and reactive to change.

As with legal pluralism, we need to distinguish between interactive governance as (1) an empirical phenomenon; (2) a normative theory; and (3) an analytical perspective (see Pierre and Peters 2000: 24). In the first instance, the issue is whether interactive governance as defined here is actually occurring, whether the blurring of traditional boundaries between government and the private sector is really happening; where, when and how. Is it really true that the traditional role of the state is changing from a governing state to 'an enabling state' (Pierre and Peters 2000: 12)? Interactive governance is not necessarily a recent phenomenon. Neither does it have to be the true and only representation of how societal sectors are steered. This is ultimately an empirical question. A comparative study of fisheries governance systems in Europe, in which I participated (Hoof 2005; Mikalsen and Jentoft 2008), showed a lot of variation among countries with regard to government–industry interaction. In some countries, fisheries governance is indeed structured according to an interactive model, where user-organisations have an active role in regulatory decision-making and where considerable governance functions are delegated to the sector. This is done in harmony with a legislative framework that defines the mandates, rights and responsibilities that user-organisations have in the governance system. In Spain, for instance, this occurs where regions are granted considerable autonomy within the governance system. In other countries, such as in Scandinavia, consultative arrangements between government and industry are common. All over the world, co-management has become a popular remedy to what is seen as widespread governance malfunction (Wilson et al. 2003).

In the second instance, as a normative theory, interactive governance argues that the move from government to governance is a progressive one; governing should indeed become (even) more interactive and participatory than it is currently. In fisheries, for instance, many would argue that the current governance system led by government is too top-down in many cases, too hierarchical, and that is a reason why it so often fails (Gray 2005). This is because central government does not have the capacity and the contextual knowledge it needs to govern effectively. It must therefore involve stakeholders in decision-making and in power-sharing. Several additional arguments are put forward in support of such a shift.

First, as already indicated, governance has potentially useful merits. According to Jessop (1998: 36) 'the state gives up part of its capacity for top-down authoritative decision making in exchange for influence over economic agents and more effective overall economic performance', in other words a governability achievement. It may also make governance more effective as it broadens the information base and makes governors more sensitive to the specificities of local contexts. A more interactive and cooperative form of governance should make governing systems able to employ a broader set of tools, and make governors capable of dealing with both macro and micro issues. The same argument would apply to legal processes. This is also why in most instances government is a multi-scalar legislative system.

Then there is the issue of legitimacy and trust, which is a prerequisite for governability and hence the effectiveness of governing systems. There are, of course, many ways to make people abide by rules, repression being one (Held 1987). Governing would, however, be less costly if people were to follow rules voluntarily. This is more likely to happen if people are allowed to see why rules sometimes are necessary. Opening governing systems to broader participation would thus facilitate the transparency and experiential learning that would enable people to do that. Moreover, participation is, as Sen (2009) argues, also about social justice. People who have stakes in the outcome have a right to be recognised, and direct involvement of stakeholders in the process is a way to do so. The causal chain is therefore that justice is good for legitimacy, which is good for compliance and ultimately for governability.

Finally, it could be argued that interactive governance is a good thing in itself in so far as it institutes a more democratic form of governance. This is true regardless of whether interactive governance is living up to all its promises. As with democracy, interactive governance comes with the risk of abuse. It may, as already mentioned, be corrupted by power. However, the remedy is hardly to abandon democracy, but to make it work better. Accommodating for legal pluralism may be one of the remedies (Jentoft et al. 2009). This means ensuring that legal norms and orders that are 'out there' are represented 'in here' when decisions pertaining to, for instance, fisheries and coastal management are deliberated and decided on. If legal norms are too tacit to be expressed and integrated directly, they can be represented by involving those who embody them. Co-management would only provide the beginning of the answer of how to do this. The solution must also be found in the details of the organisational set-up; for instance who gets to be represented and how, and therefore whose normative orders are recognised. If the diversity of legal norms is to be taken into consideration, representation must be structured to ensure that the legal pluralisms that exist and are relevant for decision-making in particular instances are represented at the table. It is also therefore reasonable to assume that the legitimacy of co-management would largely depend on its contextualisation and its ability to learn and adapt (Armitage et al. 2008). For this, co-management must also pay as much attention to communicative processes as to institutional design.

Finally, it would be naive to assume that more interactive governance is always better, and that blurring the boundaries between government, civil society and markets is always a good thing. Each party has distinct roles, functions and capacities. There is something that only each of them can do. For instance, the state cannot (and should not) replace what a family does, or a business enterprise cannot perform the roles of the former two. Still, these boundaries are not written in stone; things are constantly moving on the borders between what the parties do. How we look at these boundary issues largely depends on where we start – from a situation where government is largely absent or from a situation where government is omnipresent. Interactive governance theorists, on the one hand, commence primarily from the latter situation, where the hierarchical, command and control governing approach of the state has inherent deficiencies that interactive governance may compensate for. They share the search for new approaches to the functioning of the state and its changing borders with other societal entities, in this case with market entities that advocate Public Management (Eliassen and Kooiman 1987), later New Public Management (Christensen and Lægreid 2002; Pollitt and Bouchaert 2011), and most recently Public Governance (Osborne 2010), each with varying emphases of the normative and empirical features of public and private functions and their boundary traffic. New Public Management is predominantly concerned with movement along the state–market axis, and it is normatively arguing for outsourcing of public functions, privatisation etc. Interactive governance and other governance theorists are equally concerned about what is occurring on the state–civil society axis when they talk about the need to involve stakeholders and their representative organisations in governance.

Legal pluralists, on the other hand, often start from the bottom-up, from a situation where state government is, or used to be, more or less absent, and is interfering in situations that are already governed by indigenous, informal or unofficial law, as did colonial powers. Certainly one may imagine situations and spheres of life where society needs to be protected against government. In fisheries, for instance, it can be argued that communities in many instances are better left alone to handle their collective choice issues. They do not necessarily find themselves in a legal vacuum or anarchy even if the government is not present. Instead, they work according to rules that they have developed and are able to enforce themselves – thereby contributing to legal pluralism and governability. Bavinck's (2001) study of the panchayat system of the Pattinavar fishers of South India is a case in point. Government interference is therefore not necessarily enhancing governability but may well lead to the contrary; for instance by reducing the capacity of local people to manage their fishery by their own initiatives, values and norms (Wiber and Milley 2007). Therefore governance raises 'the question of the relation between state intervention and societal autonomy' (Offe 2009: 555), and the essentials of creating a truly mutually constructive governing interaction.

In the third instance, interactive governance as an analytical perspective, given that in reality governance is less hierarchical, more interactive and institutionally hybrid than we often tend to believe, and that a move towards more interaction should be supported for reasons given above, we need a conceptual framework by which we can analyse interactive governance both as a reality and as a potential governing enhancement. It is perhaps primarily as an analytical perspective that interactive governance theory may have something to offer legal pluralism. What this perspective entails conceptually is summarised below.

Applying interactive governance theory to legal pluralism

Interactive governance is developed into a comprehensive conceptual framework by Kooiman (2003) and later applied by Kooiman et al. (2005) and Bavinck et al. (2013) for fisheries. The framework is richer than what is possible to depict and explain in a short chapter like this. I will therefore concentrate on those aspects that I find particularly relevant from a legal pluralism perspective.

Governance systems

Interactive governance operates with a three-system model: a system-to-be-governed and a governing system, between which there is interaction that may take various 'modes' (hierarchical, co- or self-governance). In fisheries, the system-to-be-governed, on the one hand, is partly natural and partly social – comprising ecosystems, natural resources in those ecosystems, as well as various categories of resource users and their institutions. The governing system, on the other hand, consists of institutions and steering mechanisms, among which legal rules play a prominent part. Interactive governance emphasises that there are limitations to how governable these systems are, and that it is essential to understand the nature of these limits, where they sit and how they can possibly be overcome (Jentoft 2007b). Are such limits, as Mayntz (1994: 13) mentions, due to 'an implementation problem', a 'knowledge problem within the governing system' or a 'motivation problem' at the receiving end of the governing interventions, i.e. within the system-to-be-governed?

According to interactive governance theory, these limits are, as Figure 10.1 illustrates, related to four properties that are common to all systems. These systems tend to be characterised by (1) *diversity*, and thus, there is no single formula for addressing governability, and any measure would need to be tailored to context. The normative order is obviously also part of that specific context, and any

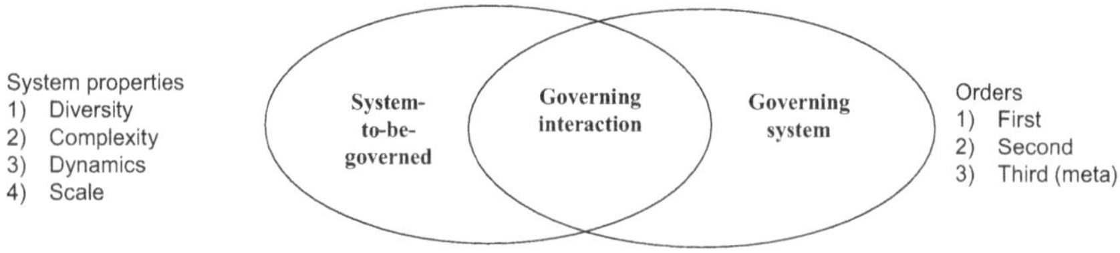

Figure 10.1 Interactive governance systems model.

Source: Author.

governability analysis would naturally need to detect and describe whatever normative orders exist and how individuals need to adapt to them. Legal pluralism does after all stem from sociological pluralism (Rouland 1994). This pluralism may cause problems for people who must adapt to it. For instance, a fisher who has to move out of and into legal systems that apply to the different communities and fishing grounds as he moves with the fish has an information problem. How is he supposed to know about them? What if he breaks rules unknowingly?

Complexity (2) refers to the way system components are linked, such as in trophic chains or social networks. Complexities may, of course, also be of a legal nature. Not only are activities such as fishing, aquaculture, transport, tourism etc. competing for space and resources in the coastal zone but they are also subject to separate legal measures that are often poorly harmonised, in direct conflict, and thus turn coastal zone management into more of a legal battleground than it needs to be (see for example Cicin-Sain and Knecht 1998; Buanes and Jentoft 2005; Sanchirico et al. 2010).

Dynamics (3): we live in a world where targets of governance are constantly moving; it is essentially a process that is interactive, and hence fluid. Similarly the legislation that underpins governance is not stable. 'There is no legal system that does not change at all' (Benda-Beckmann, K. von 2001: 20). Thus dynamics is a key governability aspect both as a problem and a solution. The governability problem is enhanced by the fact that the system-to-be-governed and the governing system are changing at a different pace and the governing system tends to lag behind. Fisheries resources may therefore be depleted before management authorities are able to respond. This has been pointed out as the problem with the so-called 'roving bandits' – those fleets that move around the world fishing out unregulated fish stocks and are gone the moment management authorities are ready to intervene (Berkes et al. 2006). The need for adaptive governance as a governability enhancement measure is therefore pretty obvious but perhaps not fully attainable for the simple reason that law is not meant to be unstable or flexible, and that legal reform is cumbersome and takes time.

Finally, there is the issue of (4) *scale*. The governance challenge is not only that legal systems are diverse, inherently complex and often unstable, but also that they exist at different levels, as with state and community law, which may or may not be in conflict (Tamanaha 2008). How are they to respond if local rules are in conflict with national legislation (Gezelius 2002)? This is a problem for both the governing system and the system-to-be-governed. For the governing system it is likely to generate low compliance and high transaction costs. For the fisher it represents a dilemma. Whether he chooses to abide by local or state law, he will be a law-breaker. This issue is addressed in the fisheries management literature as well as in the legal pluralism literature. When Vanderlinden (1989: 151) talks about the individual as the 'converging point' of legal pluralism, this is, as far as I understand, what he is thinking about. Similarly, when Ambler (2001: 41) raises the question whether 'it is possible to balance the intended universalism of statutory law with the particularism of customary law', he is alluding to the same dilemma but also suggesting that the answer might be affirmative.

Governance orders

Interactive governance also distinguishes between three 'orders' of governance, between which there are linkages and interactions (Figure 10.1). The first order (1) is about the decision-making that occurs on a day-to-day basis and is often of a routine nature. There are rules and guidelines for the procedures regarding how these actions should occur, but which are also supposed to be consistent with norms and principles at a higher order. In fisheries, for instance, these are harvesting and processing rules related to where, how, when and how much to fish and how to secure a good quality product. Since such rules are predominantly about technical matters that require a lot of specialised expertise, they lend themselves for delegation to administrators and practitioners who, once the basic principles and institutional framework are established, have the normative foundation and guidelines they need for implementation. Such principles and institutional designs, according to interactive governance theory, occur at the second and third order of governance. At these orders, decisions are of a political nature, and therefore require a different kind of knowledge than that of the technical specialist, be it a lawyer or a business manager (see Jentoft 2006).

The second order (2) concerns institutions. In the quoted definition of interactive governance, Kooiman and Bavinck (2005: 17) talk about caring for those institutions that enable 'the formulation and application of principles guiding those interactions'. This is also what interactive governance theory labels 'second order' governance. Notably, interactive governance not only emphasises the problem-solving capacity of institutions but also their 'opportunity creation', their facilitation; they make things possible, they empower. Institutions are about norms and rules that are inscribed in their role repertoire (Scott 2001). Hence they are legal systems in their own right.

Governance systems are typically complex networks of institutions, often in the shape of formal organisations with their own distinct boundaries, structures, cultures and mandates. Both within the governing system as well as in the system-to-be-governed, there is a diversity and fluidity of organisations. The fisheries industry is no exception to this rule. Understanding governability in this sector will therefore require in-depth analysis of these organisational networks. As a whole these institutional networks embody a legal pluralism, which often confronts members with conflicting values, norms, directives and mandates, thus easily leading to role conflict and normative confusion. In other words, understanding how legal pluralism works within institutional networks and organisational designs is essential for revealing the limitations and opportunities of governability.

The third order (3 – meta order) governance is about the governing of governance, i.e. those values, images and principles that underpin governance at lower orders and that are essential for understanding what directions governance takes: which goals are prioritised, why certain tools are preferred to others, what criteria constitute good governance and why. Interactive governance argues that these questions are not outside or prior to governance, but central to it. They should therefore be subject to similar interactive processes as those which occur at lower orders; they should be brought out in the open, deliberated and decided upon rather than playing the shadow role, as they often do (Kooiman and Jentoft 2009). It is essential to constructive communication that stakeholders know which position people come from when they argue about concerns that are important in the process and why certain things are left out, why governance in action is often suffering from particular biases. Schattschneider's (1960) perception of organisation as the 'mobilisation of bias', i.e. that it is inherent to organisations that some issues and concerns are included and some are left out, would also apply to governance institutions, including those organisations whose responsibility it is to uphold the law. It is essential for any governability assessment to investigate how and why certain values, images and principles are codified as law while others are not, which would inevitably involve the analysis of power and culture. It is, as Bavinck (2005) argues, important to recognise that not all conflicts among stakeholders in coastal settings are about interests. They are often about disparate ethics, values and worldviews, and how to best include these issues in terms of constitutional and operational rules that governors negotiate. How stakeholders argue when they negotiate these rules would therefore be of special interest. Do they for instance invoke state or customary law, or perhaps universal governance principles? In fisheries and coastal governance there is an increasing influence of principles that are negotiated at a global level. The United Nations Food and Agricultural Organization's Code of Conduct for Responsible Fisheries is meant to inspire and inform governing institutions on how to promote more ecologically and socially sustainable and just fishing practices (www.fao.org/fishery/publications/ccrf/en). There is also a trend where fishing rights are perceived not just as a management tool but also as a human rights issue, given the way fishing rights interfere in social relations and people's ability and opportunity to sustain their livelihoods (Allison et al. 2012). This also raises the issue of universal versus local perceptions of justice, and how human rights are recognised principles within customary law. From an interactive governance perspective meta-order governance of local, indigenous law requires a similar critical assessment as that instituted by the state. As K. von Benda-Beckmann (2001: 40) maintains:

> Taking legal pluralism seriously, taking local law seriously, is not the same as endorsing every rule, or even any rule at all ... To take it seriously means to acknowledge that it is there, that it affects people's behaviour, and that it also affects the way legislation is implemented.

Still, contrary to the role of the analyst, it is the role of governors to make value judgements, i.e. either to endorse or reject such rules. But when they do so, interactive governance argues normatively that they need to be explicit with regard to why they choose one over the other, i.e. what meta-governance criteria they are using.

Shifting perspectives

The system-to-be-governed can also be seen as a governing system in itself – and vice versa. One might here, for instance, think of a marine protected area (MPA). Those who inhabit the area to be protected may already have their own governing system of roles, rules and routines when the government decides to establish a formal MPA (Jentoft et al. 2007). In this case, we see one governing (legal) system being imposed on another governing system (see Pospisil 1971: 125) who talks 'about different legal levels that are superimposed one upon the other'). It is also well-established through ethnographic research that fisheries communities as systems-to-be-governed may have their own governing capacity, and thus may potentially be in no real need of exocratic governance, i.e. governing by some external authority such as the state. Instead they have the capacity to operate according to principles, norms and rules that are self-generated, often spontaneously, and often, but certainly not always, as a tacit legal system. The fisheries social science literature is full of examples of such self-governance by institutions that are indigenous to the community. Again, Bavinck's (2001) study of the panchayat system in South India provides an example. Social researchers should, however, look at indigenous legal systems critically; they may be far from perfect either from a functional or a justice perspective. Indeed, they may suffer from some of the same deficiencies as state law, including the inability to be sufficiently adaptive to changing circumstances.

The governing system as that of the state is obviously also a legal system. It is not only imposing the law on the system-to-be-governed, be it a community or an industry, but it also works according to the rule of law, and must be assessed accordingly, i.e. as a system-to-be-governed. An issue here is the classic question of 'who governs the governors?'. Who are those people? Do they operate according to the rule of law? What are the rules, how are they instituted in the first place, how are they enforced, and to what extent do they actually promote good governance, such as facilitating transparency and inhibiting corruption etc.? The same applies to governing interactions (see Figure 10.1), i.e. the ways in which the governing system and the system-to-be-governed communicate with each other. Interactive governance would argue that in many instances, but not necessarily all, the 'co-' mode (such as in co-management) is a well-suited mechanism for assisting good communication, but co-management systems are also legal systems: they work according to rules that determine how representation of stakeholders is to be arranged and how decision-making shall take place. What legal norms exist, how consistent and how flexible are they? What images and values underpin them? Which rules are instituted and apply at which order of governance? Is it necessarily always true that local law is 'ad hoc, pragmatic and free to achieve quick and inexpensive resolutions' as Guillet (1998: 65–66) describes for the evolution of water property rights of northwestern Spain? I think we are better served if we take this position as an issue for empirical research.

Conclusion

If, from a governance perspective, we want to assess the limits of governability of fisheries and coastal systems, which we need to do in order to understand why governance mechanisms often fail and what can be done to prevent it, legal pluralism is an issue that stands out. Is legal pluralism part of the problem or the solution – or both? Interactive governance provides a conceptual framework for such an analysis. It is, of course, not the only way to investigate governance and legal pluralism, but one worth exploring in my view. Specifically, the task would be to search for the diversity, complexity, dynamics and scale of normative orders in their particular contexts, trying to understand how these properties of the governing system, the system-to-be-governed and the governing interactions limit and enable social action in general and those directly and indirectly affecting fisheries and coastal governance.

Assessing legal pluralism for the sake of understanding (analytical) and enhancing (normative) governability would involve the investigation of the normative orders that are operative in the system-to-be-governed, the governing system and in the governing interactions, as well as their linkages and the interactions surrounding them. This calls for a rather comprehensive assessment, and interactive governance offers an array of hypotheses and concepts that are detailed, tested in the literature and ready to be applied. Notably, interactive governance and governability theory is still a work in progress. It needs further elaboration, operationalisation and empirical application. For this it would certainly benefit from drawing on the thinking on legal pluralism. But as I have tried to convey in this chapter, I also believe that the reverse is true.

Note

1 This chapter is a slightly revised version of my paper published in *Journal of Legal Pluralism*, 2011, no. 64. Before that it was presented at the Conference on Legal Pluralism in Natural Resource Management Amrita University, Coimbatore, India, 29–30 April 2012.

References

Allison, E.H., B.D. Ratner, B. Åsgaård, R. Willmann, R. Pomeroy and J. Kurien (2012) 'Rights-based Fisheries Governance: From Fishing Rights to Human Rights', *Fish and Fisheries*, vol. 13, pp. 14–29.

Ambler, J. (2001) 'Customary Law and Natural Resource Management: Implications for Integrating State And Local Law in Asia', *Tai Culture. International Review of Tai Cultural Studies*, vol. VI, nos. 1–2, pp. 41–62.

Ansell, C. and A. Gash (2007) 'Collaborative Governance in Theory and Practice', *Journal of Public Administration Research and Theory*, vol. 18, pp. 543–571.

Armitage, D., F. Berkes and N. Doubleday (2008) *Adaptive Co-Management: Collaboration, Learning, and Multi-Level Governance*, Vancouver: University of British Columbia Press.

Bavink, M. (2001) *Marine Resource Management. Conflict and Regulation in the Fisheries of the Coromandel Coast*, New Delhi: Sage Publications.

Bavinck, M. (2005) 'Understanding Fisheries Conflict in the South – A Legal Pluralist Perspective', *Society & Natural Resources*, vol. 18, pp. 805–820.
Bavinck, M., R. Chuenpagdee, S. Jentoft and J. Kooiman (eds) (2013) *Governability of Fisheries and Aquaculture: Theory and Applications*, Dordrecht: Springer.
Benda-Beckmann, F. von (2001) 'Legal Pluralism and Social Justice in Economic and Political Development', *IDS Bulletin*, vol. 32, no. 1, pp. 46–56.
Benda-Beckmann, F. von (2002) 'Who's Afraid of Legal Pluralism?', *Journal Legal Pluralism*, vol. 47, pp. 1–44.
Benda-Beckman, K. von (2001) 'Legal Pluralism', *Tai Culture. International Review of Tai Cultural Studies*, vol. VI, nos. 1–2, pp. 18–40.
Berkes, F., T.P. Hughes, R.S. Steneck, J.A. Wilson, D.R. Bellwood, B. Crona, C. Folke, L.H. Gunderson, H.M. Leslie, J. Norberg, M. Nyström, P. Olsson, H. Österblom, M. Scheffer and B. Worm (2006) 'Globalization, Roving Bandits, and Marine Resources', *Science*, vol. 311, pp. 1557–1558.
Berman, P.S. (2007) 'Global Legal Pluralism', *Southern California Review*, vol. 80, p. 1155.
Blacket, A. (2001) 'Global Governance, Legal Pluralism and the Decentered State. A Labour Law Critique of Codes of Corporate Conduct', *Indiana Journal of Global Legal Studies*, vol. 8, no. 2, pp. 401–447.
Buanes, A. and S. Jentoft (2005) 'Challenges and Myths in Norwegian Coastal Zone Management', *Coastal Management*, vol. 33, no. 2, pp. 153–167.
Buanes, A. and S. Jentoft (2009) 'Building Bridges, Institutional Perspectives on Inter-disciplinarity', *FUTURES*, vol. 41, no. 5, pp. 446–454.
Christensen, T. and P. Lægreid (2002) *New Public Management: The Transformation of Ideas and Practice*, Aldershot: Ashgate Publishing.
Cicin-Sain, B. and R.W. Knecht (1998) *Integrated Coastal and Ocean Management: Concepts and Practices*, Washington, DC: Island Press.
Donahue, J.D. and R.J. Zeckhauser (2011) *Collaborative Governance: Private Roles for Public Goals in Turbulent Times*, Princeton, NJ: Princeton University Press.
Eliassen, K.A. and J. Kooiman (eds) (1987) *Managing Public Organizations: Lessons from Contemporary European Experience*, London: Sage Publications.
Folke, C., T. Hahn, P. Olsson and J. Norberg (2005) 'Adaptive Governance of Social-ecological Systems', *Annual Review of Environment and Resources*, vol. 30, pp. 441–473.
Fukuyama, F. (2011) *The Origins of Political Order. From Prehuman Times to the French Revolution*, New York: Farrar, Straus and Giroux.
Gadamer, H.-G. (2003) *Truth and Method*, New York: The Continuum International Publishing Group.
Gezelius, S.S. (2002) 'Do Norms Count? State Regulation and Compliance in a Norwegian Fishing Community', *Acta Sociologica*, vol. 45, no. 4, pp. 305–314.
Gray, T. (ed.) (2005) *Participation in Fisheries Governance*, Dordrecht: Kluwer.
Griffiths, J. (1986) 'What is Legal Pluralism?', *Journal of Legal Pluralism*, vol. 24, pp. 1–55.
Guillet, D. (1998) 'Rethinking Legal Pluralism: Local Law and State Law in the Evolution of Water Property Rights in Northwestern Spain', *Comparative Studies in Society and History*, vol. 40, pp. 42–70.
Held, D. (1987) *Models of Democracy*, Cambridge: Polity Press.
Hoof, L. van (ed.) (2005) *Sharing Responsibilities in Fisheries Management Vol. 1 and 2*, Report from the EU project: Sharing Responsibilities in European Fisheries Management (Q5RS-2001-01998), The Hague: Agricultural Economics Institute (LEI).
Jagers, S., D. Berlin and S. Jentoft (2012) 'Why Comply? Attitudes among Swedish Fishers towards Harvesting Regulations', *Marine Policy*, vol. 36, pp. 969–976.

Jentoft, S. (2006) 'Beyond Fisheries Management: The *Phronetic* Dimension', *Marine Policy*, vol. 30, pp. 671–680.

Jentoft, S. (2007a) 'In the Power of Power: The Understated Aspect of Fisheries and Coastal Management', *Human Organization*, vol. 66, no. 4, pp. 426–437.

Jentoft, S. (2007b) 'Limits of Governability? Institutional Implications for Fisheries and Coastal Governance', *Marine Policy*, vol. 31, pp. 360–370.

Jentoft, S. and A. Eide (eds) (2011) *Poverty Mosaics: Realities and Prospects in Small-Scale Fisheries*, Dordrecht: Springer-Verlag.

Jentoft, S., T. van Son and M. Bjørkan (2007) 'Marine Protected Areas: A Governance System Analysis', *Human Ecology*, vol. 35, pp. 611–622.

Jentoft, S., M. Bavinck, D. Johnson and T. Kaleekal (2009) 'Co-management and Legal Pluralism: How an Analytical Problem Becomes an Institutional One', *Human Organization*, vol. 68, no. 1, pp. 27–38.

Jessop, B. (1998) 'The Rise of Governance and the Risk of Failure: The Case of Economic Development', *International Social Science Journal*, vol. 155, pp. 29–45.

Kickert, W.J.M. (2001) 'Public Management of Hybrid Organizations: Governance of Quasi-Autonomous Executive Agencies', *International Public Management Journal*, vol. 4, pp. 135–150.

Kjær, A.M. (2004) *Governance*, Cambridge: Polity Press.

Kooiman, J. (2003) *Governing as Governance*, London: Sage Publications.

Kooiman, J. (2008) 'Exploring the Concept of Governability', *Journal of Comparative Policy Analysis*, vol. 10, no. 2, pp. 171–190.

Kooiman, J. and M. Bavinck (2005) 'The Governance Perspective', in Kooiman, J., M. Bavinck, S. Jentoft and R. Pullin (eds), *Fish for Life: Interactive Governance for Fisheries*, Amsterdam: Amsterdam University Press, pp. 11–24.

Kooiman, J. and S. Jentoft (2009) 'Meta-governance: Values, Norms and Principles, and the Making of Hard Choices', *Public Administration*, vol. 87, no. 4, pp. 818–836.

Kooiman, J., M. Bavinck, S, Jentoft and R. Pullin (eds) (2005) *Fish for Life. Interactive Governance for Fisheries*, Amsterdam: Amsterdam University Press.

Linke, S., M. Dreyer and P. Sellke (2011) 'The Regional Advisory Councils: What Is their Potential to Incorporate Stakeholder Knowledge into Fisheries Governance?', *AMBIO*, vol. 40, no. 2, pp. 133–143.

Long, R. (2010) 'The Role of Regional Advisory Councils in the European Common Fisheries Policy: Legal Constraints and Future Options', *International Journal of Marine and Coastal Law*, vol. 25, pp. 289–346.

Mayntz, R. (1994) 'Governing Failures and the Problem of Governability: Some Comments on a Theoretical Paradigm', in Kooiman, J. (ed.), *Modern Governance: New Government–Society Interactions*, London: Sage Publications, pp. 9–20.

Meinzen-Dick, R.S. and R. Pradham (2002) 'Legal Pluralism and Dynamic Property Rights', CAPRI Working Paper no. 22, Washington, DC: International Food Policy Research Institute.

Meinzen-Dick, R.S. (2009) 'Property Rights for Poverty Reduction?', DESA Working Paper no. 91, New York: United Nations Department of Economic and Social Affairs (www.un.org/esa/desa/papers/2009/wp91_2009.pdf).

Mikalsen, K.H. and S. Jentoft (2008) 'Participatory Practices in Fisheries Across Europe: Making Stakeholders more Responsible', *Marine Policy*, vol. 32, pp. 169–177.

Offe, C. (2009) 'Governance: An "Empty Signifier"?' *Constellations*, vol. 16, no. 4, pp. 550–562.

Osborne, S.P. (ed.) (2010) *The New Public Governance? Emerging Perspectives on the Theory and Practice of Public Governance*, London: Routledge.
Ostrom, E. (1993) *Governing the Commons. The Evolution of Institutions for Collective Action*, Cambridge: Cambridge University Press.
Pierre, J. and B.G. Peters (2000) *Governance, Politics and the State*, London: Palgrave Macmillan.
Pimentel, D.T. (2010) 'Can Indigenous Justice Survive?', *Harvard International Review*, 1 August. (http://hir.harvard.edu/archives/2683).
Pollitt, C. and G. Bouchaert (2011) *Public Management Reform: A Comparative Analysis: New Public Management, Governance, and the Neo-Weberian State*, Oxford: Oxford University Press.
Pospisil, L. (1971) *Anthropology of Law: A Comparative Theory*, New Haven: HRAF Press.
Rhodes, R.A. (1996) 'The New Governance: Governing without Government', *Political Studies*, vol. XLIV, pp. 652–667.
Rouland, N. (1994) *Legal Anthropology*, London: The Athlone Press.
Sanchirico, J., N.J. Eagle, S. Palumbi and B.H. Thompson, Jr. (2010) 'Comprehensive Planning, Dominant Use-Zones, and User Rights: A New Era in Ocean Governance', *Bulletin of Marine Science*, vol. 86, no. 2, pp. 249–259.
Schattschneider, E.E. (1960) *The Semi-Sovereign People: A Realist's View of Democracy in America*, Chicago: Holt, Rinehart and Winston.
Scott, W.R. (2001) *Institutions and Organizations*, London: Sage Publications.
Sen, A. (2009) *The Idea of Justice*, London: Penguin.
Sousa Santos, B. de (2006) 'The Heterogeneous State and Legal Pluralism in Mozambique', *Law & Society Review*, vol. 40, no. 1, pp. 39–75.
Stoker, G. (1998) 'Governance as Theory: Five Propositions', *International Social Science Journal*, vol. 50, pp. 17–28.
Tamanaha, B.Z. (2008) 'Understanding Legal Pluralism; Past to Present, Local to Global', *Sydney Law Review*, vol. 30, pp. 375–411.
Vanderlinden, J. (1989) 'Return of Legal Pluralism; Twenty Years After', *Journal of Legal Pluralism*, vol. 28, pp. 149–157.
Wiber, M. and C. Milley (2007) 'After Marshall: Implementation of Aboriginal Fishing Rights in Atlantic Canada', *Journal of Legal Pluralism*, vol. 55, pp. 163–186.
Wilson, D.C., J. Raakjær Nielsen and P. Degnbol (eds) (2003) *The Fisheries Co-management Experience: Accomplishments, Challenges and Prospects*, Dordrecht: Kluwer Academic Publishers.
Woodman, G.R. (1999) 'The Idea of Legal Pluralism', in Dupret, B., M. Berger and K. al-Zwani (eds), *Legal Pluralism in the Arab World*, The Hague: Kluwer Law International, pp. 3–20.
Zips, W. and M. Weilenmann (2011) 'Introduction: Governance and Legal Pluralism – and Emerging Symbiotic Relationship', in Zips, W. and M. Weilenmann (eds), *The Governance of Legal Pluralism: Empirical Studies from Africa and Beyond*, Wien: LIT Verlag GmbG & CoKG, pp. 7–34.

Index

For Product Safety Concerns and Information please contact our
EU representative GPSR@taylorandfrancis.com Taylor & Francis
Verlag GmbH, Kaufingerstraße 24, 80331 München, Germany